Contract Law

Contract Law

Fourth edition

Mary Charman

WILLAN
PUBLISHING

Published by

Willan Publishing
Culmcott House
Mill Street, Uffculme
Cullompton, Devon
EX15 3AT, UK
Tel: +44(0)1884 840337
Fax: +44(0)1884 840251
e-mail: info@willan.publishing.co.uk
Website: www.willan.publishing.co.uk

Published simultaneously in the USA and Canada by

Willan Publishing
c/o ISBS, 920 NE 58th Ave, Suite 300,
Portland, Oregon 97213-3786, USA
Tel: +001(0)503 287 3093
Fax: +001(0)503 280 8832
e-mail: info@isbs.com
Website: www.isbs.com

First edition published 2001
Second edition published 2002
Third edition published 2005
Fourth edition published 2007

ISBN 978-1-84392-358-9 paperback

British Library Cataloguing-in-Publication Data

A catalogue record for this book is available from the British Library

Project managed by Deer Park Productions, Tavistock, Devon
Typeset by Pantek Arts, Maidstone, Kent
Printed and Bound by TJ International, Padstow, Cornwall

Contents

Table of Statutes

Table of Cases

Preface to the fourth edition

The study of any area of law can appear somewhat daunting to a new student and presenting material in an accessible way, while retaining academic integrity, has become a significant feature of each edition of this book. This new edition is no exception and the book aims to be a complete text for students of Contract Law at A-level as well as those on other courses in further and higher education. The frequent revision programme means that the book is up to date with regard to examination specifications and this edition incorporates the new OCR four-module requirements, including both new source materials for the Special Study paper and examples of the new-style dilemma questions.

As before, the book includes opportunities to make connections between areas of law and to consider the moral, ethical and social issues found within the law. The reminders within the text prompt you to think about issues, to consider whether outcomes are fair to individuals and to consider the way in which justice is achieved within the broad context of the society in which we live. Many of these issues are raised in 'boxed' questions, indicating points at which you could stop and consider answers for yourself before moving on to the next section. At the end of each chapter is an updated set of questions, including some from recent A2 examination papers, for you to practise, with suggested outline answers at the end of the book. A whole section towards the end examines the general context of the law of contract, and the specific ways in which a synoptic overview is assessed by the major examination boards have been updated. The aim is twofold: to help you to achieve success in examinations and to present a context in which contract law may be set in order to acquire skills for life and to extend the value of study.

Many students have found the key skills section useful in assembling their portfolios, finding that generally those students who achieve a qualification at an advanced level do have such key skills in order to undertake their studies. At A-level there are specific requirements for this qualification, so to aid you in achieving this as smoothly as possible, a section is included to suggest some ways in which these skills can be demonstrated through your 'normal' study of contract law, and in fact to show how the assessments can complement and enhance each other.

It is obviously important that a law textbook keeps up to date, since the law itself is a living and changing entity, reflecting the society in which we live. This book is based on the state of the law at the time of publication, including recent cases and statutes. Try to read quality newspapers and legal journals, visit courts and legal practices, and make full use of the internet. The opinion of others is valued as a resource in both forming an individual view and in assessing the current state of the law. I have suggested further resources which you may like to investigate to help broaden your knowledge and to become aware of new law as it develops.

I hope that this book helps you not only to acquire the knowledge that you need to pass examinations, but that it will encourage you to be enthusiastic in your study of Contract Law for its own sake, so that you really want to find out more because you are genuinely interested. Most of all, I wish you well in your studies and examinations, and hope that you are indeed successful.

Acknowledgements

I would again like to acknowledge gratitude to the A-level examination board OCR for allowing the reproduction of examination questions. I would also like to thank Brian Willan and the production team for their continuing expertise, support and extreme patience, and my family for again putting up with the domestic difficulties that writing seems to produce.

1 Principles of the law of contract

Have *you* made a contract today, or this week? If you have not studied the law of contract at all, then your answer may well be 'no', since the law of contract may conjure up images of long, complicated forms for the sale of houses, loan agreements, exchange of businesses, etc. However, contracts exist in much more humble settings, beginning with everyday actions such as buying a packet of crisps or making a bus journey, and so the law concerning it has simple foundations. Yet this basic law of everyday contracts with which we will be concerned during much of this book, covers all kinds of situations from simple shopping to large commercial deals, and the cases which lay down the rules are equally wide in the matters which they cover.

Note: The particular area of contracts concerning the sale of land operates within this general framework of the law of contract, but is also covered by further law specific to land, which is outside the scope of this book. ('Land' covers not just the ground, but things growing in it, flowing through it, and attached to it, such as houses and other buildings.)

> Can you think of some situations during the last few days when you might have made a contract?

Contracts are made by ordinary people in everyday situations, often many times during a day. Examples include buying a magazine, parking a car, doing the family shopping, entering competitions. Most of these events take place quite smoothly without any awareness of a contract having been made. It is usually not until disputes occur that the question of a possible contract arises.

Why do we need a law of contract?

The majority of people generally honour most of their promises as a matter of principle. However, situations do arise where conflicting interests lead to dispute, and then an established system of some sort is needed to resolve the problems and to attempt to prevent injustice.

It is easy enough to imagine a situation where an intention to trade dishonestly leads to a contract dispute, but problems may also arise when two or more people have honest, but differing, views of a situation. For example, those involved may have used similar language while understanding completely different things in an agreement. Equally, an arrangement may have begun amicably, a subsequent difference of opinion colouring a person's view of the situation.

In theory, at least, it would be ideal if problems with contracts could be sorted out by referring to the intentions of those involved. However, most contracts are not written, and it is obvious that no court can look into a person's mind, so English law looks for an objective test of agreement. It attempts to look at the conduct and communications between the parties involved, as if through the eyes of an ordinary reasonable person, to see if the outward signs of a contract exist. A good illustration of this is found in the following case.

Smith v Hughes (1871) Here a buyer wanted some old, mature, oats for his horse, and, after inspecting a sample, thought he had obtained these at a reasonable price. In fact the seller thought that new oats were required, and sold him less mature oats at a fairly high price (old oats were worth more than new oats). When the error was discovered the question arose as to what had really been intended.

Since the court could not investigate what had taken place in the parties' minds, they based their decision on the evidence of what was intended, that is that the two parties had been quite happy with the sale of what they had seen in the sample in front of them.

Blackburn, J said of this objective approach,

> If, whatever a man's real intention may be, he so conducts himself that a reasonable man would believe that he was assenting to the terms proposed by the other party, and that other party, upon that belief, enters into the contract with him, the man thus conducting himself would be equally bound, as if he had intended to agree to the other party's terms.

Are all promises enforced by law?

No. If a friend promises to bring a CD along for you to listen to, and forgets, this would not be a breach of contract. Even though the friend's promise is made honestly and seriously and intended to be binding, it was probably not the intention that it would form a legal agreement enforceable in court. Happily, the law takes this view too, as the promise itself may not contain the essential elements which are considered to be part of a contract. An obvious example is two members of a family, or a group of friends, making social arrangements – but more about this later.

Generally, the type of promise which the law will enforce is where something is to be gained on each side, such as goods for money, goods for goods, or exchange of services, although other less obvious bargains may be enforceable. So, in contract law, a court will look for a *promise given for a promise*, as opposed to a gratuitous (or one-sided) promise.

The form of a contract

Apart from a few exceptions (such as the sale of land) a contract may take any form. It may be oral or in writing, and may be made as a casual statement or accompanied by anything from a handshake to an elaborate ceremony. Often the form of agreement is suggested by the value of the contract in money terms, although this is not always the case, and it is certainly not a legal principle. However, buying a newspaper would not normally take place in the same manner as an agreement to deal in gold bullion!

The basis of contract law

The main aim of the law of contract is to ensure that these agreements are made in a fair way, and to enforce them, whether it is on behalf of the owner of a large company or a consumer buying a bar of chocolate. The rules of contract law are built on fairness and reasonableness, as cases have been decided in court, and on top of these Parliament has formed statutes where issues are of general concern.

As issues have come before the courts in the form of broken, misunderstood or non-existent contracts, the law has developed the rules which we apply to contracts today. The situation is gradually changing as more legislation is passed, often in an attempt to protect the consumer, who may otherwise be at a disadvantage in negotiating arrangements. Some examples are the Sale of Goods Act 1979 (as amended) and the Unfair Terms in Consumer Contracts Regulations 1994.

However, the principle that contract is a 'case law' subject remains true. The law of contract does not, in general, give rights and impose duties (as do some other aspects of law). It works by limiting the obligations that people may impose on themselves and others, within a general freedom to contract. The case of *Felthouse v Bindley* (1862) shows that obligations cannot be imposed on another party. In this case an uncle proposed to buy his nephew's horse. The uncle wrote to the nephew saying that if he did not hear otherwise, he would assume that the horse was his. It was held that this could not amount to a contract without some communication from the nephew, as a contract cannot be imposed on a person in this way (even if they are happy with it).

Some aspects of *Felthouse v Bindley* appear a little harsh. Do you think that the outcome is justified? What if someone wrote to you offering to buy your hi-fi, and stated that unless you let them know otherwise they would assume that there was a contract between you? Should you be under an obligation to reply?

So, exactly what is needed to form a valid contract? The rest of this book will address that issue, and will also look at ways in which courts deal with problems that may arise once a contract is formed.

Part 1

The formation of a contract

Is there agreement?

To form a binding contract, the essential requirement is that the parties are like-minded over the basis of their contract. We say that there should be *consensus ad idem*, which is a meeting of minds, and to a pure theorist that is all which should be required. The problem lies in finding evidence of this agreement. It is a little like convincing a teacher or an examiner of your knowledge of the law (or anything else). Evidence is required of your knowledge in an agreed way.

Through case law a pattern has evolved of finding evidence of agreement, and it is by requiring the parties to have communicated in some way, one of them making an offer and the other making an acceptance. In most cases this is not too difficult, although it will be seen in Chapter 2 that there are a few difficult and non-standard cases.

The benefit obtained or 'bargained'

If offer and acceptance were the only requirements, we could in theory have some very one-sided agreements. If I offer to give you a present of £20 next week, and you agree to this, we have an offer from me and an acceptance from you. If I then do not give anything at all next week, I will have broken my promise. Is this something that the law should enforce? The law is quite strict on not generally enforcing one-sided promises, feeling that it becomes very much a problem of morals when people break such promises.

The law will, however, enforce an agreement if something has been bargained by both parties, and both sides have contributed to the agreement in a recognisable way, for example by paying in exchange for goods. This does not have to be the actual handing over of goods, so a promise to pay could be given in exchange for the promise to hand over goods. This exchange is known as consideration, and is another requirement in forming a contract.

The intention to be bound by the agreement

A third requirement is that the parties do really intend to be bound by whatever they agree. In a shopping context this is likely to go without saying, as a seller is unlikely to intend to give away goods without really expecting payment! However, if I offer to pay for my friend's drink if he buys my sandwich, I do not seriously expect to sue him if he only buys his own sandwich. To distinguish between serious contracts and social agreements the law requires an element of legal intention in forming a contract.

Capacity

A further factor to consider in the legality of a contract is whether the parties are of the standing required by the law to make a binding agreement. If a child in a playground agrees to sell one of his toys, this would not normally be binding. The law requires a legal capacity to contract, and generally adults over the age of 18 are said to have this. A further formation requirement examined in this part of the book, then, is the capacity to contract.

If all four of these requirements are present, then there will normally be a binding contract.

2 Offer and acceptance

A contract is an agreement between two parties imposing rights and obligations which may be enforced by law. The courts need some kind of evidence of this agreement, so they look, through the eyes of a reasonable person, for external evidence of it. To help identify evidence of agreement, it is conventionally analysed into two aspects: offer and acceptance.

Figure 2.1

Offer

An offer can be defined as follows:

An expression of willingness to contract on certain terms, made with the intention that it shall become binding as soon as it is accepted by the person to whom it is addressed.

Offers can be one of two types:

- Specific – made to one person or group of people. Then only that particular person or group of people can accept.
- General – made to 'the whole world' (or people generally), particularly seen in the cases of rewards and other public advertisements.

The following is probably one of the best known cases in contract law, and it involves a general offer, made to the 'whole world'.

Carlill v Carbolic Smoke Ball Company (1893)
In the *Illustrated London News* in November 1891 appeared what was to become a notorious advertisement. It read,

£100 reward will be paid by the Carbolic Smoke Ball Company to any person who contracts the increasing epidemic, influenza, colds or any diseases caused by taking cold, after having used the ball three times daily for two weeks according to the printed directions supplied with each ball .... One Carbolic Smoke Ball will last a family several months making it the cheapest remedy in the world at the price – 10 shillings post free.

Recent winters had been hard, influenza epidemics sweeping the country and resulting in many deaths. Mrs Carlill, like many others, must have been impressed by the advertisement and acquired a smoke ball from her chemist. Unlike many others, however, when the smoke ball failed to prevent her from getting influenza (despite its use as directed from November to January), Mrs Carlill claimed her £100. When the company refused to pay she sued them. It was held that Mrs Carlill could successfully recover the £100. An offer to the whole world was possible, becoming a contract with any person(s) who accepted the offer before its termination. Mrs Carlill had accepted by her actions, and had turned the offer to the world into a contract with her personally. The Carbolic Smoke Ball Company were therefore bound to give her the money promised in the advertisement.

Imagine life in 1893. The fear of influenza was immense, and a remedy would appear attractive. The price of 10 shillings would be high (this could have be a person's wages for a week at that time). Do you think, therefore, that a customer like Mrs Carlill would have considered the advertisement to be taken seriously, as a genuine offer?

The Carbolic Smoke Ball Company, in defending its claim, put forward various defences, and in rejecting them one by one the court laid down important legal principles:

1 The Company claimed that promise was a mere advertising puff, not intended to create legal relations (see Chapter 4 on this issue). However, the Court of Appeal dismissed this argument because:

   (a)   The company had made a specific statement of fact, capable of forming part of a binding contract: If you use our product and catch 'flu, we will give you £100.

   (b)   The advert had also stated that '£1000 is deposited with the Alliance Bank, Regent Street, showing our sincerity in the matter'. The court felt that people generally would interpret this as an offer to be acted on.

2 The company argued that a 'contract with the whole world' was not legally possible.

Bowen LJ said that this was not a contract with the whole world, but an offer made to all the world, which was to ripen into a contract with anybody who performed the necessary conditions.

3 The company claimed that as Mrs Carlill had not notified them of her intention to accept the offer there was no contract.

The Court of Appeal held that the company had waived the need to communicate acceptance because the advert indicated that the action of using the smoke ball was what was required of the offeree, rather than an oral or written response. In this the court recognised the existence of unilateral contracts.

4 The company argued that there was no consideration to make the promise binding.

The Court of Appeal said that Mrs Carlill's use three times daily was consideration, also the benefit received in promoting sales.

Apart from the various points of law dealt with by this case, it had other interesting implications, in that it probably had a strong influence on commercial thinking in advertising practice. Whereas it had been acceptable until this time to make unsubstantiated claims over products, Victorian advertising in similar style was greatly curtailed, and later years saw the arrival of consumer protection legislation. As for the Carbolic Smoke Ball Company, they went into liquidation in 1895.

A recent case found acceptance of a general offer to take place in a similar way, involving action in response to a written poster.

> *Bowerman v ABTA* (1996)
> Notices on the wall in a travel agency were held to amount to an offer that anyone booking a holiday with this agency would be covered by membership of the Association of British Travel Agents. Acceptance was the act of booking a holiday with this agency by a client.

So, while most offers require verbal or written acceptance (forming what are known as bilateral contracts), with general offers the performance of some act may be valid acceptance (forming a unilateral contract).

An offer may be:

- express – either verbal or written, or
- implied – from conduct or circumstances. Sometimes nothing is said at all, but an offer is obvious from the actions. This is probably the situation when making a journey on a bus. The case of *Wilkie v London Passenger Transport Board* (1947) involved a discussion as to how and where a contract was formed in a bus journey. Clearly there was a contract, but exactly where offer and acceptance took place was debatable. It was

largely implied by the actions of the parties, rather than anything said specifically on each bus journey.

> Think about your actions when you travel on a bus. What part of your conduct, or the conduct of the bus company, could amount to an offer?

Offers and 'non-offers'

Faced with the task of establishing whether or not a contract exists between two parties, the court normally looks first at the statements and negotiations between the parties to see if a binding offer has been made. Sometimes what appears to be an offer is, in law, an invitation to others to make an offer, or an invitation to treat. Although many given situations may at first sight appear to be debatable, enough cases have passed before the courts over the years for certain 'rules' to be laid down.

So, initial negotiations could amount to:

- an offer – which is capable of acceptance, or
- an invitation to treat, which is an invitation to others to make or negotiate an offer – and therefore not open to acceptance.

Generally, displays in shop windows are not offers, but merely invitations to treat. This was established in the case of *Timothy v Simpson*, but confirmed in the following more recent case.

> *Fisher v Bell* (1961)
> A seller was accused of 'offering for sale' a flick-knife, contrary to the Restriction of Offensive Weapons Act 1959. The knife was on display in his window, and the court held that this was an invitation to treat, not an offer.

A similar situation arose shortly afterwards in *Mella v Monahan* (1961) regarding obscene publications in a shop window, with the court again holding the window display to be an invitation to treat, not an offer.

So if the customer makes the offer in this situation, it is up to the seller to accept or reject the offer. This follows through the idea that there is freedom to contract, and means that the seller has a right to refuse to sell an item to a particular customer. This could occur, for example, if a customer mistakenly thought that a display item was for sale, or if a person asking a landlord for alcohol was already very drunk, or if a seller just did not like a customer. This was expressed by Winfield in 1939 as follows:

> A shop is a place for bargaining and not compulsory sales.... If the display of such goods were an offer, the shopkeeper might be forced

to contract with his worst enemy, his greatest trade rival, a reeling drunkard or a ragged and verminous tramp.

> Do you think that this law is widely known? Does it make any difference in practical terms? It is likely, in practice, that most sellers will want to maintain good customer relations, and most retailers will not refuse to sell to people because of personal dislike.

It should be noted that:

- A shopkeeper might incur criminal liability under the Trade Descriptions Act 1968.
- The law is not the same in some other countries.

The idea of an invitation to treat was applied to supermarkets, which of course is very relevant to modern shopping habits, in the following case.

> *Pharmaceutical Society of Great Britain v Boots Cash Chemists Ltd* (1953)
> Boots were accused of selling goods without the supervision of a pharmacist under the Pharmacy and Poisons Act 1933. Boots had opened a shop in supermarket style, the customer taking products from displays and paying for them at a cash point. It was established that there was a registered pharmacist at the cashier point. The court held that the display of goods amounted to an invitation to treat, the customer making an offer by taking them to a cashier, and the cashier accepting by some action which indicated willingness to sell. There was therefore no offence, since the 'sale', that is the offer and acceptance, took place at the cash point where a pharmacist was situated.

> What about goods and services described in advertisements? Would such an advertisement amount to an offer?

In many situations the court has held that the advertisement of goods or services is an invitation to treat, the customer making the offer. These situations include the distribution of circulars, the posting of timetables, auctions, tenders and where goods are mentioned in the small advertisements section of newspapers. This last situation arose in the following case.

> *Partridge v Crittenden* (1968)
> The appellant had inserted in the classified section of a periodical a notice advertising 'bramblefinch cocks and hens, 25s each'. He was charged with

▶

unlawfully offering for sale a wild live bird contrary to the provisions of the Protection of Birds Act 1954, and was convicted. The divisional court quashed the conviction, saying that as the advertisement was an invitation to treat, there had been no 'offer for sale'. Lord Parker said in his judgment, 'I think that when one is dealing with advertisements and circulars, unless indeed they come from manufacturers, there is business sense in their being construed as invitations to treat and not offers for sale.' He went on to explain that if the advertisement was an offer, then the seller may well find that he had contracts with a large number of people when he only had a limited supply of birds for sale. The problem of exhausted stocks is a practical reason for the law being this way round.

So, for displays of goods in shop windows, classified advertisements, catalogues, circulars and timetables, the following general 'shopping' principles apply.

'Shopping' principles
- *The display or advertisement is an invitation to treat.*
- *The customer offers to buy the goods at a particular price.*
- *This offer can then be accepted by the seller in some action, for example by a verbal statement or by entering the price in a cash register.*
- *This offer and acceptance may then be a binding contract.*

However, this does not mean that all advertisements are automatically invitations to treat. We have seen already in *Carlill v Carbolic Smoke Ball Company* that some advertisements are general offers, especially where the main terms are included in the advertisement and all that remains is for the customer to take action. This could arise in a sale, for example, where a shop window display contains an advertisement which says, 'Any CD player at £5 for the first 10 customers inside the shop on 1st January'. If a customer is one of the first ten customers in the queue, and wished to buy a CD player for £5, they would presumably be regarded by the court as accepting the offer made by the shop in its advertisement. A similar kind of situation arose in the case which follows, regarding a sale of fur coats.

Lefkowitz v Great Minneapolis Surplus Stores (1957)
Here the advertisement stated, 'Saturday 9am sharp; 3 brand new fur coats worth $100. First come, first served, $1 each.' The seller refused to sell to one of the first three customer because he was a man, and they intended to sell to women. It was held that the man had accepted the terms of the offer in the advertisement and was entitled to the coat for $1.

A further problem arises where the two parties are not in a traditional 'shopping' situation, but are negotiating individually. How do the courts decide when their statements have become firm enough for one of them to have made an offer? The issue arose in the following case.

> *Gibson v Manchester City Council* (1979)
> Gibson wanted to buy his council house under a scheme run by the Manchester Council. The council wrote that 'the Corporation may be prepared to sell the house to you' at a certain price. Gibson completed the necessary form and returned it, but this was followed by an election and change of council policy on house sales. The council refused to sell, and when the case went to court it was held that the council's proposal was an invitation to treat, followed by an offer from Gibson on the form which was rejected by the council, therefore not forming a binding contract of sale.

This is one logical view of the negotiations, but another equally logical view may produce an opposite result, and this may well be more in line with the expectations of both Gibson and the council as it was at the point of negotiations – the original parties to the contract. The court was not prepared to view the negotiations as a whole, and was very precise in identifying an invitation to treat, leading to an offer followed by an acceptance. It is not always easy to be as precise as this in real life situations, and the approach taken was quite different in the case of *Trentham Ltd v Archital Luxfer* (1993) – see p. 22.

The issue of whether a party has made an offer or invitation to treat enters a new arena with the increase in trading on the internet. See further discussion of this at the end of the chapter, p. 40.

Termination of an offer

Various events may bring an offer to an end, but only an unconditional acceptance will result in a contract. The diagram on page 14 summarises the various ways in which an offer may terminate.

Acceptance

This will normally mean that the offer is no longer available to anyone else, as the stock may be exhausted, such as where a person has a bicycle for sale.

Refusal

An offeree may refuse an offer, in which case the offer ends, so it cannot be accepted later by the offeree.

Counter-offer

Sometimes a reply from an offeree comes in the form of a new proposal, or counter-offer. It may simply be that the offeree is not happy with one or more of the terms and makes changes accordingly. Since this is not an agreement to all the terms of the offer, it is not an acceptance (p. 20), and is known as a counter-offer. It is really a new offer, which is then open to acceptance or termination in some other way. The effect of a counter-offer is to destroy the original offer. An example would be if Jack offers to sell a bicycle to Jill for £70, and Jill says 'I'll give you £68 for it'; here, there would be no contract, even though Jack and Jill may be quite close to agreement. Further, if Jack did not want to accept £68, Jill could not subsequently insist on being allowed to buy the bicycle for the original price of £0, because her counter-offer cancelled Jack's original offer. In the following case this kind of bargaining situation arose over buying a farm.

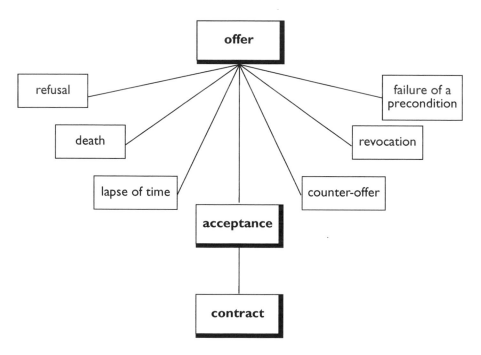

Figure 2.2

Hyde v Wrench (1840)
An offer was made to sell at £1000. The buyer refused this, but offered to pay £950. When this was not accepted by the seller, the buyer then tried to insist on buying at £1000, but the seller had decided not to sell him. It was held that he was not obliged to do so, since in making a counter-offer of £950 the buyer had at the same time refused the original offer, thereby terminating it.

In this case there were no external signs of agreement at any stage, in contrast to *Brogden v Metropolitan Rail Co* (1877), where both parties thought that a valid contract existed and indeed behaved as if that was so, until the time of the dispute. These are good examples of the necessity of looking at the situation and the actions of the parties objectively.

The following, more recent, case shows an interesting variation of a typical counter-offer situation.

Pickfords v Celestica (2003)
An offer was made to carry out work using lorries, the price quoted being £890 per lorry used. Then a second offer was made as a total price of £98,760 for the whole work, regardless of the number of lorries. The second offer was seen by the court as cancelling the first one, in a similar way to a counter-offer, and eventually the carrying out of the work was held to amount to acceptance.

Battle of forms

An extension of the counter-offer situation arises in modern business negotiations where both parties deal with standard form stationery. Both have their own terms set out, often on the back of printed quotations, invoices, delivery notes, etc. If one party's terms differ substantially from the other's, on whose terms are the parties dealing? The view taken by the courts is that the last party to send a piece of paper containing such terms, before the actual performance takes place (often delivering goods), lays down the terms. This has turned into the saying that 'he who fires the last shot wins'. This situation arose in *Butler Machine Tool Co Ltd v Ex-Cell-O Corp (England) Ltd* (1979) where the buyer and seller of a piece of machinery clearly had their own, quite different, standard terms. Lord Denning suggested in this case that basing everything on the chance of being the party to fire the 'last shot' in this way was not satisfactory, and that the courts should look at the whole picture painted by the parties' actions in deciding whether there is really a contract, and exactly what terms have been agreed. His views were largely based on an approach suggested in *Gibson v Manchester City Council* (1979) (see p.13 above). However, this was not the eventual decision of the court in Gibson, and his views are not therefore really representative of the law on this, sensible though they may appear, and the 'last shot' rule still remains.

Request for further information

The distinction between a counter-offer and a request for further information is sometimes difficult to make. It is important because of the effect on the original offer.

- A counter-offer (as seen above) terminates the original offer.
- A request for further information leaves the original offer open until withdrawn by the offeror.

An enquiry of this kind arose in the following case.

Stevenson v McLean (1880)
Following an offer to sell iron, the buyer sent a telegram asking whether credit terms would be available. As this did not change any existing terms, but merely asked for more information on the agreed price, it did not constitute an offer which could be accepted and was held not to be a counter-offer but an enquiry.

This must be a borderline case, but it does not fit in with the proposition that a counter-offer must be:

- definite enough to accept just like an original offer
- a change of terms – not just adding new information to the original ones.

Lapse of time

An offer may lapse due to the passing of time. This can occur when:

(a) It is stated in the offer that it is open for a specific time, for example, 'You have until Friday to let me know your decision'. If acceptance, refusal or revocation do not take place before Friday, then the offer will lapse on that day.

(b) No specific time limit is stated in the offer. In this case the offer is open for a 'reasonable time'. It is left to the courts to decide exactly what is a reasonable time, and their decision will depend on the individual circumstances and the nature of the goods. The following case is an example of an unreasonable time delay.

Ramsgate Hotel v Montefiore (1866)
An offer to buy shares was made in June and an attempt was made to accept in November. It was held that after five months the offer had lapsed. This is a fairly predictable decision, given the time span. It would be more difficult if the acceptance had not been such a long time after the offer.

So how long after the offer would the courts find that it had lapsed? They would probably take into account such factors as the nature of the goods (strawberries would not be treated in the same way as books or a house), the market demand for the goods, and whether prices for the item normally fluctuated greatly, as they do when selling shares, for instance.

Death

The death of an offeror will obviously, in some circumstances, mean that a contract becomes impossible to complete, as in the case of a personal service or artistic performance (such as an offer to paint a portrait or sing or dance). Where the offer is not of a personal nature, such as an offer to sell someone a piece of furniture, then there seems no reason why it should not remain open for acceptance and be honoured by the estate of the deceased offeror. The case of *Bradbury v Morgan* (1862) suggests that in general the death of an offeror may not cause an offer to lapse, particularly if the offeree accepts in ignorance of the death. The law regarding the death of an offeree is not clearly decided, but there seems no reason why the offer should not be accepted by the estate, as in the case of the death of the offeror, given the right circumstances.

Revocation

An offer can be revoked, or withdrawn, by the offeror at any time before it is accepted. This must be communicated to the offeree before acceptance takes place. The offeror has taken the responsibility of starting the negotiations, and cannot simply change his mind. This is illustrated in the following cases.

Byrne v Van Tienhoven (1880)
The defendant, trading in Cardiff, wrote to the plaintiff, in New York, offering to sell goods. On the day when the offer was received, the plaintiff telegraphed acceptance, but, three days before, the defendant had sent a letter withdrawing the offer. However, this did not arrive until after the acceptance had been confirmed by post. It was held that there was a binding contract on acceptance, and the revocation was of no effect as it was not communicated until after acceptance had taken place. So an offer can be revoked, but the revocation must be communicated to the offeree before acceptance.

Confetti Records v Warner Music UK (2003)
The recording company, Warner, produced an album from music sent to them by Confetti. It was then held too late for Confetti to revoke their offer.

Revocation via a third party

It appears from the following case, *Dickinson v Dodds* (1876), that the communication does not have to come from the offeror himself. Consider the following facts.

> *Dickinson v Dodds* (1876)
> Dodds offered to sell a house to Dickinson, the offer to be left open until Friday. Dickinson decided to buy the house on the Thursday, but during that afternoon heard from another person that Dodds had agreed to sell the house to someone else. On the Thursday evening Dickinson nevertheless delivered a letter of acceptance to Dodds. It was held that Dickinson's acceptance was not valid, as he knew 'as plainly and clearly as if Dodds had told him in so many words' that the offer had been revoked. The courts placed importance on the fact that there was no 'meeting of minds', as Dickinson did not attempt to accept until after the time when he knew that Dodds did not want to sell to him.

Several issues arise from this case, and it has been criticised as leaving unanswered various questions. Firstly, the issue of whether the source of information needs to be reliable. If not, this could obviously put the offeree at a disadvantage. Treitel, a leading authority on contract law, has suggested that the finding in *Dickinson v Dodds* is really that revocation is valid when made by any reliable third party.

Secondly, it is clearly possible to revoke an offer even though a time limit is specified, providing this is communicated to the offeree. The time limit merely has the effect of terminating the offer if it has not already been revoked. Authority for this comes from *Routledge v Grant* (1828) and was discussed in 1975 by the Law Commission (Working Paper No. 60, 'Firm Offers'). It seems particularly hard on an offeree who has depended on the offer being open and has taken action based on this. Obviously if money had been paid to keep the option open, the situation would be different, as there would be valid consideration.

> Is there any reasonable way in which the parties and the courts could decide who is a 'reliable' source?

Revocation in unilateral contracts

Normally a general offer made 'to the whole world' can be withdrawn by giving the withdrawal as much publicity as the original offer, and of the same type. It will normally be accepted that the revocation cannot practically be brought to the attention of every reader of the original offer.

There is no direct English authority on this but it was raised as an issue in the following American case.

Shuey v US (1875)
The case concerned a reward for the apprehension of a criminal. The plaintiff was not given the reward because he had not actually 'apprehended' the criminal, but it was also said that the notice had been revoked because 'the same notoriety was given to the revocation that was given to the offer'.

Figure 2.3

So if, in the case of *Carlill v Carbolic Smoke Ball Company* the Company had wanted to revoke their offer, they would simply have needed to place notices in the newspapers in which they had previously advertised the offer, saying that it was now withdrawn.

How many promotional offers have you seen recently? Have you ever seen a revocation of a unilateral contract? Do you think that this law actually operates in practice, or do members of the public assume that if a notice is no longer on display the offer it contained has ended?

Revocation during an ongoing act of acceptance

Problems may occur when an offeror attempts to withdraw an offer while a person is in the process of accepting (remember, accepting is often by conduct in unilateral contracts). An example of the problem is found in the following case.

Errington v Errington (1952)
A father bought a house on mortgage, and promised that if his son and daughter-in-law paid all of the mortgage instalments, the house would be theirs. The couple paid the instalments, but when the father died his widow tried to obtain possession of the house. She was

prevented by the court, who said that the paying of the mortgage by the couple was an ongoing act of acceptance. When the couple had completed the mortgage payments they would be entitled to the house, and while they continued to pay revocation was not possible. This seems to be a very fair position.

Lord Denning used, as an illustration of the reasonableness of his decision, the example of an offer of money to walk from London to York.

- If acceptance was binding on completion, and revocation was possible up to the moment of completion, then payment would be due on arrival in York. It would be unfair on the walker if the offeror then revoked as the walker was near to York.

- If acceptance was binding at the first moment of the act of acceptance, then payment would be due as the walker left London. This could then be unfair on the offeror if the walk was not completed.

- Lord Denning concluded that acceptance here was a continuing act, with payment enforceable on completion of the walk. While the walk was taking place, however, revocation would not be possible. This is the principle that he applied to the couple in *Errington v Errington*.

Failure of a precondition

If a main term of an offer, which is vital to the contract, is not fulfilled or is substantially altered, then the offer is no longer capable of acceptance. This arose in the following case.

Financings Ltd v Stimson (1962)
Between the defendant's offer to buy a car and the plaintiff's acceptance, the car was stolen and badly damaged. The plaintiff did not know and signed an agreement. This was held not to be acceptance, since the precondition that the car was in a certain state had failed, and there was therefore no valid contract.

Acceptance

Acceptance is the second 'half' of a contract. If Bill offers Ben a bag of sweets for 20p, and Ben says 'I accept', clearly a contract has been made. Similarly, if Ben offers Bill 20p for his bag of sweets, and Bill says 'I accept', that is also a contract. Clearly it does not matter, when dealing one to one in this way, who starts the negotiations. What the law is really saying is that there must be evidence from both sides of genuine agreement between the parties – the old idea of *consensus ad idem*, or meeting of minds.

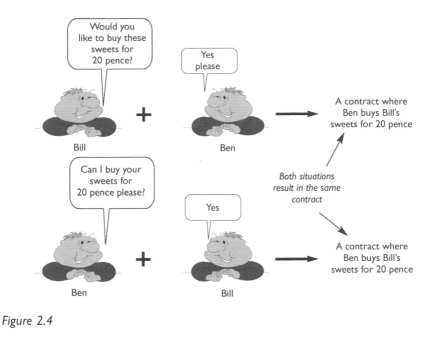

Figure 2.4

Agreement to all the terms of an offer by words or conduct.

Acceptance must fit the terms of the offer exactly, otherwise it could lead to more negotiations, for example a counter-offer, but not to a contract. However, it is sometimes difficult to see when acceptance takes place, as it does not always need to be communicated in words – it may be by conduct. The negotiations between parties may have covered a long period of time and be contained in much paperwork, and then it is especially difficult to pinpoint the exact moment of acceptance. This is seen in the following case.

Brogden v Metropolitan Rail Co (1877)
Brogden supplied the railway company with coal regularly, without a formal contract. Each time the railway company needed coal an order was placed and it was delivered. The company paid and both parties were happy with the arrangements. The railway company eventually created a written contract, and sent a copy to Brogden, who made amendments to the document, signed it and returned it. On arrival at the railway company's office it was placed in a drawer, and the supply of coal continued. When a dispute subsequently arose the parties referred to the document. On investigation it was found that there was an offer from the railway company, followed by a counter offer from Brogden, with acceptance not immediate, but probably by the placing of an order and taking delivery of coal. The acceptance was not, then,

> the mental agreement to the counter-offer, but the external evidence of
> the agreement, by the actions later.

A similar approach was taken in the following more recent case.

> *Trentham Ltd v Archital Luxfer* (1993)
> The case concerned contracts to carry out carpentry work on a building
> project. The contract was said to take into account the 'reasonable
> expectations of sensible businessmen', not the 'unexpressed mental
> reservations of the parties'. It was also important that in this situation
> the work was actually being carried out, whether or not offer and
> acceptance were apparent and easily identifiable.

The decision in these cases, that a contract did exist, even though it could
not be said with certainty when it was formed, illustrates how a court looks
through the eyes of a 'reasonable man' to see if a contract has been made.

This objective approach should always be remembered when looking at
problems of contract law, and particularly when looking for an acceptance.

> If the courts were prepared to find that a contract existed in the cases of
> *Brogden* and *Trentham*, why do you think that they are so precise about
> looking for offer and acceptance in other cases?

Communication of acceptance

Just making a mental decision to accept an offer is not normally enough.
The offeree must show in some positive way an intention to accept.
Sometimes this will mean that acceptance has to be communicated to the
offeror in a prescribed way.

Prescribed acceptance

If the offeror stipulates that an offer must be accepted in a certain way, then
he is not bound unless acceptance is made in that way. So if an offeror asks
for acceptance to be sent to a particular place, acceptance sent somewhere
else will not be binding. Similarly, if he requests acceptance in writing, oral
acceptance will not bind. However, it may be different if the offeror only
suggests a method of acceptance. The principle emerged from the
following case, *Yates Building v Pulleyn* (1975), that unless the offeror

clearly stipulates that the prescribed mode of acceptance is the only way to accept, then another method may be binding, provided that it is does not put the offeror at a disadvantage.

> *Yates Building v Pulleyn* (1975)
> The offeror asked for acceptance to be by letter using registered or recorded delivery. The letter was sent by normal delivery, but it made no practical difference to the offeror, since the letter was delivered on time, so acceptance by this method was held binding.

No prescribed acceptance

If no method of communicating acceptance is stipulated, the starting-point is that acceptance is made using the same method of communication as the offeror. However, any reasonable way of replying will normally form a contract, the responsibility being on the person accepting to ensure that communication is effective. Lord Denning gave some examples in the following case.

> *Entores Ltd v Miles Far East Corporation* (1955)
> He said that if two people are walking along either side of a river and a message shouted is obliterated by the sound of a passing aircraft, it is necessary to repeat the message until the person speaking is sure that the message is heard. Similarly if a telephone line goes dead, it is necessary to redial and ensure that the message has been received. The burden on communication of acceptance is therefore firmly on the offeree in normal circumstances, and acceptance is effective on receipt. In *Entores* a Dutch company accepted an offer by an English company, and the issue arose of where the contract was formed. It was held to have been formed in England, since that is where the acceptance was received by telex.

Waiver of communication of acceptance

One of the principles that came out of *Carlill* was that as far as a general offer is concerned the offeror is at liberty to waive communication of acceptance (that is, to say that communication is not needed on this occasion). Waiver may be:

- specifically expressed by the offeror, or
- implied (as in *Carlill*) – the nature of the advertisement implied that a person buying and using the smoke ball as prescribed who then contracted 'flu would obtain a reward. The company clearly did not

expect the user to contact them and tell them that the product was being used or that a bout of 'flu seemed to be starting!

- By conduct, as in *Day Morris v Voyce* (2003) where a seller of property was held to have accepted an estate agent's offer to market the property by letting the agent go ahead with advertising it and showing potential buyers around.

Silence

Silence alone is not a valid acceptance. The following case, already discussed in Chapter 1, is the usual authority for this.

Felthouse v Bindley (1862)
An uncle wanted to buy his nephew's horse, and after discussion over price, wrote saying, 'If I hear no more about him, I consider the horse is mine at £30.15s'. The nephew did not reply, but was clearly happy about the arrangements as he told the auctioneer that the horse was sold. The auctioneer mistakenly sold the horse to a third party, and the uncle sued the auctioneer to recover the horse. The court held that there had been no communication of acceptance by the nephew to the uncle, and therefore there was no contract between the two of them.

Various issues arise in this case. Clearly, if A offers B £500 for B's car, and B says nothing on the subject, there is no valid contract. Similarly, if B writes a letter to A, offering to sell the car, and A does not reply, there is no contract. If, however, A lets someone else know that he is about to buy the car, and later goes to collect it, the sale will no doubt proceed as if communication had taken place. It was probably the presence of the third party which influenced the decision in *Felthouse v Bindley*. An innocent genuine third party (a *bona fide* third party) is given high priority generally in law, and there is no reason why the eventual purchaser, who paid good money for the horse, should suffer. It could also be argued that the offeror, in this case the uncle, started this round of negotiations, and took on board the risk of not knowing whether the contract had been concluded by the wording of his letter.

There is also an important principle that an offeror should not be able to limit an offeree's freedom of action, nor impose on him an unwanted contract. For instance, it would not be fair if an offeror stipulated that an offer would be considered accepted if the offeree arrives at his place of work in the morning, or by doing some other necessary everyday act.

The case does, however, contradict the idea that acceptance may be by conduct, which could be a silent but clear act indicating agreement. Future case law may throw more light on this, but the present position is that, particularly in the case of a bilateral contract, silence alone is insufficient as acceptance.

> Think about the facts of *Felthouse v Bindley*. Is it right that silence can never be used as acceptance, even if the offeree clearly intended to accept, and there is evidence of this in subsequent conduct (notifying the auctioneer, for instance)?

The general theme of *Felthouse v Bindley* was taken up in statute in 1971. Clearly a contract should not be imposed on any person who does not wish it, and this seems totally reasonable. It would be wholly unreasonable to send someone an item in the post and to be able to enforce a demand for payment. This did in fact happen a lot before the passing of the Unsolicited Goods and Services Act 1971. This Act supports the concept of freedom to contract, stating that a recipient of unsolicited goods can treat them as an unconditional gift if

- the goods are kept unused for 28 days and the seller informed that they are not wanted, or
- the goods are kept as new for six months unused.

This statute has been very effective with a huge decrease in 'inertia' methods of selling. Consumers can additionally rely on s. 24 of the Consumer Protection (Distance Selling) Regulations 2000. Under this section unsolicited goods sent to consumers become an unconditional gift immediately and it is an offence to demand payment for such goods.

Ignorance of an offer (the 'reward' cases)

Generally, if a person performs whatever is specified as acceptance, but is totally unaware of the offer, there is not a binding contract. This might easily arise in a 'reward' case. What if, for example, a person returns a dog, not knowing that a reward had been offered for it? Is there an obligation to hand over the reward money? There may well be a moral obligation, but in law the answer will generally be no. The act which amounts to acceptance must be done at least in part in response to the offer.

On the other hand, if a person knows of an offer, it does not matter that the act of acceptance is performed for some motive other than gaining the reward. The case of *Williams v Carwardine* demonstrates this.

Williams v Carwardine (1833)
The defendant gave information which led to the arrest and conviction of the murderers of a man called Carwardine. The defendant was the ▶

dead man's wife, who had offered a reward for the information. The plaintiff had given the information 'to ease my conscience and in the hope of forgiveness thereafter'. She was in fact ill and feared that she would soon die. It was held that her motives were largely irrelevant. She had given the information with knowledge of the reward, and had therefore made a valid acceptance of the offer.

This contrasts with the situation where there is absolutely no knowledge of the offer. The following Australian case falls somewhere between the two.

R v Clarke (1927)

In this case the defendant knew of a reward for information leading to the arrest and conviction of the murderers of two police officers. He gave the necessary information, but admitted as evidence in court that he had only done so to clear himself of possible charges. He had no thought of claiming any reward, and had actually forgotten about it at the time of giving the information. However, he decided to claim the money that was obviously available, since he had known of it, and had provided the necessary information. The evidence that he gave that he had forgotten about the reward was considered by the court to be the same as never having known of the offer, and the High Court of Australia dismissed his claim for the reward.

It has been suggested that the above two cases can be distinguished because Clarke was not even partly motivated by the reward, but it must in practice be extremely difficult to differentiate objectively between these two instances, especially as they depend largely upon evidence given at the time of the hearing. The decision in *Clarke* could be criticised on practical grounds, since if Clarke had lied and had said that he really had thought about the reward when he gave the information, he would have been entitled to it. He was, then, penalised for telling the truth! It is also difficult to accept the argument that forgetting a fact is the same as never having known of it. Of course, the case of *Clarke* is not technically binding in the United Kingdom since it is Australian, and there is not really a direct authority exactly on this point.

Forgetting the reward	=	Never having known of the reward	DOES IT? Do you agree?

So the legal points emerging from these cases can be summarised as follows:

• Responding to an offer with mixed motives can form a valid acceptance (*Williams v Carwardine*).

- If a person does not know of an offer he cannot claim to have accepted it, even if he performs what appears to amount to an acceptance (*R v Clarke*).
- If it is clear that a person had forgotten about an offer, this may be considered the same as not having known about it (*R v Clarke*).

Acceptance via the post

Firstly, it should always be considered whether it is reasonable to use the post to accept an offer. Each case is different, but the following factors should be considered:

- Whether the offer was made by letter. If so, then it is usually acceptable to reply by letter, unless the offer specifically says that the post may not be used – see *Yates Building v Pulleyn* (see p. 23 above).
- Whether the offeror states that acceptance can be made by post, even though the offer may have been made in some other way.
- Whether previous negotiations, or 'course of dealings', between the parties have established that it is normal to reply by post.

If one of these situations apply, then it will generally be considered reasonable to accept by post. On the other hand, if the offer has been made in some other, more direct way, for example by telephone, by word of mouth, or in some other form indicating a fast reply, then postal acceptance would not normally be considered reasonable, unless the offeror says so. Also, it would not be reasonable to post an acceptance if the offeree knows that postal delays are likely through strikes, floods, etc. Cases will clearly depend on their own facts, as each will be slightly different, but one example came before the court in the following case.

Henthorn v Fraser (1891)
An offer was made in person, but it was held reasonable to accept by post, given that the two parties worked in Liverpool, but one lived in Birkenhead, and a reply in person would have involved travelling, including a return ferry-trip across the river Mersey. It was said by Lord Herschell that use of the post would be reasonable where 'it must have been within the contemplation of the parties that, according to the ordinary usages of mankind, the post might be used as a means of communicating the acceptance of an offer'. So it is important to establish whether acceptance by post is reasonable in a particular case, because the postal rule will then apply.

The postal rule

Acceptance by post is effective as soon as it is posted.

This is an attempt to solve the problem of balancing the offeror's need to know whether he is bound, and the offeree's need to know that he has done what is needed to accept an offer. The following case was the first example of its use.

Adams v Lindsell (1818)
The defendants wrote offering to sell to the plaintiffs some fleeces of wool, asking for a reply 'in course of post'. The letter containing the offer was misdirected, and late in arriving, but when it did arrive the plaintiffs posted an immediate acceptance back to the defendants. However, when no reply was received by the expected time, the plaintiffs sold the wool to someone else. It was held that a valid acceptance had been made when the plaintiffs posted their reply, leaving the defendants in breach of contract. This seems particularly harsh on the defendants (although they did misdirect their letter in the first place).

Consider the position of the plaintiffs if they had not misdirected their letter. Are parties generally aware of the consequences of entering into postal negoatiations? is the postal rule a fair rule?

The fact remains that one party or another has to bear the burden of the delay in a letter of acceptance taking some time if sent by post. The court takes the view that the postal rule is reasonable since it is the offeror who starts negotiations, and therefore can bear the responsibility of this delay. The offeror could, if needed, follow up the offer with an enquiry by a faster means. The postal rule is essentially one of convenience, and it is easier to prove posting than to prove receipt of a letter. However, it has been applied fairly rigidly, at times operating harshly in favour of the offeree. In *Household Fire Insurance v Grant* (1879) a letter of acceptance was lost in the post and never arrived, but the court still held the acceptance binding. What if a letter of acceptance is posted but is wrongly addressed? There is no English case law exactly on this point, but it would seem logical that the postal rule would not then apply, acceptance in these circumstances being effective when it is received by the offeror. It was held in the case of *Re London and Northern Bank* (1900) that a letter is posted when it is correctly addressed and stamped, and placed into an official post-box or into the care of a person authorised to receive mail.

More recently, decisions in this area of law show that the courts do acknowledge that the postal 'rule' is a rule of convenience, rather than fixed law. In the case of *Holwell v Hughes* (1974) it was held that where an offer requested 'notice in writing', the postal rule did not apply, because it was obviously important to the offeror to receive communication of acceptance in writing in front of him. In such cases a person who specifically asks for receipt of the acceptance would want it on a piece of paper, not (perhaps) in a distant post-box.

Another example of this is to be found in the recent case of *Pretty Pictures v Quixote Films* (2003) where the parties envisaged a signed written contract forming acceptance. The sending of an e-mail was not, therefore, enough in this case to form a contract.

It should be noted, then, regarding acceptance, that:

- Acceptance generally should be communicated to be valid (this applies to communications in person and telephone calls).
- The postal rule is an exception to this general rule.
- An offeror is always free to say specifically that the postal rule will not operate in a particular contract (or in some other words which lead to the same conclusion, as in *Holwell v Hughes*).

Other methods of communicating acceptance

> How will other methods of communication be viewed by the courts? Should they, too, be subject to the postal rule, or does communication need to be received?

Ways of informing a person of acceptance now abound, but case law is surprisingly thin in this area. Apart from the post and telephone, acceptances by telegram and telex have been the subject of decided cases.

Telegrams and telex

Telegrams were the method of communication in *Cowan v O'Connor* (1888). These are treated in the same way as letters. This is probably because a telegram has several features in common with a letter.

It is a third party (the Post Office) who take the responsibility of delivering them, not the sender (as with letters). They are faster than letters, but not instantaneous, and there is no acknowledgement of receipt.

Telex enables a message to be dispatched from an office by a teleprinter, operated like a typewriter, with special codes, using a modem and the telephone system, and almost instantaneously received in another office, even abroad. Because it is virtually instantaneous, it was held in the case of *Entores* (see p. 23 above) that telex should be treated like a telephone call, in that the communication has to be received for acceptance to be valid. Again, some similarity can be found between the two, since a telex is relatively instantaneous, receipt is acknowledged and the message is not entrusted to a third party (apart from its travel along telephone lines). This Court of Appeal decision was upheld by the House of Lords in *Brinkibon Ltd v Stahag Stahl* (1982). The outcome is reasonable in the light of the examples given in *Entores* as it is immediately obvious to the sender of a telex when something has gone wrong, so it should be the duty of the sender to try again to ensure that the message is correctly received.

Other modern methods of communication

Modern methods of communication obviously present a problem legally. So far we have decided cases concerning letters (*Adams v Lindsell,* etc.), telegrams (*Cowan v O'Connor*) and telex (*Entores* and *Brinkibon*). However, technology is developing fast, and it is quite common now to communicate by, for example, fax, computer modems, e-mail, text messages on mobile telephones and pagers, and courier services. It is difficult to predict exactly how these would be viewed by the courts as fitting in with existing principles of offer and acceptance, but a pattern of reasoning does seem to emerge.

Certain methods may treated as letters. This will apply to telegrams. Providing it is reasonable to communicate in this way, and a reply in writing is not specifically requested, the postal rule will apply. It would seem reasonable to suggest that a reply by courier might also come within this category, since it is handed over to a third party for delivery, and there is some time delay (which is the chief reason for devising the postal rule).

Other methods may be treated as telephone calls. This will apply to telex. Because of the almost instantaneous reply, these must be communicated. It would seem reasonable to suggest that fax, computer modems and e-mail might come within this category, as they, too, can result in an almost instantaneous communication with acknowledgement of receipt.

In summary, the following guidelines might be applied to a modern method of communicating to try to decide which approach may be appropriate:

- Is the method relatively instantaneous?
- Is the communication entrusted to a third party for delivery?
- Is there acknowledgement of receipt?

You could now apply the above principles to each of the various modern methods of communication with which you are familiar, to see if it should be treated like a letter or like a telephone call.

When is acceptance 'received'?

On top of all the other problems with acceptance, we have further difficulties with actual receipt of so many different methods of communicating. If, for example, a telephone message is left on an answering machine, is it received at that point, or when the owner of the telephone eventually plays back the machine and listens to the message? What about a fax or telex machine, or an e-mail account, which can also take messages during the whole of the night and day, and is often set up specifically for that reason, especially in companies who have international contacts?

Cheshire and Fifoot, the authors of a leading textbook on contract law, suggest that, at least in a business context, it is reasonable to assume that a letter which arrives in office hours is 'received' when it arrives, whether or not it is opened immediately. The issue was discussed in *The Brimnes* (1974) where it was suggested (*obiter*) that it is the responsibility of the recipient to look for messages which are delivered during normal office hours.

Recall of acceptance

One point which sometimes arises regarding postal acceptance, and on which there is no direct authority, is whether an offeree can recall his acceptance (for example, by telephone or telegram) after he has posted it, but before it reaches the offeror. According to the postal rule, acceptance takes place as soon as the letter is posted, making a valid contract. It would appear that the offeror cannot then go back and attempt to withdraw, even if it is by a speedier method. However, it is also true to say that allowing withdrawal of acceptance would not at this stage disadvantage the offeror (see comments in *Yates Building v Pulley*n) since he does not know of it.

The Scottish case *Countess of Dunmore v Alexander* (1830) seems to indicate that a postal acceptance may be retracted by a faster method of communication. However, in the South African case of *A to Z Bazaars v Minister of Agriculture* (1974) it was held that such an attempt was not effective.

Certainty in a contract

The terms of a contract must not be vague and the law does try to bring together the intentions of parties, so there must be agreement over the central, core, issues of a bargain. The following three cases relate to this point.

Guthing v Lynn (1831)
A promise to pay more money to the seller of a horse if it proved to be 'lucky' to the buyer was held to be too vague to be legally enforceable.

Scammell v Ouston (1941)
It was held that the expression 'on hire purchase' alone was uncertain. Hire purchase varies between suppliers and it was impossible to decide what the parties had actually agreed. If, however, the central issues of a contract are clear, a court may overlook minor vague or uncertain terms. They did so in the following case.

Nicolene v Simmonds (1953)
The plaintiff ordered some iron bars at a definite price from the defendant. He wrote 'I assume that we are in agreement and the usual conditions of acceptance apply.' A dispute arose over the quality of the iron and the defendant argued that there was no enforceable contract because the words 'usual conditions of acceptance' were too vague. It was held that the words were vague and meaningless, but as they involved a subsidiary matter, all main points being agreed, they could be ignored.

Auction sales

The advertisement of an auction is not an offer to hold it, but an invitation to treat. The court stated in *Harris v Nickerson* that the advert was merely an invitation to prospective buyers to come and make bids at an auction if it was held.

Harris v Nickerson (1873)
A buyer travelled to an auction sale only to find that the goods which he wanted had been withdrawn from sale. He sued for his costs of travelling to the auction, but failed, since there was no contract to hold the sale or to have individual items for sale on the day. This is no more than an advertisement for a sale which is to take place in a shop.

The display of goods and the auctioneer's request for bids at the beginning of an auction is not an offer, but an invitation for bids from prospective buyers. This could be likened to a shop window (the 'window display' of the auctioneer). The bids themselves are the offers, each bidder making an offer to buy which is accepted by the auctioneer bringing down his hammer. The contract then formed is between the bidder and the owner of the goods, who is simply making use of the services of the auctioneer. Until the hammer comes down the bidder is free to retract his bid, and the auctioneer is also free to withdraw an item from the sale.

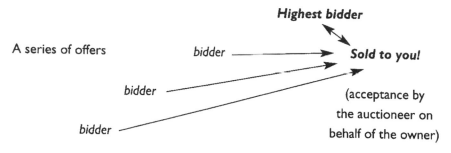

Figure 2.5

The principles of sale by auction were clearly stated by the court in *Payne v Cave* (1789) and the case law principles were restated by statute in the Sale of Goods Act 1979 s.57(2). The law of selling by auction is really an application of the normal rules of offer and acceptance, in a shopping situation. The following, then, are the rules:

- *The display of goods and the auctioneer's call for bids are an invitation to treat.*
- *The bids themselves are a series of offers, the eventual highest bona fide (genuine) bid forming the offer which stands.*
- *The fall of the auctioneer's hammer (or some other customary sign) is the acceptance.*
- *The contract is between the highest bidder and the owner of the goods, the auctioneer acting on behalf of the seller.*
- *Until the fall of the hammer a bidder is free to withdraw a bid – this is really revocation of an offer before acceptance.*

Auctions (and individual items) advertised 'without reserve'

This is where there is no minimum (reserve) price on the articles for sale, so the auctioneer will accept the highest *bona fide* (genuine) bid. There is really a second, or collateral, contract between the auctioneer and the bidders, that whoever becomes the highest *bona fide* bidder will be entitled to the goods, whatever the highest bid may be. What if the auctioneer does not accept this bid?

Warlow v Harrison (1859)
In an auction without reserve the highest bidder for a horse turned out to be its owner. He was not, therefore, the highest *bona fide* bidder as the owner of goods is not allowed to bid unless this is declared at the beginning of the sale. The case failed on a technicality, but the court laid down (*obiter*) the principles of the separate, or collateral, contract.

▶

The main contract (if one is made) is between the highest bidder and the owner of the item, but there is a second contract between the auctioneer and the highest *bona fide* bidder.

Barry v Davies (2000)
The auctioneer withdrew two machines, worth £14,000 each, from a sale advertised 'without reserve', refusing to accept a bid of £200 each. The bidder sued on the collateral contract and was awarded damages of £27,600.

In an auction without reserve, then, acceptance of the auctioneer's offer to sell is made by becoming the highest bidder. The auctioneer is in breach of contract not to sell to that bidder. However, if the sale is cancelled altogether, he can not be sued (see *Harris v Nickerson*, on page 32).

It pleasing that the opportunity has arisen for the court to review the existing cases concerning questions, and in *Barry v Davies* it was said that the decision in *Warlow v Harrison*, although not technically binding on the court, was worthy of 'very great respect'.

Tenders

A tender is where goods are to be sold or work undertaken, and the person proposing it wants to investigate whether there are people prepared to buy the items or undertake the work. Tenders are invited which are then considered, and a buyer or a worker chosen from among the tenderers. Some principles emerge, again based on the normal rules of offer and acceptance, but modified to deal with the particular situation of tenders.

Single offer tenders

A statement that goods are to be sold by tender is not an offer for sale, and there is no obligation to sell to the person making the highest tender. It is, rather, an enquiry into the viability of a transaction. *Spencer v Harding* (1870) is an example of a single offer tender, where a sale takes place on one occasion. Those submitting tenders make offers, from which a tender may be selected and accepted, forming a contract. There is generally no obligation to choose the highest or lowest tender, or to accept any tender at all.

Standing offer tenders

Where goods or services are required on an ongoing basis, from time to time, as needed, tenders may be invited. These again amount to offers, which are known as standing offers. A tender is selected and then on each occasion when an order is placed this is an acceptance, forming a separate contract. This arose in the following case.

Great Northern Rail Co v Witham (1873)
Witham supplied coal to the rail company, in quantities and at times as required by the storemaster. It was held that Witham's tender was a standing offer, each delivery of coal formed a separate contract, and if Witham wanted to revoke the standing offer he could do so, providing it was before the next order was placed. If an order had been placed he was under an obligation to supply at the stated rate. While under the agreement, the tenderer must work or supply, as agreed, whenever required, but cannot insist on any orders at all.

A sole supplier clause is where the person inviting tenders agrees to take all requirements for particular goods or services from the tenderer. There is no obligation to place an order, but if an order is placed, it must be with the tenderer. The reason for being restricted in this way is usually financial, for example where there is an agreement to order from a particular supplier in return for a price reduction.

Try to find some examples of invitation to tender from your local newspaper's classified section.

Contracts for the sale of land

The sale of land generally is dealt with in the Law of Property Act 1925. However, much of this law involves the ordinary law of contract, and apart from statutory requirements, the courts will always be wary of reading into a situation any premature intention to be bound by the parties. This is probably due to the expense involved and the importance of the transaction. Often negotiations have been held to be simply supplying information about a possible contract (still to be negotiated).

Harvey v Facey (1893)
An enquiry was made as follows, 'Will you sell us Bumper Hall Pen? Telegraph lowest cash price, reply paid.' The reply was, 'Lowest price for Bumper Hall Pen £900.' The buyer then tried to accept, but the communications were held not to form an offer and acceptance, but merely to be preparatory negotiations.

Some non-standard situations

Multi-partite contracts

These arise where a number of people make identical agreements with one person – they may then be deemed to have made them with each other. In *Clarke v Dunraven* (1897), a yacht race was held where competitors entered by a letter to the yacht club secretary. In these letters each competitor agreed to abide by club rules, which included an obligation to pay all damages caused by fouling. The *Satanita* manoeuvred and sank the *Valkyrie*. Clarke, owner of the *Valkyrie*, sued Dunraven, owner of the *Satanita*, for damages. Dunraven claimed that he was not bound by any contract with Clarke, and therefore need not pay.

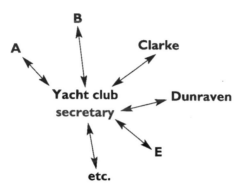

Figure 2.1

The House of Lords held Dunraven was bound by entering the race and making an individual agreement with club regarding each other compeititor. Each had accepted the rules on entry,and would be deemed to have made them regarding each other. Clarkes Claim was therefore upheld.

Do you think that this is a sensible decision? It is quite remarkable in the light of the theory which lies behind the law of contract. In the case, those who had entered the competition had not discussed any of the details of the contract with any other competitor, but were deemed to have made a contract with each of them.

Dealing with a machine

When dealing with a machine, it cannot really be possible for the customer to offer to buy and the machine to decide to accept! Therefore there has to be an exception to the normal shopping 'rules'. In such cases the owners of the machine are said to hold it in readiness for use, and thus form an offer. The buyer accepts by activating the machine in some way.

Thornton v Shoe Lane Parking (1971)
Mr Thornton parked his car at a car park which had an automatic barrier. He paid, took his ticket and parked his car. When he returned there was an accident in which he was injured and his car was damaged. He sued the car park owners, and they tried to rely on an exemption clause within the car park. It therefore became important to know the exact time at which the contract to use the car park took place. It was held that the car park owners were making an offer by having the car park ready, and holding the machine in readiness for use. The customer made an acceptance by using the machine – here by taking a ticket and paying.

This set the scene for much of today's dealings with vending machines. If a case involving one of these machines were to arise, it would no doubt be viewed that the company that owns the machine makes an offer to sell, which is accepted by the customer activating the machine in some way. This is the point of no return, and must therefore be the point at which the contract takes place.

Apply this case to a vending machine which you know, or a local car park system.

Promotional campaigns and collateral contracts

The idea of a second, or collateral, contract arose regarding auctions sales. It was also an important issue in the following case regarding a promotional campaign.

Esso v Commissioners of Customs and Excise (1976)
The case concerned the giving of 'free' coins with petrol, as part of a sales promotion by Esso in 1970. The Commissioners were responsible for collecting purchase tax (the forerunner of VAT), and they claimed that Esso were liable for unpaid purchase tax in respect of a promotional campaign where football World Cup coins were given away.

Following the win by England in the 1966 World Cup, Esso used the anticipation of the 1970 tournament to advantage in giving away almost worthless coins as collectors' items. Advertisements read, 'Going free at your Esso action station now – World Cup coins.' Motorists were thus encouraged to buy petrol from Esso stations, on the understanding that they would receive one 'free' coin for every four gallons of petrol purchased. The question arose as to whether the coins

▶

formed part of the contract of sale. If they did, then Esso would be liable for tax. If they did not, then the motorist may not be able to insist on a coin after having bought the petrol.

The House of Lords held by a majority of four to one that Esso were not liable for the tax, but the reasoning of the judges varied considerably.

- One judge thought that the coins passed under the contract of sale of petrol.
- Two judges thought that there was no legally binding contract at all concerning the coins.
- Two other judges thought that a binding collateral contact existed, whereby Esso promised that if motorists entered the premises and bought a certain quantity of petrol, a coin or coins would be transferred to them (one coin for four gallons). This was quite separate from any contract of sale (i.e. a specific quantity of petrol for the exact price).

Although the last view was a minority view on the formation of the contract, it is the view which is probably held by most judges today. The following principles therefore emerge from the case:

- The giving away of a promotional 'free' item is likely to form a collateral contract, in which the petrol company (or other seller) makes a general offer – here it was stated that if a customer used this garage and bought four gallons of petrol a coin would be given.
- This stands beside the main contract of sale, which is a certain quantity of petrol for a sum of money.
- There was legal intent (see later) despite the trivial nature of the coin. There is therefore a contract in which the customer can insist on a coin if four gallons of petrol have been purchased.
- The consideration (see later) for the coin was the purchase of four gallons of petrol.

This case applies many of the principles dealt with in this chapter, in a particular way. It is an important case, since promotional campaigns are numerous, many of them working on a similar basis to the Esso campaign. It was obviously important to the Commissioners to know where they stood over the tax issue, but it could be equally important to customers to know their position over apparently 'free' promotional goods. The goods could be more valuable, and a binding contract over then would then become important. The case is also an indication of a willingness to look at the modern commercial environment and the position of the consumer, and sets a pattern for present-day trading.

Distance trading – contracts made when the parties are not face to face

If the two parties to a contract, particularly one dealing with the sale of goods, are not dealing with each other face to face, the buyer could be at a disadvantage in not seeing the goods described by the seller. Two businesses dealing in this way could be thought to have enough resources to deal with this situation – it is in effect a business risk, and the buyer should take precautions such as asking for a sample, or later rely on remedies such as damages for breach of contract.

A consumer in a similar position is vulnerable and, following a European directive, new statutory protection now exists. *The Consumer Protection (Distance Selling) Regulations 2000* are now in force, and although they have not yet been widely used, and therefore will need some interpretation, they represent a great step forward in updating the law of Contract to cover modern methods of trading. The Regulations affect those who sell good or services to consumers (not where a business deals with a business) and apply where the sale takes place in one of the following ways:

- by telephone
- by fax
- by mail order or catalogue shopping
- over the internet
- using digital television services.

Under the Regulations the seller must give the consumer clear information about the good or services offered before the sale takes place and must give written confirmation after the sale. The consumer then has a 'cooling off' period of seven working days. This means that if the consumer changes their mind during that time, they can cancel the contract without it amounting to a breach. The Regulations do not apply to some contracts, including:

- the sale of land
- sales from a vending machine
- public pay telephones
- auction sales.

There are also partial exemptions, particularly in the areas of transport, accommodation and catering, and the right to cancel does not apply to some goods, such as perishable goods, newspapers, magazines, unsealed audio or video recordings or computer software, personalised goods, goods that by their nature cannot be returned.

Electronic trading

In addition to the difficulties which dealing at a distance may cause, trading by electronic methods (most commonly by computers over the internet) may pose further problems because of the speed and method by which the transactions take place, the facility to authorise transactions automatically which would possibly amount to acceptance, and the location of the parties. Apart from the regulations on distance trading discussed above, a further set of regulations now exists, *The Electronic Commerce (E C Directive) Regulations* 2002.

The regulations apply again to the consumer dealing with a business but also between businesses, and address such issues as broad principles of contracting electronically, online shopping, access to data, newspapers, professional services and entertainment online. According to the Department of Trade and Industry guidelines, the regulations are intended to ensure that the European Union 'reaps the full benefits of e-commerce by boosting consumer confidence and giving providers of information society services legal certainty, without excessive red tape'.

The Regulations do not change the basic common-law rules on offer and acceptance but build on them, so the principles still need to be established clearly. Is an on-line display of goods an invitation to treat or an offer? The traditional 'shopping' situation in English law would indicate that a website display is an invitation to treat, and this is in line with both case law and with Regulation 12 of the Electronic Commerce (EC Directive) Regulations 2002 which says that the customer's order *may* be the offer. However, the position is not at all clear. Wrongly priced items will present particular problems, as can be seen in the difficult situation that Argos faced when advertising Sony televisions for £3 instead of £300 in September 1999. As soon as the mistake was noticed Argos contacted customers who had tried to place an order. However, some customers had placed orders and had received confirmation. Argos argued that they had been mistaken over the price and that this should have been clear to customers – see the case in mistake of *Hartog v Colin and Shields* (p.191).

The importance of uniformity of trading principles and the need for fair dealings is clear, so the move towards this should be welcomed. However, the regulations use words that will certainly need interpretation by the courts to provide definition, such as the requirement to provide electronic acknowledgement of receipt of an order 'without undue delay' and the need to provide 'appropriate, effective and accessible technical means' to correct input errors before placing an order. An important aspect of the regulations is that they do not stipulate the way in which contracts are formed, only the principles of fairness on which they will are based. This means that the common law principles remain vital and will need further extension, by analogy, to apply to modern methods of trading.

You can find out more about the regulations on the internet at the Department of Trade and Industry website at http://www.dti.gov.uk

Summary

Offer

Definition: An expression of willingness to contract on certain terms, made with the intention that it shall become binding as soon as it is accepted by the person to whom it is addressed. Sometimes difficult to identify – *Gibson v Manchester City Council*.

An offer is further divided into two kinds:

- Specific: made to one person or group of people.
- General: made to 'the whole world' (people generally) – *Carlill v Carbolic Smoke Ball Company*.

  An offer may also be:
- Express, either verbal or written.
- Implied, by conduct or circumstances – *Wilkie v London Passenger Transport Board*.
- Distinguish between an offer, which is capable of acceptance, and an invitation to treat, which is an invitation to others to make or negotiate an offer. This is followed in the usual shopping situation by the customer making an offer, and the seller making an acceptance in some way. Examples include:
- Shop windows – *Fisher v Bell*.
- Supermarket displays – *Pharmaceutical Society of Great Britain v Boots Cash Chemists Ltd*.
- Small advertisements – *Partridge v Crittenden*. However, there are exceptions, for example *Lefkowitz v Great Minneapolis Surplus Stores*, *Wilkie v London Passenger Transport Board*.

Termination of an offer

An offer may terminate in various ways:

- Acceptance: the offer is then no longer available to anyone else.
- Refusal: the offer ends, so it cannot be accepted later by the offeree.
- Counter-offer: a new proposal from the other party – *Hyde v Wrench*; battle of forms – *Butler Machine Tool Co Ltd v Ex-Cell-O Corp (England) Ltd*; request for further information – *Stevenson v McLean*.

- Lapse of time: either a specific time or a 'reasonable time' – *Ramsgate Hotel v Montefiore*.
- Death: sometimes leaves an offer impossible to complete, but in other circumstances it may remain open for acceptance by the estate of the deceased offeror – *Bradbury v Morgan*.
- Revocation: the withdrawal of an offer before acceptance – *Byrne v Van Tienhoven*; via a third party – *Dickinson v Dodds*; in unilateral contracts – *Shuey v US*; continuing act of acceptance – *Errington v Errington*.
- Failure of a precondition: non-fulfilment of an important term – *Financings Ltd v Stimson*.

Acceptance

Definition of acceptance: Agreement to all the terms of an offer by words or conduct. Sometimes difficult to identify – *Brogden v Metropolitan Rail Co, Trentham v Archital Luxfer*.

Acceptance must be communicated, and this raises various issues:

- Prescribed method – *Yates Building v Pulleyn*.
- No prescribed method – *Entores Ltd v Miles Far East Corporation*.
- Waiver – *Carlill v Carbolic Smoke Ball Company*.
- Silence – *Felthouse v Bindley*, Unsolicited Goods and Services Act 1971.
- Ignorance of an offer ('reward' cases) – *Williams v Carwardine, R v Clarke*.
- Acceptance via the post: when reasonable to use the post – *Henthorn v Fraser*; when not overruled by the parties – *Holwell v Hughes*.
- The postal rule – *Adams v Lindsell, Household Fire Insurance v Grant, London and Northern Bank*.
- Telegrams – *Cowan v O'Connor*.
- Telex – *Entores Ltd v Miles Far East Corporation, Brinkibon Ltd v Stahag Stahl. Offer and acceptance*
- More modern methods of communicating: consider whether a method is instantaneous, via a third party and acknowledged.
- Receipt of acceptance – *The Brimnes*.
- Recall of acceptance – comments in *Yates Building v Pulleyn*.

Certainty in a contract

The terms of a contract must not be vague – *Guthing v Lynn, Scammell v Ouston, Nicolene v Simmonds*.

Auction sales

The display of goods in an invitation to treat, the bidders make the offer and the auctioneer accepts on behalf of the seller – *Harris v Nickerson*, *Payne v Cave*, Sale of Goods Act 1979 s.57(2). Auctions 'without reserve' – *Warlow v Harrison*.

Tenders

Offers are made by tenderers, and may be accepted by the party inviting the tenders – *Spencer v Harding*, *Great Northern Rail Co v Witham*.

The sale of land

This generally needs to be evidenced in writing, and the courts tend not to infer an offer as readily as with other sales – *Harvey v Facey*. Although based generally on contract law, the area is largely regulated by Law of Property Act 1925.

Non-standard situations

There are some situations which do not fit into the 'normal' picture of offer and acceptance, but where a contract has clearly taken place.

- Multi-partite contracts: where parties making identical contracts with one person are deemed to have contracted with each other – *Clarke v Dunraven*.
- Dealing with a machine, such as a vending machine or an automatic car park barrier. The offer is said to be made by 'holding the machine in readiness for use' – *Thornton v Shoe Lane Parking Ltd*.
- Promotional campaigns and collateral contracts. Often a general offer is made to give a 'free' item if a customer forms a contract of sale – *Esso v Commissioners of Customs and Excise*.

Distance trading and electronic trading

See *The Consumer Protection (Distance Selling) Regulations* 2000 for situations where the parties are not face to face, e.g. when dealing by telephone, mail order, catalogue selling or the internet. Note that for these regulations to apply trading is not done necessarily using electronic means but sometimes can include this.

See *The Electronic Commerce (E C Directive) Regulations* 2002 for situations where selling takes place by electronic means, e.g. over the internet or interactive television service.

Questions

1 Petunia wants to buy a new washing-machine, and notices the following promotional campaign in the window of a shop called Washwell, 'One Smartlook iron free of charge to any customer purchasing a Quickwash washing-machine priced at £250 or more.'

Petunia sees that the Quickwash machine is quite expensive at Washwell, but decides that the inclusion of a free iron makes it a good bargain. She therefore decides to buy a washing-machine under the promotion, but when she pays for it, the shop assistant explains that the last Smartlook iron has been given away that morning and that there are no more available at present.

On the way out of the shop Petunia sees a poster which states 'A free watch will be given to anyone spending more than £50 in our store today'. Petunia returns to the cashier to claim her watch, and is told that she should have asked before she bought the washing-machine.

Advise Petunia regarding both the iron and the watch.

2 Enrico was selected as a potential new member of a book club, Bookworms. He received a letter, addressed to him personally, stating that he had been chosen from people in the area to be given the opportunity to buy discount books direct from the supplier. The terms were that he needed only to buy one book per month from a 'large list of titles', and that the price would be 'significantly lower' than bookshops could meet. Enrico agreed to join Bookworms, but was very disappointed when the first list only contained twelve titles, none of which appealed to him. He decided to order one, however, as a gift for his sister. The following week he saw the same book in a local store at £5 less than he had paid for it.

   (a) Has a contract been formed between Enrico and Bookworms? If so, discuss whether it has been broken by either party. If this is the case, what remedies might be available.

   (b) Assuming a contract has been formed, explain how the courts will determine what the terms of the contract might be.

   (c) Consider what change(s) should be made to the 'rules' relating to the formation of a contract and explain why you think this is needed.

3 Aman, a car dealer, has a number of conversations with clients in his showroom.

   Bert states that he wishes to buy a particular Candida car on display in the showroom at £10,000, but Aman says that he could not sell it for less than £10,500. Aman says no more to Bert, but Bert assumes that the car is his for £10,500.

   Aman offers to sell a Delissimo car to Emma for £15,000 and says that she can let him know by Friday if she wants the car. On Thursday afternoon Fred pays Aman £20,000 for the same car. Emma sends Aman an E-mail on Friday to say that she wants the car.

   Aman makes an offer to sell a Grandino car, priced £22,000 to Harry who says he will think about it. Harry posts a letter to Aman the same day to say that he does want the car. Later that day Harry changes his mind and sends a fax message to Aman to say that he no longer wishes to buy the car after all.

   Consider whether Aman has made binding contracts with Bert, Emma, Fred, and Harry.

OCR 2003

4 Alex browses through a mail order catalogue of a company called Bestbuy, and is attracted by a picture of a sheepskin coat priced at £120. Alex telephones Bestbuy and orders a coat. When the parcel containing the coat arrives, Alex finds that a jumper has also been enclosed, with a letter explaining that this is 'in the hope that the client will wish to take advantage of this opportunity to purchase the jumper as the offer of the month' at a bargain price. Alex does not want the jumper.

On examining the coat Alex is dismayed to find that the sheepskin is not of the quality expected, being a darker colour than it seemed from the picture in the catalogue. Alex does not wish to keep the coat.

In desperation, needing a coat immediately, Alex visits a local clothes shop, Cuteclothes, where there is a similar coat in the window priced at £145. Alex wishes to buy the coat, but is informed that the price ticket is wrong and that the coat actually costs £160. Alex leaves the shop to seek advice.

Advise Alex as to his position in all three situations.

OCR 2004

5 Logan, a shoe manufacturer, notices an advertisement for equipment to be sold by auction. At the auction Logan finds that the item in which he is interested has been withdrawn from sale. He is angry at having wasted his time and money on this journey. Logan then places an order with Manesh via the internet on 2 May for a quantity of leather. Manesh only sees the order on 11 May. Manesh replies by e-mail immediately, agreeing to supply the leather. However, before Logan receives the e-mail he places an order for the leather with another firm. On 17 May Manesh delivers the leather and requests payment.

Nigel, an engineer, says that he will service some machines for Logan for £300, but Logan rejects this. However, finding that other engineers charge even more, Logan later contacts Nigel, claiming to accept his offer to do the work for £300. Nigel states that he is now fully booked and cannot now service the machines.

Apply the principles of offer and acceptance to each of these situations.

OCR 4-module specimen paper

6 Critically analyse the importance of making a valid offer in forming a contract.

7 'The current law on offer and acceptance establishes exactly when, where and how a contract is made, while at the same time supporting the principles of freedom to contract.'

Discuss the ways in which this law is put into practice through the 'rules' of offer and acceptance.

OCR 2007

8 'Just a person is free to form an offer in any way he chooses, he is also free to withdraw it.'

Critically evaluate the ways in which an offer to form a contract may be brought to an end.

OCR 2002

9 Consider whether the principles of acceptance are adequate to regulate the communication systems of a modern society.

A further 'dilemma' style question on offer and acceptance can be found in Part 7 of the book.

3   Consideration

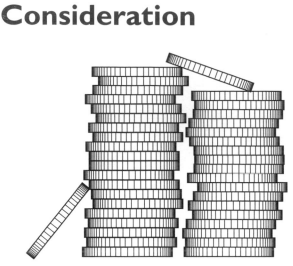

Is this a fair bargain?

All contracts require something to be given in return for something else from the other party. That 'something' is called consideration and each party to a contract must supply consideration for the contract to be valid. This is the bargaining element of a contract, where something is to be gained on each side. A classic definition of consideration, in terms of benefit and detriment (the opposite of benefit, where something is given up), was given by Lush J in *Currie v Misa* (1875), when he said:

> A valuable consideration may consist either in some right, interest, profit or benefit accruing to one party, or some forbearance, detriment, loss or responsibility given, suffered or undertaken by the other.

It is perhaps easier to think of consideration as the price paid for the contract, and this certainly fits in with the commercial concept of bargaining and gain. The House of Lords adopted Pollock's definition of consideration in *Dunlop v Selfridge* (1915):

An act or forbearance of one party, or the promise thereof, is the price for which the promise of the other is bought.

So, if A agrees to dig B's garden for £5, A's promise to dig is the price paid for B's promise to pay £5.

If I buy a kilo of potatoes for 50 pence, the potatoes are the seller's consideration, and the 50 pence is my consideration. If, however, I ask for two sacks of potatoes, to be paid for when the potatoes are delivered on Friday, what is the consideration on each side?

Executed and executory consideration

Consideration can take the form of an act or a promise, and is said to be executed, which is when the act of transfer of goods has been carried out, or executory, when a party has made a promise, but it has not yet been carried out. In the above example, A and B have both yet to fulfil their promises when the contract is made, so the consideration from both parties is executory. If C offers £20 for the return of her lost diamond ring, and D returns it in response to the offer, D's consideration would be executed, because his side of the bargain would be completed. Whether the consideration is in the form of goods which have been handed over, or is merely a promise to do something (and therefore executory), does not affect its validity. A contract based on promises is just as binding as one based on immediate delivery.

Consideration must be sufficient but need not be adequate

The words sufficient and adequate, although having very similar meanings in everyday language, have rather different meanings when applied to consideration, and should be learned (see below). For consideration to be considered sufficient, it must be of some value to the other party, however slight or trivial. If a pen is offered in exchange for a new Porsche car, however unlikely, if it is meant seriously, then that is sufficient in the eyes of the law. There is something which is of some value on each side of the bargain, and the courts do not concern themselves with the market price, or adequacy, of the bargain. This supports the idea of freedom to contract, leaving parties to make their own bargains, whether in their favour or not. The following case is the usual authority for the court's requirement of sufficiency.

Thomas v Thomas (1842)
A husband wanted his wife, when he died, to have the right to live in the house owned by him, so he formed a contract under which she paid £1 per year rent. This was held to be sufficient consideration to enforce the agreement, even though it was clearly not adequate, as it was far below the market value.

Two interesting cases follow which illustrate sufficiency and adequacy of consideration.

Bainbridge v Firmstone (1838)
The need arose to know the weight of some boilers. It was agreed that if the boilers were taken away for weighing, they would be returned in good condition. On return they were damaged, and it was held that payment

▶

should be made for this. In the contract, then, the consideration on one side was the benefit of weighing boilers, and on the other, the entitlement to having them returned in good condition. It can be seen that the benefit of weighing boilers has no real market value, but is acceptable to the courts as consideration because it is recognisable.

Chappell v Nestlé (1960)
This case went to court concerning the issue of whether Nestlé should pay Chappell royalties on records given away in exchange for chocolate wrappers (plus money for post and packing). It was held that the chocolate wrappers and the money were consideration for the record. Given the right circumstances, therefore, the chocolate wrappers alone could be valid consideration. These are obviously not adequate, having no intrinsic value (it was established in evidence that they were thrown away after receipt), but formed sufficient consideration.

Edmonds v Lawson (2000)
The agreement of a pupil barrister 'to enter into the close, important and potentially very productive relationship which pupillage involves' was held to be good consideration.

So consideration need not be adequate (generous enough to appear a fair bargain in terms of monetary value), but must be sufficient (of enough recognisable value to satisfy the courts). This is probably the most important aspect of consideration, and underpins the other 'rules' which have been developed by the courts through case law.

> Think about who 'won' in these cases. With whom do you think the court's sympathy would lie in each case?

Consideration must not be vague

While it is not necessary to be able to specify the exact value of consideration, it must be something tangible, or discernible, to be of value in law.

White v Bluett (1853)
A son's promise to cease his complaints about the distribution of his father's estate was held to be too vague to form valid consideration.

> Again, with whom do you think that the court would have sympathy here?

Consideration must move from the promisee

For a contract to be enforceable, the bargain must have been made, and the consideration provided, by the two parties involved. That is, they must have made the offer and acceptance, and they must have provided the consideration. So if A pays B £50 and B agrees to cut C's lawn, C cannot sue A. C has not provided any consideration. This is usually a three-sided matter, and a similar situation arose in the following case.

> *Tweddle v Atkinson* (1861)
> A sum of money was promised to a son and daughter-in-law on marriage. Tweddle senior paid his share but later died. The father-in-law had not given his money, so the son, Tweddle junior, sued for the agreed amount. It was held that as the son had not given any consideration for the promise of the money, the contract being between the two fathers, he could not enforce the agreement. The only person who could have enforced the agreement would have been Tweddle senior, had he been alive.

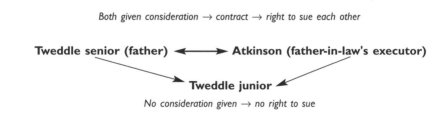

Figure 3.1

It will be seen later that this principle is very closely linked with the traditional concept of privity of contract (only those who are party to a contract can sue on it). However, this position may now be different with the introduction of the Contracts (Rights of Third Parties) Act 1999, and the implication is that the benefit of a contract may now be enforceable by a party who has provided no consideration at all, if it is made very clear that the benefit was intended for that particular person.

Past consideration

The consideration provided for a promise must be done in relation to that promise. In other words, it must be an act or promise done directly in return for the promise of the other party, and not something already completed. If the thing that is to be consideration has already been performed before the promise is made, then in the eyes of the law it will not be consideration at all.

Roscorla v Thomas (1842)
The sale of a horse had taken place, the horse being exchanged for money in the usual way. Some time after the sale, the seller told the buyer that the horse was 'sound and free from vice'. It later became apparent that the horse was not as described, but vicious and unmanageable. The buyer argued that the assurances given by the seller that the horse was 'sound and free from vice' went with the price paid by the buyer. However, the court held that the assurances were given later and could not be connected to a price already paid for the horse. The payment had already taken place, and was therefore past consideration, and not valid.

It is perhaps easier to see the concept of past consideration in the following, more recent, case.

Re McArdle (1951)
Members of the McArdle family made alterations to a house to accommodate an elderly relative. After the work was completed, other members of the family visited and were so pleased with the alterations that they offered to pay those who had done the work. Some time later the money had not been handed over, so those who had done the work sued for the amount promised. It was held that they could not insist on payment because the work had been done before the promise of the money was made. It was therefore past consideration and not valid.

Does this decision bring about a just outcome for the family?

So, if the only act or promise which could be consideration is promised after the other party's act is executed, then there is no binding contract, because past consideration will not support a contract.

However, if an act is done at the request of the promisor, and it was understood all along that payment would be made eventually, or if it was an act for which payment could reasonably be implied, then consideration which is apparently past will be valid. This is well illustrated in the following seventeenth-century case.

Lampleigh v Braithwait (1615)
A pardon was obtained from the king for a friend who had killed someone. The friend was so delighted that he promised £100 for the trouble of obtaining the pardon. When this was not paid, it was held

that it could be enforced in court because, although the amount was stated after the pardon was obtained, it was expected all along that repayment of expenses would be made, and this could be seen as a setting of the level of repayment.

Was this amount a reasonable one for expenses (take into account the date of the case)?

The following, more recent, example arose in the context of the workplace. *Re Casey's Patents* (1892) Work was undertaken and afterwards, in lieu of payment, some shares in patents were promised. When they were not handed over it was held that this could be enforced by law because it was understood that payment would be given for work undertaken.

So, if a request of the promisor carries an implication that payment will be made for the act, the later promise can then be seen as just a fixing of the level of payment. This could easily arise where an employee is asked to undertake extra work. The exact amount may be settled when the work is finished, but it is obvious that they will not be working for nothing!

Forbearance to sue

Abandoning a legal claim against someone may be good consideration. In fact this is the basis upon which vast numbers of out-of-court settlements are made, and arises very often in practice. The following are examples of consideration arising from promises not to take a certain action.

Haigh v Brooks (1839)
A sum of money was to be paid in return for an agreement to abandon a legal claim under a guarantee. It was held that this was enforceable, even though there was some doubt over the validity of the guarantee. So giving up a right to sue can be sufficient consideration, even if that right is not certain, provided

- the claim had some chance of success, and
- the person had otherwise intended to enforce the claim.

R v Attorney General (2003)
A promise of a member of an SAS patrol not to disclose details of his work, e.g. in publishing the story of his experiences, was held to be good consideration for a promise by the Ministry of Defence not to return him to his original unit, with an associated reduction in pay.

Performance of an existing duty

Generally, doing something which is already an obligation is not sufficient consideration. The cases on this fall into two categories: those where an obligation already exists under the general law of the land, and those where a duty is owed to another under a contract.

Performance of an existing duty owed under the general law of the land

> *Collins v Godefroy* (1831)
> A lawyer was obliged to appear in court by witness order, but agreed with one party that they would pay him to give evidence. It was held that he was not entitled to enforce this payment, as it was something which he was already obliged to do by law, and merely doing that did not amount to valid consideration.

However, going beyond what is strictly required by law, and doing something extra to this existing duty, can be seen as valid consideration.

> *Glasbrook Bros v Glamorgan County Council* (1925)
> At the time of this case the County Council was the administrator of the local police force and had a legal duty to ensure the keeping of peace in the area. The Council had decided that following recent strikes and disturbances around coal mines in South Wales a mobile patrol of policemen would be sufficient to keep the peace. The owners of a particular coal mine requested a large patrol to be stationed at their mine. The Council agreed, but for a sum of money. This was held to be enforceable because the Council was going beyond their existing duty in supplying more policemen than was their legal obligation.
> This decision was applied to football matches in *Harris v Sheffield United* (1987) where it was held that a request for a police presence in order to hold a match safely would result in an obligation to pay for the service.

A more recent example is in the following case.

> *Ward v Byham* (1956)
> A single mother was promised by the father of her child a regular payment of £1 per week for the maintenance of the child provided that she kept the child 'well looked after and happy'. The child would later be able to choose whether to stay with the father or mother. There was

at that time a legal obligation on a mother to maintain her child (this is managed differently now). The father defaulted on the payments and the mother claimed that a contract existed for the payment. The father's consideration was obviously the promise of the money. The father argued that the mother had not given any consideration since she was already obliged to maintain the child by law. However, it was held that in keeping the child 'well looked after and happy' she was doing more than simply maintaining, which was the legal obligation. The payment of the money was therefore enforceable.

With which party, in this case, do you think the courts would have the greater sympathy?

Legally, this must be a borderline case, and shows that very little 'extra' is needed to make payment enforceable, if the court really want to hold a contract valid. In practice there must be little difference in clarity between keeping a child 'well looked after and happy' and 'ceasing complaints', which was rejected as consideration in the case seen earlier of *White v Bluett*, and it raises the question of what the courts are really looking for.

Performance of an existing contractual duty

If a person has already made a contract to do something, this same duty cannot generally be used again as consideration to the same person. Two shipping cases can be used to illustrate this.

Stilk v Myrick (1809)
Two sailors deserted ship during a journey to the Baltic. Eight of the sailors who were left agreed with the captain to share the wages of the deserters between them in exchange for sailing the ship shorthanded. On arrival at the port the money was not paid, so the sailors sued the captain. It was held that the sailors had done no more than their contractual duty already owed to the captain in their initial agreement to sail the ship.

There may again have been a certain amount of sympathy with the captain of a ship, trying to recruit sailors in difficult circumstances. However, the decision went the other way in the following case.

Hartley v Ponsonby (1857)
Here 17 sailors deserted ship out of a crew of 36, and out of those sailors left, only a few were experienced seamen. A similar agreement

▶

was made with the captain to share the wages of the deserters between the eight sailors remaining if the ship was sailed on dangerously short-handed. On return the payment was not made. This time it was held that the sailors had gone beyond their existing duty, and that the wages of the deserters should be paid to those remaining. It was suggested, by way of explanation, that what had happened was so fundamentally different from the original agreement that the initial contract had been discharged and a new one formed.

It is important to consider the impact of the following recent case on the existing doctrine.

Williams v Roffey (1990)
The defendant builders contracted with the plaintiff carpenters to do carpentry work on some flats. When the builders found that the carpenters were in financial difficulty, unable to obtain materials and labour, and unable to finish the work, they offered extra money to ensure that the work was completed on time according to the agreement. In turn, the builders thus avoided paying a penalty under a liquidated damages clause with the owner of the flats. The carpenters continued, but the builders did not pay, so the carpenters sued to recover the money promised in the new agreement. It was held that the carpenters should succeed, as the builders made a choice to pay them, to avoid the inconvenience of having to find new carpenters, and that they had avoided the disadvantage of having to pay a penalty to the owners of the building.

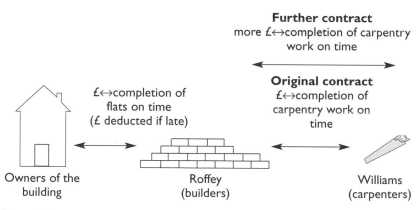

Figure 3.2

Owners of the Roffey Williams **building** (builders) (carpenters) *Figure 3.2* The case of *Williams v Roffey* has caused a huge amount of discussion in the legal world, mainly because, at least to some extent, it goes against the traditional requirement of consideration. The carpenters were due to complete the flats by a certain date in their original contract with the builders. They further bargained with the builders that they would complete by that date if more money was paid. So the carpenters could be seen to be doing no more than was their original duty, but using that to ask for more money. On the other hand, it could be argued that the builders had made a calculated choice in agreeing to pay the carpenters, and avoiding the extra payment to the owners was of practical and financial benefit to them. The case is certainly an example of the courts making a real effort to consider the commercial reality of the difficulties faced by the parties in financial crisis, and in the context of recession in their trade. However, there has been a decided unwillingness to extend the principle any further at present, and this was seen in *Re Selectmove* (1995) where the court refused to apply the arguments of *Roffey* to part payment of a debt. Following an arrangement to pay the Inland Revenue in instalments, a claim was made that interest should not be payable, as the Inland Revenue had the practical advantage of not having to go to any further trouble to recover the debt. This could be viewed at least in part as a policy decision since it involved payment to the Inland Revenue, not an individual. More recently the case of *Simon Container Machinery v Emba Machinery* (1998) followed the decision in *Roffey*, consideration being found in the practical benefit of avoiding the problems that would have been caused by the withdrawal of the other party from the contract.

Performance of an existing contractual duty owed to a third party

A promise by A to B, to do something which A is already obliged to do under a contract with a third party, C, can be good consideration.

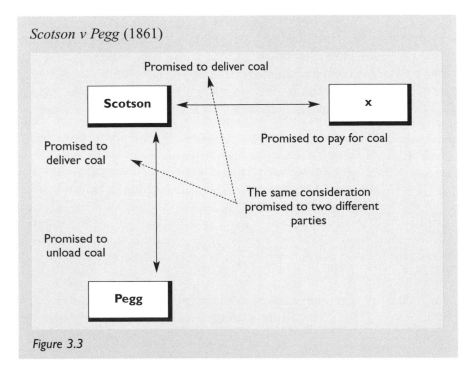

Figure 3.3

Scotson agreed to deliver a quantity of coal to a person, X, or to anyone nominated by X, in exchange for payment. X asked for the coal to be delivered to Pegg. Scotson then contacted Pegg and agreed to deliver the same quantity of coal, if Pegg could unload it. Pegg agreed, but when the coal was delivered he did not unload it. Scotson sued for this, and it was argued that his agreement with Pegg was not valid because he was offering exactly the same thing as consideration that he was obliged to do already under his contract with X. However, the court held that it was in order to offer the same consideration to two different parties, since if Scotson had not delivered the coal at all he would have run the risk of being sued twice, by Pegg and by X.

It is interesting that the argument in this case is only really viable if the consideration is executory. The mere performance of the act of delivering the coal may not alone have been sufficient consideration, because the defendant was obliged to do this anyway, but the promise of doing it to two parties imposed on him the possibility of being sued for breach of contract by two parties, and this was good consideration.

This argument was approved in the Privy Council case of *New Zealand Shipping Co v Satterthwaite* (1975), also known as *The Eurymedon* (another three-sided agreement involving stevedores), and was also accepted in principle in *Pao On v Lau Yiu Long* (1980).

Part-payment of a debt

It is clear then that consideration must normally be something beyond any existing obligation to the promisor, whether it be a duty owed under the law of the land or by a contractual arrangement. An extension of this is to say that paying part of a debt owed to someone, when it is due, is not satisfaction for the whole payment. This has become known as the rule in *Pinnel's Case*.

Pinnel's Case (1602)
A man called Cole owed Pinnel some money, and at request of Pinnel had paid him a lesser sum over one month early. Pinnel had at first said that this would end the debt, but then tried to sue for the rest. It was held that although in general a lesser sum did not satisfy the whole debt, earlier payment, at the request of the creditor, would do so, as would payment in a different place or in a different form.

The original rule was adopted and confirmed by the House of Lords case of *Foakes v Beer* (1884) where after a debt was paid following judgment, the creditor sued successfully for interest for late payment. This case was further confirmed in *Re Selectmove* (see p. 55) and *Ferguson v Davies* (1997).

The rule in *Pinnel's case*, then, still stands as good law, despite its antiquity. However, in the case itself, apart from the general rule, it was said that although just paying off less than the debt on the day due does not discharge the whole debt, the addition of something else to part of the money may do so. The following situations can therefore be regarded as exceptions to the general rule.

- *If, at the request of the creditor, something else is added to the payment.* This could arise if A owes B £200, and at B's request pays £100 together with a piece of jewellery that A likes. In the case it was suggested that an item such as 'the gift of a horse, hawk or robe'. may discharge the debt completely, provided that the other party is happy with the arrangement. The illustration is still relevant 400 years later. If someone owes some money, and the other party is happy to take part payment plus a car, hi-fi system or jacket belonging to the other instead of money, there is no reason why this should not be acknowledged as payment. It has already been established that the court do not insist on market value, so it is not relevant whether the article is an exact replacement for the sum of money outstanding.

> How far should the courts go along this line? We have seen that worthless chocolate wrappers can form good consideration. Would the same wrappers, or one small bar of chocolate, plus five pence, be satisfaction for a large original debt? Should it be? If so, why are the chocolate and five pence needed at all, since they are so trivial compared to a large debt?

- *If, at the creditor's request, the debtor pays a lesser sum before the date on which it is due.* This gives the creditor something 'extra' in terms of the time, so is regarded as good consideration. If C owes D £30, to be repaid on 15 December, but at D's request C repays £25 on 1 December in settlement, this will be regarded as ending the debt, and D will not be able to go back on the agreement and sue for the other £5.

- *If, at the request of the creditor, the method of payment is changed.* The payment may be made at a different place, or in a different form, for example if E owes F £100 to be paid at his office in London, and at F's request, E takes the money to F's home in Swindon. However, it has been held in *D and C Builders v Rees* (1965) that payment of a lesser amount by cheque rather than cash is not a great enough difference in method of payment to discharge the full debt.

- *Where there is a composition agreement with creditors.* If X is declared insolvent, and owes money to Tom, Dick and Harry, X clearly cannot repay them all in full. However, they may then agree to accept a proportion of the debts owed to them in settlement of their claims against X. This will be held binding in the courts, since if Tom, Dick and Harry have each made an agreement with X concerning each other, it would be a fraud on each other to go back on that and sue X. The situation is a little like the multipartite agreement in *Clarke v Dunraven* (see p. 36), although with this creditor's agreement Tom, Dick and Harry may have had input into exactly what is agreed regarding each other.

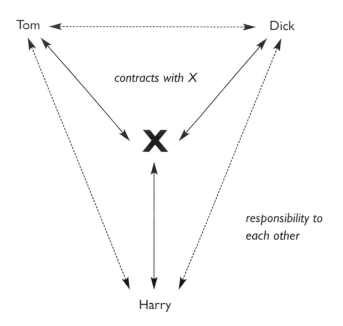

Figure 3.4

- ***Where payment of a lesser amount by a third party is accepted, the creditor cannot then sue the original debtor for the full amount.*** This arose in the case of *Hirachand Punamchand v Temple* (1911), where the plaintiff money lender agreed with Temple's uncle to accept a cheque in settlement of Temple's debt, even though the cheque was not for the full amount. The plaintiff was then unable to go back on his word and sue Temple for the rest. Again, in doing so, the plaintiff would have been in breach of the agreement with the uncle.

However it is clear from the more recent case of *Inland Revenue Commissioners v Fry* (2001) that there is not a strict rule concerning part payment by a third party. It is seen as a presumption that can be rebutted in appropriate circumstances. In this case a husband offered £10,000 instead of over £100,000 as a settlement of his wife's taxation 'in full and final settlement'. The Inland Revenue cashed the cheque and then asked for rest of the payment. The court allowed them to insist on the rest being paid and said that 'cashing a cheque gives rise to a rebuttable presumption of acceptance'.

In the case of *Bracken v Billinghurst* (2003) a builder was personally liable for debts. They were paid off by his company by sending a cheque for a lesser amount 'in full and final settlement' of the debt. The creditor then tried to enforce payment of balance, but like the moneylender in *Temple* was unsuccessful.

Promissory estoppel

The above exceptions to the rule in *Pinnel's Case* are all examples of accord and satisfaction. That is where agreement is reached over the discharge of the contract, both sides having provided consideration. A further, very important, exception to the principle is the doctrine of promissory estoppel. Estoppel is a procedure by which a court estops (or prevents) a person from saying something which they would otherwise be allowed to say. Promissory estoppel applies this procedure where a promise is made to excuse a party from contractual obligations, and where applying the law strictly may cause obvious injustice. The principle stems from the case of *High Trees*, where it was decided that where a promise was made to excuse a party from contractual obligations, with legal intent, and where it was both intended to be acted upon and was in fact acted upon, the promisor will be prevented from bringing evidence that there was no consideration.

Central London Property Trust v High Trees House (1947)
The plaintiff owners of a block of flats in London leased it to the defendant in 1937 for £2,500 per year, and the defendant in turn let out the property as individual flats to tenants. During the period of World War II it became increasingly difficult to find tenants, so the defendant was going to end the arrangements. Rather than do this, the plaintiffs agreed to reduce the payment due under the lease to £1,250 per year. As a result the defendant was able to continue with a reduced number of tenants. At the end of 1945 people were returning to London, and the flats were again full. The plaintiffs then decided to go back to the original full payment under the lease, and to test their case, sued for the full payment for the last half of 1945. It was held that the full amount should be paid for this six-month period, since the flats were fully occupied. However, Denning J also took the opportunity to make the following points (*obiter*):

- The plaintiffs were entitled to request full payment from now on.
- On the other hand, if the plaintiffs should sue for payment for the war years (up to 1945), then they would be estopped from enforcing payment. It would be inequitable to allow them to go back on a promise on which the defendant had relied in continuing with the contract.

This became known as the doctrine of promissory estoppel. It began in *High Trees* with Lord Denning (when he was a fairly new but perceptive and innovative judge) using his powers of equity to provide a suitable remedy where there was a need, and has developed since into a fully recognised doctrine. It is an example of an inspired opportunity to develop the law as a way of mitigating unfairness, as the original rule in *Pinnel's Case* (confirmed in *Foakes v Beer*) that part payment of a debt cannot discharge liability for the whole debt, can be very harsh in certain circumstances if strictly applied. Authority for Denning's proposal was found to some extent in the following House of Lords case.

Hughes v Metropolitan Railway Co (1877)
Under a repairing lease the tenants of a property were ordered to make repairs or be evicted, and were given a period of six months to do this. However, negotiations then began for the purchase of the property, but these came to nothing, so the owners sued immediately for possession. The tenants claimed that while the negotiations for purchase were taking place the notice to repair was suspended, then giving them time to make the repairs. The court agreed that the obligations to repair were suspended during this time.

Lord Cairns made a statement to the effect that in the tradition of equity, if parties are in a contractual relationship, and one promises to excuse the other from strict legal duties, 'the person who otherwise might have enforced those rights will not be allowed to enforce them where it would be inequitable having regard to the dealings which have thus taken place between the parties'.

Some important points concerning promissory estoppel:

1 In *Hughes* the rights of the landlord had been suspended, but *High Trees* took this a step further in saying that the right to rent for the 1940–45 period had been extinguished, since it would be inequitable ever to revive it, as the money could never be recovered.

2 Promissory estoppel can only be used as a defence, and not to bring a new cause of action where none already existed. In *Combe v Combe* (1951) a husband promised to pay his wife £100 per year on separation, and when he defaulted she sued him for ten years' payments, claiming to rely on *High Trees*. It was held that the doctrine could not be used to start a cause of action, where no consideration existed. It was a 'shield and not a sword'.

3 A promisor can withdraw his promise when he gives reasonable notice that he is doing so, provided that the promisee is able to resume his

original position. This could have been done in *Hughes*, but not in *High Trees* for the period of the war years.

4 It was stated quite clearly in this case that promissory estoppel does not strike at the roots of the doctrine of consideration. Consideration is still essential to the formation of a contract, but not necessarily vital to its variation.

So, to assess the circumstances in which the doctrine of promissory estoppel will operate, the following conditions are necessary:

- There must be an existing legal relationship between the parties. In *High Trees* this was the contract for the lease of the property between the owner of the property and the defendant.

- The plaintiff deliberately waived his legal rights against the defendant. In *High Trees* the owners chose to reduce the rent (in fact, on this occasion it was in their interests to do so). In *Baird Textiles Holdings v Marks and Spencer* (2002) it was said that the statement of waiver must be very clear. Here it was held to be too uncertain and the claim of estoppel failed.

- The defendant gave no consideration for the waiver of contractual rights. In *High Trees* there was no stated consideration to reduce the rent – it was a one-sided gesture. However, it could be argued now, in the light of *Williams v Roffey*, that in *High Trees* the benefit of not having the property standing empty, and having a reduced rent instead of none at all, was a benefit to the owners (remember in *Williams v Roffey* the benefit to the builders was not having to look for new carpenters and avoiding the payment of a penalty to the owners of the building).

- The defendant altered his position as a result of the waiver, so that it would be inequitable to allow the plaintiff to succeed merely by lack of consideration. In *High Trees* the defendant certainly would not have continued with the lease at full rent. Since he had relied on the reduction, and there was no way that he could have recovered the rent for the war period, it would now be inequitable to ask him to pay full price for that period.

Promissory estoppel is still a developing doctrine, with its origins in equity. This means that the usual principles of equity apply, and this is seen in the following case.

> *D and C Builders v Rees* (1966)
> The plaintiff builders did work for the defendant family. When it was not performed satisfactorily the defendant paid part of the amount

▶

requested by cheque, and the plaintiff sued for the rest. The defendant claimed promissory estoppel, arguing that in accepting the cheque the builders had agreed to payment of part of the debt. The court, however, felt that the builders had been held to ransom, being forced to take what they could, and awarded judgment in their favour. In the circumstances it would have been inequitable to allow the defendants to succeed in a claim of promissory estoppel, as the whole idea of equity is to do justice (he who seeks equity must do equity).

Promissory estoppel has yet to be explored fully in the light of decided cases, and some issues remain a little uncertain. Debate has taken place about whether original rights are extinguished or merely suspended. Lord Denning favoured the former view in the case of *Alan v El Nasr* (1972), where he said that the creditor's strict legal rights were not to be enforced later, basing this on the argument that the other party may be unable to pay, having altered his position as a result of the promise. A more cautious view is generally taken by the majority of the judiciary, the House of Lords favouring the suspension of rights (as in Hughes) in the case *Tool Metal Manufacturing Co Ltd v Tungsten Electric* (1955). The Privy Council expressed the view in *Emmanuel Ayodei Ajayi v Briscoe (Nigeria) Ltd* (1964) that the promise only becomes final and irrevocable if the promisee cannot resume their original position. This seems a reasonable position, since the whole doctrine is based on equity, and perhaps will provide a reconciliation of these opposing views.

Consider the following situation. Jim borrows money from Kate, but then finds that he cannot work for the next few weeks because his mother is seriously ill in Japan and he needs to visit her. On hearing this Kate says 'I will let you off the rest of your debt, if it means that you can visit your mother with an easy conscience.' Jim is very grateful and goes to Japan. Six weeks later he returns to England and wins the lottery. Should Jim be able to rely on promissory estoppel, or should Kate now be able to enforce full payment?

Another issue which has caused debate is whether the promisee must have acted to his detriment to use the doctrine as a defence successfully. This was an important factor in *Hughes*, but again Lord Denning posed an alternative view in saying in *Alan v El Nasr* (1972), and more recently in *Brikom Investments Ltd v Carr* (1979), that the element of detriment is not strictly necessary.

Summing up, perhaps it is reasonable to say that the present position is that:

* Rights are probably extinguished in the situation of a single complete act (such as the payments for the war years in *High Trees*), where the promisee is unable to return to his original position.

* However, with an ongoing agreement (as in the post-1945 payments in *High Trees*) the original position can be restored with notice.

* It is probably not necessary for a promisee to have acted to his detriment, provided that he has done something which he would not otherwise have done in reliance on the promise.

The current state of the doctrine

The traditional requirement of consideration is still alive, as can be seen by some recent cases. Some doubt was placed over it by the rise of promissory estoppel – interesting itself, since it is based on a series of *obiter dicta,* which, of course are not technically binding – and a further blow was dealt by the case of *Williams v Roffey*. This case, however, does not so much challenge the doctrine's existence, just the way in which it is measured or found. It is certainly true that in previous case law there is some inconsistency – compare *Ward v Byham* with *White v Bluett*. Are they not both too vague to provide consideration if the court is really looking for something recognisable? Yet one contract was valid, the other not.

There are other anomalies, and the doctrine has had a fair amount of criticism over the years. As far back as *Couldery v Bartrum* (1881) Jessel MR said:

> According to English Common Law a creditor may accept anything in satisfaction of his debt except a less amount of money. He might take a horse, or a canary or a tom-tit if he chose, and that was accord and satisfaction; but by a most extraordinary peculiarity of the English Common Law, he could not take 19s 6d in the pound; that was nudum pactum.

Professor Atiyah would agree, suggesting that if we have offer and acceptance, and providing legal intent is present, there is no need for strict consideration. However, others, like Professor Hamson, would say, just as forcefully, that the doctrine is, along with offer and acceptance, part of an 'indivisible trinity' of contract. Perhaps the courts are now acknowledging that consideration is needed, if by that we mean a two-sided bargain, but perhaps adding on to that argument the kind of commercial realism found in *Williams v Roffey*. We await further developments.

Summary

Definition

- *Currie v Misa:* 'A valuable consideration may consist either in some right, interest, profit or benefit accruing to one party, or some forbearance, detriment, loss or responsibility given, suffered or undertaken by the other.'
- *Dunlop v Selfridge*: 'An act or forbearance of one party, or the promise thereof, is the price for which the promise of the other is bought.'

Sufficiency and adequacy

Consideration must be sufficient but need not be adequate – *Thomas v Thomas* (£1 per year ground rent), *Chapple v Nestlî_* (chocolate wrappers), *Bainbridge v Firmstone* (weighing boilers).

Other 'rules' of consideration

- Consideration must not be vague – *White v Bluett*.
- Consideration must move from the promisee – *Tweddle v Atkinson*.
- Consideration must not be past – *Roscorla v Thomas, Re McArdle*, but may be valid if it is expected that payment would be made – *Lampleigh v Braithwait, Re Casey's Patents*.
- Forbearance to sue may amount to consideration – *Haigh v Brooks*.
- Consideration must not be illegal – *Foster v Driscoll*.

Performance of an existing duty

A duty owed under the general law

- An existing duty is not generally valid consideration – *Collins v Godefroy.*
- Doing more than the existing duty may be valid consideration – *Glasbrook v Glamorgan*.
- Very little 'extra' is needed – *Ward v Byham*.

A duty owed under a contract

- Where an existing duty is owed under a contract, performing the task which is already the subject of a contract cannot normally form consideration – *Stilk v Myrick*.
- Adding something extra, with the agreement of the other party, may amount to valid consideration – *Hartley v Ponsonby*.
- Sometimes, however, the court may modify the rules to reflect practice in a modern society – *Williams v Roffey*.

Part-payment of a debt

* Paying part of a debt is not normally good consideration – *Pinnel's Case,* confirmed in *Foakes v Beer*.

* However, some exceptions exist.

Questions

1 Alan and Beth decide to extend and redecorate their house, to improve the accommodation which elderly Aunt Carrie occupies, and to provide space for the family's hobbies. Pleased with the result, they hold a small party. Aunt Carrie's accountant, David, is impressed with the work on the house, and offers to pay £1000 towards it, in order to help support Aunt Carrie. Alan and Beth thank David, and look forward to receiving the money. Two weeks after the party it has not arrived. Edmund, a wealthy local businessman, who has loaned Alan and Beth £500 towards the cost of the improvements, is also impressed with the work and tells the couple that they need not repay the loan. They thank him, saying that they will now be able to go for a short holiday, and take Aunt Carrie with them. However, on return from their holiday, they find a letter informing them that Edmund requests the payment of £500 after all.

  Advise Alan and Beth concerning the money from David and the loan from Edmund.

  OCR 2001/2 specimen

2 Jake is developing a leisure centre in time for the summer holiday trade and he contracts with Kanbild to undertake the installation of a swimming-pool. Kanbild contracts with Mariner to supply pipes to build the pool. Kanbild begins work in January, but in May he informs Jake that he will not be able to complete the work because of the steep increase in the cost of materials. Jake agrees to pay £2000 more than was originally agreed, so that Kanbild can obtain the materials needed and complete the pool on time. When the work is finished Jake refuses to pay the extra £2000. Six months after Mariner supplied the pipes, he has still not been paid by Kanbild. Both Kanbild and Mariner are now requesting payment from Jake.

  Advise Jake whether he must pay Kanbild the extra £2000 and Mariner for the pipes.

  OCR 2000

3 Evaluate the 'rules' which the courts might take into account when deciding whether consideration is sufficient to form a binding contract.

4 'The language of benefit and detriment is, and I believe long has been, out of date. So is the idea that consideration must be an economic benefit of some kind. All that is necessary is that the defendant should, expressly or impliedly, ask for something in return for his promise ......' (J. C. Smith in *The Law of Contract* quoted in 'Alive or Dead', *The Law Teacher*, 13).

  Explain and comment on the doctrine of consideration in the light of the above statement.

  WJEB 2001/02 specimen

5 Critically consider whether there are any circumstances in which the payment of part of a debt may be considered to have satisfied the whole debt.

6 To what extent may an act which has already taken place form the basis of valid consideration?

7 Consider the circumstances in which the performance of an existing duty may form valid consideration.

OCR 2002

8 The principles of consideration have developed through a need for justice in individual cases. It is time that they were reviewed in the context of a modern society. Discuss this view of the way in which the 'rules' of consideration have developed.

OCR 2003

A further 'dilemma' style question on consideration can be found in Part 7 of the book.

4   Legal intent

Did he really mean *to form a contract?*

In forming a contract, in addition to looking for an offer, acceptance and consideration, the court looks for a genuine intention to be legally bound. Without legal intent (or intention to create legal relations) an agreement may appear to contain the elements of a contract, but will not be enforceable legally. It is reasonable for the court to look for this requirement, since in many everyday situations people who have formed some kind of agreement would not expect or intend to create a contract, and would not wish to be bound by one, for example in social arrangements. On the other hand, it is quite easy to form an agreement, even in the course of business dealings, without actually saying or writing very much, but with a definite intention to be bound by it; for example in shopping, where it is often a matter of the customer handing over goods to be wrapped, the seller fully expecting to receive money for them. It is important here that the court can identify some legal intent, rather than just a general matter of trust. The cases concerning this issue fall into the following two categories:

• social and domestic arrangements
• commercial agreements.

Social and domestic arrangements

There is a general presumption that social and domestic arrangements are not intended to be legally binding.

Why do you think that this is needed?

Suppose that one person offers to cook and in return his friend agrees to provide drinks for the occasion. If the meal is ready but the drinks have been forgotten, no one would seriously suggest going to court to enforce the agreement. It is merely a social arrangement, and not a situation which would, in the intentions of the parties or in view of most people, have legal intent. It would be absurd if valuable court time was taken up with such issues, and so the law must have a way of deciding that this kind of disagreement does not become a legal battle – hence the presumption. This situation is mainly concerned with arrangements within families, but also extends to other relationships. Cases will often turn on their own facts, but a fair number have been brought before the courts. Atkin LJ explained the legal position in the following case.

Balfour v Balfour (1919)

There are agreements between parties which do not result in contracts within the meaning of that term in our law. The ordinary example is where two parties agree to take a walk together, or where there is an offer and acceptance of hospitality. Nobody would suggest in ordinary circumstances that those agreements result in what we know as a contract, and one of the most usual forms of agreement which does not constitute a contract appears to me to be the arrangements which are made between husband and wife.

In this case Mr Balfour was a civil servant returning to his posting in Bombay. His wife had been unwell and decided to stay in Britain. He promised to pay her £30 a month in consideration of her supporting herself without calling on him for further maintenance. When Mr Balfour defaulted on the payments, his wife claimed that he was bound by the promise to pay. It was held that no legally binding contract existed. It was a domestic arrangement, not intended to create legal relations. In any case, the courts were particularly loathe to investigate matters arising between husband and wife.

It should be remembered, however, that the general presumption may be rebutted, or overridden by a evidence that there really was a contract. Social changes may also contribute to decisions in cases, and this is seen in the following case.

Merritt v Merritt (1970)

The facts were very similar, in that a husband and wife, living apart, agreed that if the wife completed the mortgage payments, the husband would transfer the house to her. This was held to be enforceable, rebutting the presumption of no legal intent.

Lord Denning explained the decision in *Merritt v Merritt* in this way,

In all these cases the court does not try to discover the intention by looking into the minds of the parties. It looks at the situation in which they were placed and asks itself: Would reasonable people regard this agreement as intended to be legally binding?

Lord Denning is really saying that looking on from the outside, as the court is when making a judgment, it would be difficult to decide whether the parties intended in their minds that what they said should be legally binding. In addition there is often very little concrete evidence about what the parties intended, so that is why the court makes a presumption that in these situations the parties do not have legal intent.

However, in *Merritt v Merritt*, the husband and wife were legally separated, and the court therefore saw enough in that fact to differentiate between this case and *Balfour v Balfour*. Another factor could well have been changes in society during the period 1919 to 1970, making it more commonplace for a husband and wife to make these arrangements.

In the case of *Darke v Strout* (2003) it was held that the formality of a letter of agreement to child maintenance was enough to rebut the presumption between family members.

Why do you think that the outcome of *Merritt v Merritt* was different from *Balfour*.

Problems may arise in this context between other family members, such as parent and child, as in the following case.

Jones v Padvatton (1969)
A mother provided a house for her daughter whilst she was studying for her bar exams. The Court of Appeal later held that the agreement to let her continue there was a family arrangement and not legally binding, so refused to allow reprossession by the mother.

This contrasts with the decision in *Webb v Webb* (1997) where a father was held to have intended legal relations in handing over a flat to his son, after the son 'sided' with his estranged wife.

The following two cases involved other family relationships, and in both cases the presumption was rebutted.

Simpkin v Pays (1955)
The defendant, her grand-daughter, and the plaintiff (a lodger at the defendant's house), entered a fashion competition each week in a Sunday paper, each filling in a line, and the entry being sent in under the defendant's name. They won a prize of £750 and the plaintiff sued for a third share as agreed. Here, in contrast to the decision in *Jones v Padvatton,* it was held that there was a legally binding contract, and the plaintiff was entitled to a third share. The presence of the lodger, amongst other things, had the effect of rebutting the presumption of this being merely a domestic matter.

Parker v Clark (1960)
Two elderly couples were relatives. The Clarks lived in a large house and invited the Parkers to share it, making very clear and detailed arrangements about who was to pay various bills, and what would happen to their property when they eventually died. Later a dispute arose and the court held that the arrangement was binding, particularly in view of the Parkers having taken the 'drastic and irrevocable step' of selling their own home.

Do you think that the Parkers and the Clarks would have expected this agreement to be legally binding (think about the evidence – what arrangements did they make?)

In the next case *Buckpitt v Oates*, the plaintiff and defendant were merely friends, but since the social circle has changed over a period of time, and ease of transport and communications means that members of families are much more widely spread now, it seems logical to extend the presumption concerning domestic arrangements to friends as well as strict family. Of course, this creates some uncertainty, and means that cases will depend more on individual facts, in order to determine whether there is legal intent.

Buckpitt v Oates (1968) The plaintiff and defendant were friends, both 17, and in the habit of riding in each other's cars. The plaintiff sustained an injury through the defendant's negligence, on a journey where he had paid the defendant ten shillings towards the petrol. Despite the contribution to the fuel, it was held that this was a friendly arrangement, or a 'gentlemen's agreement' to go on the trip. This gave rise to no legal obligations or benefits, except those which the general law of the land imposed or implied. Of course this particular situation would be different today, since there is compulsory passenger insurance, but it is important in showing a willingness of the court to extend the presumption beyond the strict family, and also to reflect what the parties probably did intend.

Commercial agreements

In commercial agreements the general presumption is that parties do intend to create legal relations, although, again, this may be rebutted. However, it is more difficult to rebut this presumption and very clear evidence will be needed. It is very important in a commercial context to remember that most contracts are formed in situations where at least one of the parties is expecting to make some commercial gain – often money. Provided that these contracts are made in a fair way, it is reasonable to expect that the law will support the agreements. So, if a person orders a piece of furniture from a shop, and it is delivered, it is reasonable that the law would make the customer liable for payment. Equally, if the furniture shop obtains more items from a manufacturer, the owners of the shop are, in turn, legally liable to pay the manufacturer under the terms of the agreement with them. This supports the commercial expectations of the person in business, but what about the consumer?

> If you bought a new toothbrush which was advertised as 'sold with a smiley sticker', and when you paid for the toothbrush you were told that there were no stickers left, would you expect to be able to force the seller legally to compensate you? What if you bought a new computer and you were promised a free printer?

The courts took a contextual approach to rebutting the presumption in *Edmonds v Lawson* (2000). A pupil barrister argued that the agreement concerning pupillage was made in a commercial context and therefore a binding contract. If this was so, then the presumption of legal intent would bring the contract within employment legislation and subject to the minimum wage. The court held that the presumption would apply, but would be rebutted because of the context of pupillage where payment was traditionally not made.

Honourable pledge causes

It is important that the consumer, an individual buying from a person in business, is protected from exploitation by a commercial venture. We can see here two sides to agreement, and the law merely aims to see that fairness exists between them. That is generally the reason for the presumption regarding commercial agreements. Sometimes, however, a party may successfully rebut the presumption, although the courts will require very clear evidence to deny legal intent.

> *Rose and Frank Co v Crompton Bros* (1925)
> Both parties were in business, and they formed an agreement in which one acted as agent for the other to sell paper. In their written negotiation they included a statement that they had not entered into a 'formal or legal agreement', but had only made a 'definite expression and record of the purpose and intention' of the parties. When later a dispute arose, the House of Lords accepted this statement, and concluded that there was no intention to create legal relations in their negotiations. It is at least arguable that if the parties had gone to the lengths of writing all of this down, then it could hardly be claimed that the agreement was not a formal one. However, the outcome was in accordance with the parties' expectations, which was probably at least part of the reasoning behind the court's decision.

The kind of statement found in *Rose and Frank v Crompton* is known as an honourable pledge clause, one in which the parties bind each other in honour but not in law. Honourable pledge clauses are allowed by the court, with some reluctance on occasions, and the House of Lords re-examined the issue in the following case.

> *Edwards v Skyways* (1964)
> Skyways claimed that the term *ex gratia* meant the same as legally unenforceable, and this would have enabled the company to avoid a payment to a pilot who had been made redundant. The court did not agree, and emphasised that there was a very heavy burden on any party claiming that the presumption in a commercial contract had been rebutted.

The opportunity to restate the extent of this burden of proof arose in the Court of Appeal in the following case.

> *Kleinwort Benson v Malaysian Mining Corporation* (1989)
> The trial judge found that a 'letter of comfort', which was really a letter giving support to a credit arrangement, did have legal intent, being written in a commercial context, and followed the normal presumption that such agreements were intended to be binding. However, the Court of Appeal, somewhat reluctantly, held that the letter did not carry an intention to be bound.

In the case of *Carlill v Carbolic Smoke Ball Company*, seen earlier, it was argued that there was no intention there to create legal relations, but the argument failed as a defence. The court decided that the evidence showed that the company had really led the public to believe that any contract was intended to be binding. So why does the court decide that some parties really mean to be bound, but not others? One important difference between *Rose and Frank v Crompton and Carlill* may be that when one party is a consumer there is a greater need to give protection to the expectations of that party. This argument has a lot of merit, and is certainly in line with the bulk of statutory protection now given to consumers.

Imagine shopping for a new video recorder, and in the High Street you notice that two shops have the same model advertised. In one of them the price is slightly higher than the other, but the shop with the higher price also says in the shop window that a portable television will be given 'free' with each video recorder purchased. Would you be willing to buy your video recorder from this shop, if you knew that there was little chance of obtaining the television?

In the case of *Esso v Commissioners of Customs and Excise*, seen earlier, the courts were willing to find that legal intent existed between a consumer and Esso, even over something as trivial as a 'free' metal coin with hardly any monetary value. This is fair, since the consumer would certainly have expected to receive a coin, and if the 'free' item was worth more in monetary terms, it would be important the agreement was enforceable legally.

However, there are examples to be found of such honorary pledge clauses which have been upheld, even against a consumer. When pools coupons are completed, for example, ready for entry into the pools competition, it is likely that the consumer really believes that, should the form contain a winning entry, the law will generally enforce payment. In most cases, however, the coupon will contain a clause which allows the pools company to refuse to honour the agreement. The cases of *Jones v Vernons Pools* (1938) and *Appleson v Littlewoods* (1939) are both situations where the pools company refused to pay and the claimants were unable to enforce payment via the courts. More recently, and somewhat surprisingly, these decisions were reinforced in the case of *Halloway v Cuozzo* (1999).

The following is a typical honourable pledge clause found in a football pools coupon, and it is often written in very small print at the end of a form.

This agreement is binding in honour only, and neither the organisers nor their agents intend this to form an agreement enforceable in a court of law.

Figure 4.1

> ˙Do you think that the average player of these competitions understands the significance of these clauses?

There is now a fair amount of legislation controlling unfair practice in consumer contracts, and if a similar case should revisit the courts it is possible that the practice of honourable pledge clauses may fall foul of the Unfair Terms in Consumer Contract Regulations 1999. It is certainly against the spirit of the European Directive which led to the regulations, and the courts should look for an opportunity to outlaw the practice.

One business-like situation where it is presumed that legal intent exists is when employers and trade unions meet to discuss pay settlements or working conditions. In order to facilitate collective bargaining, it is presumed that any agreements made are not intended to be binding unless this is expressly stated in writing. This principle was applied in the case of *Ford Motor Co Ltd v Amalgamated Union of Engineering and Foundry Workers* (1969).

The existence of legal intent is therefore an important element in the formation of a contract. The presumptions operate to prevent social arrangements turning inadvertently into legally binding contracts, but, on the other hand, to ensure that the reasonable and realistic intentions of the parties are supported by law. It has been argued by academics, notably Atiyah, that as there are at present three major formation requirements (offer and acceptance, consideration and legal intent), consideration is not strictly necessary. If this line was to be pursued by the courts, legal intent would play an even greater role in the formation of a contract. In that situation, it would be even more important that the parties honour their obligations when they clearly set out to form a legally binding agreement, and the presumption of legal intent is one way of ensuring that this happens.

Summary

An intention to be legally bound (or to 'form legal relations') is required as a formation element of a contract, in addition to offer, acceptance and consideration.

Social and domestic arrangements

The presumption and its rebuttal

A presumption exists in social and domestic situations that there is no legal intent and that arrangements are not therefore enforceable.

* The presumption can be rebutted by evidence that the parties were serious in their intention to be legally bound.

- Presumption followed – *Balfour v Balfour, Jones v Padvatton, Buckpitt v Oates.*
- Presumption rebutted – *Merritt v Merritt, Simpkin v Pays, Parker v Clark.*

Commercial agreements

The presumption and its rebuttal

Any agreements made in a commercial context are presumed to have legal intent, and therefore be binding.

The presumption can be rebutted, but very clear evidence will be needed for this to succeed: *Edwards v Skyways.*

- Presumption followed – *Carlill v Carbolic Smoke Ball Co, Esso v Commissioners of Customs and Excise.*
- Presumption rebutted – *Rose and Frank v Crompton Bros, Jones v Vernons Pools, Appleson v Littlewoods, Kleinwort Benson v Malaysia Mining Corporation.*
- Presumption of no legal intent in collective bargaining (unless clearly evidenced in writing) – *Ford Motor Co Ltd v Amalgamated Union of Engineering and Foundry Workers.*

Questions

1   Logan invites two friends, Maurice and Nesta, to his house for the evening, on the basis that he will provide the drinks if they bring the food. The friends arrive, but they have felt tired during the day, so although they have plenty to drink there is no food. Logan is disappointed, but decides to buy some food instead.

   The friends see an advertisement for fast delivery of burgers, with 'free dessert with each burger meal'. Logan orders three burger meals, but when he pays the delivery girl he is told that they are not giving free desserts any more because they are busy.

   Logan produces a football pools competition form for the three friends to complete and enter together, and they do so, each paying towards the entry fee and agreeing to share any money which they may win.

   The friends prove to be lucky, and find a week later that they have won £1500 on the football pools entry. However, the football pools organisers are refusing to pay out at all this week due to low funds.

   Advise Logan regarding the supply of food for the party, the free desserts and the winnings from the football pools competition.

2   Franco is an amateur jazz musician who plays regularly with a group of friends at various locations. At Christmas Franco agrees with the manager of Grandstore that the group will play seasonal music at the entrance to the store to attract customers during the holiday period.

Franco and his friends play for the agreed time each day for three weeks and then send Grandstore an invoice for payment. Grandstore replies, without paying Franco, stating that the agreement to play was not intended to be binding, but 'in the spirit of providing a happy Christmas environment and an opportunity for an amateur group to practise in public'.

On another occasion, after performing, Franco buys some concert tickets, at £30 each, for himself and for his neighbour, Hilary. Franco has in the past bought tickets for Hilary, knowing that she enjoys the kind of music to be performed, and on these occasions Hilary has paid Franco. Franco gives Hilary the ticket and asks her for £30.

Hilary at first agrees to pay, but later says that she does not really want this particular ticket. Advise Franco whether he can claim payment from Grandstore and from Hilary.

OCR 2003

3 'In the context of today's society, the need for contracts to be enforced is more important than ever before.' Critically consider this view of the need to establish an intention to create legal relations.

OCR 2004

4 'The proof of legal intent is an essential element in the formation of a valid contract.' To what extent can this claim be justified?

OCR 2002

5 'An intention to be legally bound is a requirement in forming a contract; the presumption for or against this intention can give much needed protection.'

Analyse the reasons for requiring an intention to be legally bound in the light of the above statement.

OCR 4-module specimen paper

A further 'dilemma' style question on legal intent can be found in Part 7 of the book.

5   Capacity

Proof of Age ID Card

Forename.
George

Surename.
Smith

Expiry date.
25-02-2010

D.O.B.
21/3/1989

Card No.
1298560012595

123568258   56984   256984135474

Is he over 18?

We have established that the essential 'ingredients' of a contract are agreement in the form of offer and acceptance, consideration and legal intent. One further requirement for a contract to be valid, is the status of the people or parties to the contract. An agreement may well exist between anybody, but to be able to sue on it in law, the makers of the agreement must have full capacity. In general the law assumes that most adults have this contractual capacity, and are therefore competent or able to contract, but there are some exceptions to this general freedom to sue and be sued. These are:

- corporations (registered business organisations)
- persons of unsound mind and drunkards
- minors.

In addition, sovereigns and diplomats have a general diplomatic immunity, and cannot be sued in British courts unless they voluntarily agree to this.

We will concentrate mostly on minors, but it is useful to briefly consider why the restrictions exist. Generally the restrictions in the law of capacity exist to protect people, there being certain groups in society who, for various reasons, may be more vulnerable than others in forming contracts.

> Who do *you* think are the more vulnerable members of society, as far as the formulation of a contract is concerned?

Corporations

Corporations, themselves are protected by the incorporation procedure in company law, which gives them limited liability to others. However, there is a need to protect the shareholders and investors from the improper use of their money, and third parties who deal with corporations. The capacity of a corporation is limited by the instrument (usually a document) which creates it, so in the case of a chartered corporation, the limitation will be found within the charter. Similarly, with a statutory corporation, the limitation will be found in the statute, and a registered company is limited by the registration procedure (although the effect of this has been lessened by the Companies Act 1989, when a person contracts in good faith with a company director).

Mental disability and intoxication

The law also protects those of unsound mind and those who are drunk at the time of making a contract. Under the Sale of Goods Act a drunken person or one of unsound mind will be liable for the reasonable cost of necessaries (see below), and would also be liable if the contract was ratified (confirmed), later, when in a more rational state of mind. Generally if a person is suffering from mental disability or is drunk at the time of making a contract, the contract is voidable, if he can prove that:

Do you think that the law should give those who are drunk the same protection as those who suffer from mental disability?

- he did not understand the nature of the transaction, and
- the other party was aware of this.

It could be argued that in the case of intoxication, the second condition is almost always likely to be satisfied if the first one has been established, because if a person is so drunk that they do not know what they are doing, it is likely to be apparent to the other party. This may seem to be an easy way out of an unwanted contract for a person who is drunk, but remember that the evidence must support both of the conditions above, and that the law is then designed to protect a person who has been taken advantage of by the other party while in such a state. More sympathy may be felt toward those who suffer from mental disability or involuntarily intoxication, such as a 'spiked' drink, but the law does not seem to distinguish between this and voluntary intoxication. Regarding the knowledge of the other party, the Privy Council said in *Hart v O'Connor* (1985) that where one party is unaware of the incapacity of the other, and the state of the afflicted party is not apparent, then the contract will be regarded as a contract between two parties of sound mind. In this case a sale of land was held binding because the buyer did not realise that the seller suffered from a mental disability.

The situation in *Hart v O'Connor* is in practice unlikely to arise often, and is an example of the courts taking an objective and reasonable approach, and looking for external evidence of agreement. The law here is in line with criminal law, where a defence of intoxication may only be used in limited circumstances. In both cases the court must be convinced of the genuineness of the arguments, and it is unlikely that much sympathy would be felt towards a party using deliberate excessive drinking to escape an unwanted contract.

The principles regarding those with mental disability are now restated in s. 7 of the Mental Capacity Act 2005.

Diplomats and sovereigns

This category of limited capacity exists to protect those who work on behalf of their country, and to enable international relations to proceed unfettered by problems of ignorance of foreign law. In practice it is only seen actively in minor incidents, apart from an isolated group of more high profile cases.

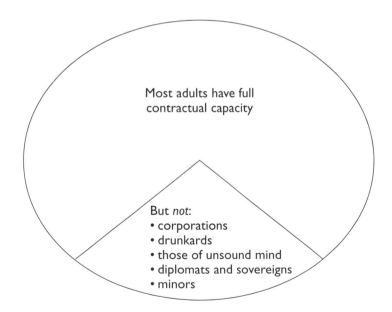

Most adults have full contractual capacity

But *not*:
• corporations
• drunkards
• those of unsound mind
• diplomats and sovereigns
• minors

Figure 5.1

Minors

The final category of those protected by the law of contractual capacity is minors, and this is the category of capacity which this chapter will focus on. A minor is a person under 18, although as recently as 1969, before the Family Law Reform Act was passed, a person under 21 was referred to as an 'infant'. The above Act lowered the age of majority to 18 and introduced the term minor.

A somewhat paternalistic approach is taken in contract law, by restricting the minor's capacity to contract. However, if there was no protection at all for minors, there would surely be criticism in the other direction, namely that the law was too harsh on young people. The Law Commission suggested in 1982 that minors should be bound from the age of 16, rather than 18, which is a reasonable argument given that a 16-yearold can legally marry, have children and enter into employment. However, a cautious approach has prevailed, perhaps because of the involvement of commercial pressure in a modern consumer-orientated society.

At what age do you think that a minor should be liable for contracts, and why?

The aim, then, is to protect minors from their own inexperience and perhaps from unwise transactions, whilst not being too hard on any adult dealing fairly with a minor. A minor can enforce a contract against the other party, providing it is an adult, but there is a general presumption that contracts with minors are unenforceable. However, some contracts with a minor are valid, and therefore enforceable.

Necessaries

A minor will be liable for a contract for the sale of necessaries. If all contracts with minors were unenforceable, retailers would be reluctant to sell to them on credit under any circumstances. So, to enable a minor to obtain basic essentials for ordinary living, the law regards a minor as being bound under a contract for the sale of necessaries sold and delivered to them. The term 'necessaries' covers more than just items needed to stay alive, such as shelter, food and clothing, but those things which are essential *and* suited to the minor's position in life. So a minor who is in a relatively high social position will be liable for payment for more than a minor in a lower position financially.

Should the law discriminate by linking 'necessaries' to a person's social status, or should a wealthy person be liable for the same purchases as a poorer person?

There is a twofold definition of necessaries, therefore, dependant on both social status and a genuine need.

The Sale of Goods Act 1979 s.3(3) defines necessaries as, 'goods suitable to the condition in life of the minor and to his actual requirements at the time of sale and delivery'.

This distinction does appear somewhat discriminatory, but if it were not so, a person who was wealthy and could well afford to pay for purchases would 'escape' with the same liability as a much poorer person. The question must arise as to how a retailer is to establish a person's social status (assuming that he is aware of the law and has first of all established the age of the customer).

The operation of the twofold definition of necessaries is illustrated in the following case.

Nash v Inman (1908)
A Cambridge university undergraduate, the son of a wealthy architect, ordered 'eleven fancy waistcoats' from a Savile Row tailor. He did not pay for them, relying on the fact that he was not of full capacity. The incident arose at a time when such waistcoats were normal student clothing at Cambridge, and this, coupled with the status of the client, persuaded the court that such items could be necessaries. However, it was found that the student's father had already provided him with plenty of clothing, including waistcoats, and therefore they were not actually required. The law at the time, then, protected the student very well, but was rather harsh on the tailor, who received no payment at all. We will see later that the position may be different should a similar situation arise at the present time.

How easy is it now to obtain credit as a minor? Should it be more difficult, or should credit be easily available?

Despite suggestions by the Law Commission that the definition of necessaries be made clearer and narrower, no action has yet been taken, and the principles used in *Nash v Inman* are still the starting-point in deciding exactly what is a necessary. So to enforce a contract against a minor, it must be shown that the goods in question are both necessary and actually required at the time, having regard to the individual situation.

Chapple v Cooper (1844)
Some useful observations were made in this case which give further guidance on what may amount to a necessary. Alderson B said,

> Things necessary are those without which an individual cannot reasonably exist. In the first place, food, raiment, lodging and the like. About these there is no doubt. Again, as the proper cultivation of the mind is as expedient as the support of the body, instruction in art or trade, or intellectual, moral and religious information may be a necessary also. Again, as man lives in society ... his clothes may be fine or coarse according to his rank; his education may vary according to the station he is to fill; and the medicines will depend on the illness with which he is afflicted .... Thus, articles of mere luxury are always excluded, though luxurious articles of utility are sometimes allowed.

What purchases could be 'luxurious articles of utility' and therefore treated like necessaries?

Two examples follow from the same Victorian period as *Nash v Inman*.

Peters v Fleming (1840)
An expensive watch-chain was supplied on credit, and it was left to the jury (which was more usual in civil cases at that time) to decide whether it was a reasonable purchase for this particular student, and therefore whether it was a necessary. It was considered reasonable for a student to have a watch, and therefore a watch-chain was needed.

Wharton v MacKenzie (1844)
An undergraduate, this time from Oxford, obtained supplies for dinner parties. It was held that fruits, ices and confectionery could not be treated as necessaries without further justification. So the application of necessaries to a person's social standing will be a matter of fact on each occasion.

> Think of some things which you have bought recently, and try to decide if they would be regarded by the court as necessaries.

Necessaries may take the form of services, although these have not been defined by statute in the same way as goods. The term includes contracts for education, training, employment, and legal and medical expenses, and also applies to the spouse and children of a minor.

> *Chapple v Cooper* (1844)
> A young widow was sued successfully for the funeral expenses for her late husband, as these services were regarded as necessaries.

However, if a contract for services is particularly onerous on the minor, it will not be binding, however necessary the services are to him.

> *Fawcett v Smethurst* (1914)
> A minor hired a vehicle to transport his belongings – a service which would almost certainly be considered a necessary. However, in this case is was held not to be binding, since a clause in the contract would have made the minor liable for cost of repairs to the vehicle, whether his own fault or not.

So, we can see that the following position emerges regarding necessaries:

- basic requirements for survival, such as basic shelter, food and clothing, normally *will* be necessaries, and the minor will have to pay a reasonable price for them
- more luxurious items which have a utility value *may* be regarded as necessaries, such as a car which is used to reach the work place or college course, and, again, the minor will have to pay
- items which are merely luxuries, such as jewellery, will *not* normally be regarded as necessaries, and the contract will be unenforceable against the minor
- similar principles apply to services, providing the agreement is not too onerous on the minor.

Beneficial contracts of service

A second type of contract which may be valid against a minor, is the beneficial contract of service, really an extension of the statement of Baron

Alderson in *Chapple v Cooper* (see p. 82). Often this takes the form of a contract of employment, education or training for a minor.

Why, as a matter of policy, should the law be concerned with beneficial contracts of service?

It is really an extension of the idea of necessaries, as it is regarded as essential that a minor learns a skill or trade in order to support himself. It is obviously of major concern economically that minors develop the skills and in an environment which enables them to learn a trade or profession, and that they are able to form satisfactory contracts of employment. With these contracts the courts take the view that an oppressive contract is unenforceable against a minor, but that if a contract is, on the whole, beneficial to the minor, then it will be binding, even though an individual clause may not be to his advantage.

The approach taken by the courts is illustrated in the following contrasting cases.

De Francesco v Barnum (1889)
A 14-year-old girl formed a 7-year agreement to train as a stage dancer. It was said that she was entirely at the disposal of her stage master, as he did not guarantee her any work, she could not accept any other work without his agreement, and she could not marry or travel abroad during this time. The contract was held to be on the whole oppressive, rather than beneficial, and therefore unenforceable.

Aylesbury FC v Watford AFC (1977)
Lee Cook, a 17-year-old footballer, was contracted to Aylesbury but allowed to treat the contract as not binding on him so that he could form a new contract to play for Watford. A restraint of trade clause in his original contract was held to be too onerous and the contract not therefore, on the whole, for the minor's benefit.

Clements v London & NW Rail Co (1894)
A young porter joined a private insurance scheme, but in return gave up certain statutory rights as an employee. The court held that despite the benefit which had been given up under the contract, he had received greater benefit from the employer, so it was on the whole to his benefit, and therefore enforceable.

Doyle v White City Stadium (1935)
A young boxer was held bound by a contract in which he was subject to the rules of the British Boxing Board of Control. This meant that he

lost his 'purse' – the prize money from a fight – but the contract was seen to be on the whole beneficial to him, despite this one clause which was disadvantageous, because of the training which he received.

Chaplin v Leslie Frewin (1966)
A contract made by the son of Charlie Chaplin to write his autobiography was held binding, as it enabled the minor to begin to earn his living as an author.

Roberts v Gray (1913)
When a billiards player agreed to take a minor on a world billiards tour, providing his lodging and travelling arrangements under the contract, this was viewed by the court as 'a kind of education'. The minor later changed his mind and claimed the contract unenforceable, but was held liable in damages.

On the other hand, trading contracts with a minor will not be enforced.

Mercantile Union Guarantee v Ball (1937)
A contract of hire purchase by a minor running his own haulage business was held unenforceable. Although this is a measure to protect the minor, it could be seen as putting a young person who wishes to run his own business at a disadvantage, for example as a market trader or other retailer, compared with a similar minor who is employed. It is an example of the courts looking after the interests of the minor, by preventing him from taking financial risks, without the necessary experience, and it could be argued that this is not necessarily a bad position, given that the age of majority is now 18.

Voidable contracts

A third type of contract with a minor which may be binding is where a minor enters into an agreement of continuing obligation. This is a contract of an ongoing nature, such as the renting of accommodation. In this case the contract will be regarded as valid, unless the minor repudiates it before reaching 18, or within a reasonable time afterwards. This leaves a workable arrangement for those dealing with a minor, but gives the minor an opportunity to 'escape' if he later regrets his action.

In the case of *Edwards v Carter* (1893) Lord Watson explained the position as follows. 'If he [meaning the minor] chooses to be inactive, his opportunity passes away; if he chooses to be active, the law comes to his assistance,' meaning that the minor has an opportunity to excuse himself from the contract, otherwise it will be presumed binding on him. In this case, a marriage settlement was made for a young man who made a further agreement to invest any money which he later acquired into the same settlement. He reached adulthood, and then inherited money from his father. He regretted having made the commitment to invest it and repudiated the agreement. It was held that the repudiation was too late, and the agreement was binding.

Is a minor's contract enforceable?

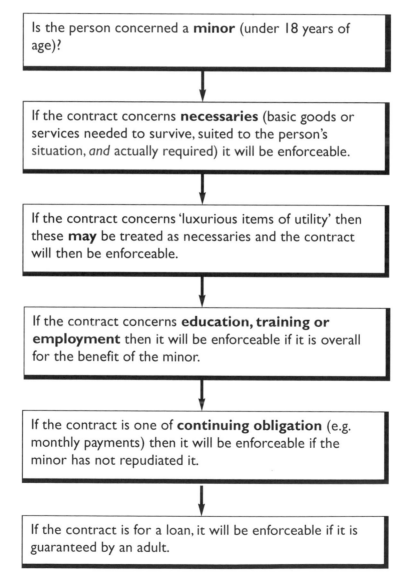

Is the person concerned a **minor** (under 18 years of age)?

If the contract concerns **necessaries** (basic goods or services needed to survive, suited to the person's situation, *and* actually required) it will be enforceable.

If the contract concerns 'luxurious items of utility' then these **may** be treated as necessaries and the contract will then be enforceable.

If the contract concerns **education, training or employment** then it will be enforceable if it is overall for the benefit of the minor.

If the contract is one of **continuing obligation** (e.g. monthly payments) then it will be enforceable if the minor has not repudiated it.

If the contract is for a loan, it will be enforceable if it is guaranteed by an adult.

Figure 5.2

Exactly what is a reasonable time is not clear, and will be a decision of the court given the particular circumstances. It was argued in *Edwards v Carter* that the effect of the agreement did not have an impact on the minor until he inherited the father's estate. This does seem a reasonable claim, but what if the inheritance had not been received until ten years later? A further argument could be raised over the level of legal knowledge of the minor. If the presumption is that such an agreement is binding, the only protection for the minor depends on his knowledge of the legal right to repudiate.

The effect of repudiating a voidable contract is that the minor's obligations end, but he is not entitled to recover money already paid, unless there is a complete lack of consideration. In *Steinberg v Scala* (1923) a minor repudiated a contract for shares. All obligations between the minor and the company ended at this point, but she could not recover the original cost of the shares. The position regarding money due up to the time of repudiation is less clear, and even academic authorities differ on the issue. It is possible that the minor may be liable for debts incurred up to the time of repudiation.

The Minors' Contracts Act 1987

All of these common law measures seem to leave the minor in a very protected and somewhat privileged position. Indeed, until recent years, the law was regarded as being particularly harsh in some circumstances on an adult who contracted with a minor, especially given that there is a great difference in the experiences of various young people. In a case where a minor had knowingly taken advantage of an adult, using the law of contractual capacity to his benefit, there appeared to be injustice arising out of a law which aimed to protect. However, with the passing of the Minors' Contracts Act 1987 this imbalance has been somewhat remedied. The Act does not remove the protection given to a minor, but improves the position of the adult dealing with him.

The two main provisions are:

- where a minor enters into a contract for a loan, guaranteed by an adult, the guarantee is enforceable against the adult (s.2)
- where a minor unjustly acquires goods under an unenforceable contract, the court may order restitution (handing back) of the goods, or of 'other property' representing the goods (s.3).

Loans

The common law position is unchanged, in that a straightforward repayment of a loan under a contract with a minor is unenforceable. Before 1987 a guarantee was also unenforceable, but now, where an adult guarantor agrees to repay the loan if the minor defaults, this is now enforceable against the guarantor.

How can the protection of minors be balanced against fairness towards adults who deal with them?

Restitution

We saw that in *Nash v Inman* the tailor was left in an unfortunate position of receiving no payment for the eleven waistcoats which the student had been wearing. In order to address this position, section 3 of the Minors' Contracts Act 1987 gives the court a discretionary power to insist on the handing back of goods under an unenforceable contract with a minor (note that the statute says that the court 'may' order restitution, not that they always will). This means that if the minor has been exploited by an adult, the court may well feel that it is just not to order restitution. However, in the event that a minor has taken advantage of an adult, using the law to escape from obligations, then restitution will go some way to providing a remedy for the other party. The courts have the final decision to make on this, but they are the ones who will be in knowledge of the facts of the case.

In addition, where the minor has exchanged goods acquired in this way for other goods, these may be the subject of the restitution order. For example if a minor has bought a car on credit, and has sold it, using the money to buy a motor-cycle, the court may order the minor to hand over the motor-cycle to the seller of the car.

The provisions on restitution do raise some problems. Restitution of goods which hold their value, such as antique jewellery, is satisfactory for the seller, as he receives back what he has lost. However, restitution of clothing which is now second-hand, and of very low monetary value, is less satisfactory. It could be argued that where the court feels that restitution is necessary in such cases, because on the facts it is evident that a minor has manipulated the law to his own ends, then some payment could be ordered. However, there is no provision for such an order at present. Furthermore, in some contracts restitution is not possible, such as in a contract for services or consumable items, such as a meal.

A further problem arises where the original goods acquired by the minor are now represented by money. If they have been sold and the money is kept intact, for example in a labelled envelope, there should not be a problem. However, if the money is used with other money to buy a more expensive item, or is paid into a bank account which contains other money, and from which withdrawals have been made, difficulties exist. No detailed ruling exists at present, so it will no doubt be up to the courts to use their discretion in such cases.

On the whole, despite the problems raised, the power of restitution does give the courts the possibility of providing a just outcome in more situations than before the Minors' Contracts Act was passed.

General concerns

Is the law of contractual capacity now satisfactory? Are there any other groups of people who are vulnerable, yet still unprotected?

One particular group of people unprotected by the law of capacity is the elderly, who may be subject to consumer pressure. There is some protection in consumer law (which applies to all consumers), and they will generally elicit the sympathy of the court, but as a matter of law there is no specific provision regarding contracts with elderly people.

Some general problems still arise with the law of capacity in contracts. Like many other areas of law it is not widely known. This has been addressed by statute concerning corporations (really the subject of in-depth study in the area of company law), but regarding minors it remains a problem. Obviously large organisations will be well aware of their position in law when dealing with minors, and will develop policies based on it.

How old are you then, sir?

Figure 5.3

This leaves the small retailer at a disadvantage, although this, arguably, is a wider problem of access to the law generally.

A further difficulty is that in the absence of formal identity cards, such as are carried in some other European countries, it is very difficult for a retailer to identify a minor, without causing offence, and therefore potentially losing custom. However, in pursuing the general aim of protecting minors, the combination of common law and statute now maintains a reasonably balanced approach, so as not to leave an adult dealing with a minor in an unreasonable position.

Summary

Most adults have full capacity. The following have limited capacity in forming contracts, for various reasons:

- Corporations (organisations, such as universities and companies): limited according to the instrument creating the corporation (e.g. a statutory corporation by the statute, a limited company by the articles of incorporation) – to enable businesses to trade with limited liability.
- Diplomats and sovereigns – to facilitate international diplomatic relations and travel.
- Those who are drunk or of unsound mind – for protection when vulnerable.
- Minors – for protection from inexperience.

Minors

Definition

- A minor is a person under eighteen years of age – Family Law Reform Act 1969. Identity may be a problem, without any official documentation.

Liabilities

- Necessaries, in other words, things needed to exist, suited to the position in life of the minor, and required at the time must be paid for by a minor – Sale of Goods Act 1979 s.3, *Nash v Inman, Peters v Capacity Fleming, Wharton v MacKenzie*. Necessaries may include 'luxurious items of utility' – *Chapple v Cooper.*
- Contracts of education, training and employment (beneficial contracts of service) will be binding if on the whole for the benefit of the minor and not oppressive – *Clements v London & NW Rail Co, Doyle v White City Stadium, Roberts v Gray, De Francesco v Barnum, Mercantile Union Guarantee v Ball.*
- Voidable contracts (those of continuing obligation) may be repudiated before or around the eighteenth birthday – *Edwards v Carter, Steinberg v Scala*.

Legislative measures

- Guarantees for loans may be enforceable against an adult guarantor – Minors' Contracts Act 1987 s.2. Restitution may be ordered (minor may have to hand back property unfairly acquired or property representing it – Minors' Contracts Act 1987
- s.3. Problems arise regarding goods exchanged for money, and the section can obviously not apply to goods which have been consumed.

Questions

1 Anna, aged 17, obtains a loan from Brillbank and enrols for a course in underwater photography at Countyshire College, payment being on a monthly basis. She is hoping to make her career in this field. Anna then visits her local bookshop, Dreamread, and buys a quantity of books on credit. Most of these are for her course, one is about pop music and one is entitled 'Stylish Swimming'. On the way home Anna is also tempted to subscribe to a mobile telephone service from Evertalk. Two months later, Anna decides that the course is not helping her at all and no longer wishes to attend classes. She has only made one of the monthly payments. Dreamread demands payment for the books and Anna wishes that she had not taken on the mobile phone subscription. On top of all this, Anna's bank overdraft has grown so Brillbank is now asking for repayment of the loan. Advise Anna regarding outstanding payments to Brillbank, Countyshire College, Deamread and Evertalk.

OCR 2003

2 Ben is a 17 year old student at Campshire College, following a course in media studies. Whilst shopping at Downtown Stores he is persuaded by a sales assistant that a computer would be useful to him, so he agrees to buy one on credit. He also decides to buy on credit from the same store an expensive digital camera for his planned holiday abroad. The bus service to Campshire College is terminated by the local authority, so Ben decides to buy a car in order to attend lectures. He obtains the money for this by a loan from Evergreen Bank, guaranteed by his mother. Ben later experiences financial difficulties, and is unable to pay either the credit payments to Downtown Stores or the loan repayments to Evergreen Bank. In addition he sells the camera to a friend, retaining the proceeds in his bank account ready to pay for his holiday. Advise Ben regarding the payments for the computer, the camera and the loan repayments to Evergreen Bank.

3 Critically assess the amount of protection which the law gives to a minor who enters into a contract with an adult.

4 Consider whether the law of contractual capacity is satisfactory for the society in which we live. Are there any areas which are in need of reform?

5 Minors are clearly in need of protection in the formation of a contract, but not at the expense of fair-minded adults with whom they may be dealing.' How far does the law of contract support this view?

6 Discuss the reasons why limits are placed on the contractual capacity of certain parties within society.

OCR 2004

Part 2

The contents of a contract

Is this what I agreed?

We have seen in Part 1 of this book that to form a binding contract, the essential requirement is that the parties are like-minded over the basis of their contract. This includes the detailed terms which make up the contract.

For example, if a person visits a store and agrees to buy a carpet, both the seller and the buyer may be quite clear on which carpet is required, and how much is to be paid, but they may have quite different expectations over the delivery date. In this case it would be important to have a contract to refer to, in order to determine exactly what was decided. Of course, it would only be fair to include such terms if they were put in at or before the point of agreement. It would be wrong for one party to be able to slip in a date of delivery afterwards which was unacceptable to the other. So we say that terms must be incorporated into a contract in a fair way.

Sometimes a consumer (an ordinary person, buying from a person in business) will not think about a term which could be quite important at a later stage, and therefore be at a disadvantage when dealing with a business. To help prevent this, Parliament has passed statute law to imply some terms into every consumer contract. This process will be examined in this part of the book, and some of the terms implied can be found in Part 5 on Consumer Protection.

The different types of terms found in a contract

The terms within a contract are clearly not all of the same importance. Referring back to the carpet example, the price of the carpet is obviously of vital importance to the buyer, whereas it is of lesser importance whether the fitting is carried out by two or three people, providing the task is done. The distinction between different types of terms in a contract will be examined here.

That's not covered – it was worded very carefully!

Sometimes one party to a contract tries to avoid or restrict liability for something which may well be thought to be part of the agreement. When this arises in a consumer contract, it could be very unfair.

If, for example, in the carpet sale mentioned above, the buyer found that one week after the carpet was fitted the part coloured red began to disintegrate, a remedy would certainly be needed. It would be most unfortunate if, on complaining to the seller, a term was found in their contract which the buyer had not noticed, and which stated that 'no responsibility will be taken for damage or deterioration caused by dyes'. Happily, this type of exemption clause, which could be extremely unfair on a consumer, is now very restricted, and is the subject of debate in this part of the book.

Who exactly made this agreement?

The relationship between the two parties, or people, involved in forming a contract is known as privity of contract. Traditionally only those two parties could enforce the agreement. This could cause problems, for example, where one person makes a holiday booking on behalf of another, but does not want to take legal action when something goes wrong. This issue of privity is another aspect of a contract which is considered in this part of the book.

6   Incorporation of terms

'What exactly did we agree?'

We have seen that a contract may be written or oral or a mixture of both. If a problem arises, it may become necessary to know exactly what its terms are. This may seem obvious in the case of a written contract, but it could be, for instance, that a crucial term was forgotten to be included, or that some terms were more important than others. With an oral contract, it is necessary to discover what was in fact said. A contract may be partly oral and partly written, for example where a ticket is bought for a train or bus, where much of the negotiating was spoken face to face, but with the ticket subject to a set of standard written terms. Here, as in other areas of contract law, the court attempts to look through the eyes of a reasonable person to give effect to the intentions of the parties.

Terms and representations

We need to know whether a statement is incorporated as a term of the contract, or a mere representation – that is an observation made during the course of negotiations. The importance of this is that the remedies available for breach of a term of a contract are different from those for misrepresentation. Various guidelines have been developed by the courts to help decide whether a statement is really a term of a contract or a representation.

A representor with special knowledge

Generally more importance is placed on representations made by someone who has expert knowledge on a subject than on a similar statement made by an amateur. The following two cases illustrate this. In the first case the defendant was an individual selling his car to a dealer. In the second case the defendant was a dealer.

Oscar Chess v Williams (1957)
The plaintiff sold his Morris car to the defendant car dealer. The registration document stated that the car was a 1948 model, but it was later found to be a 1939 model, for which the dealer had paid more than he would have done had he known the real age. However, it was held that the age was not a term of the contract, since the car dealer who was the buyer had the skill and experience to put him in a position to know the real age of the vehicle.

Dick Bentley Productions Ltd v Harold Smith (Motors) Ltd (1965)
A dealer sold a car to a customer which was stated to have done 20,000 miles when it had really done 100,000. This was held to be a term of the contract because the dealer was in a position to know whether the mileage was accurate.

> Why would the courts hold a car dealer more responsible than an individual for statements made about a car?

Special importance placed on the issue by the representee

A representee may make a special enquiry about an aspect of the negotiations, or make it clear that a particular fact is important. The enquiry may well be influential in having this issue considered a term of the contract.

Bannerman v White (1861)
Because a buyer particularly asked if some hops had been treated with sulphur, this was taken to be a term of the contract of sale. When the hops were later found to have been treated with sulphur the buyer was entitled to repudiate the contract.

Distance of time between statement and contract

This may be significant, but it must be a matter of circumstances and reasonableness. If a statement was made a long time before the contract was formed, it is less likely to be considered a contractual term.

Routledge v McKay (1954)
Statements made about a motor-cycle over a week before the sale were held not to be terms of the contract of sale.

Strength of inducement

A casual remark is less likely to be regarded later as a term of the contract than a statement made with much persuasion. Contrast the following two cases.

> *Ecay v Godfrey* (1947)
> The defendant described the boat he was selling as 'sound', but suggested that the buyer obtain a private survey. Because of this, the statement was held not to be a term of the contract of sale.
>
> *Schawel v Reade* (1913)
> The seller of a horse claimed that it was sound and that the buyer need not look for anything. He said, 'If there was anything the matter with the horse I would tell you.' The claim was held to be a term of the contract of sale.

Incorporating terms into oral contracts

It would obviously be unfair if one party to a contract was allowed to claim that he had contracted on certain terms unknown to the other party – the essence of a contract is agreement. The terms of an oral contract must therefore be apparent to both parties before any contract is actually made. A term will usually be considered to be incorporated into a contract if:

- the affected party knew of the clause, or
- reasonable steps have been taken to bring the term to his notice.

In deciding whether a party has had reasonable notice of a term, the courts look at the extent, or degree, of the notice, and at the point in time at which the notice was given.

The degree of notice

or

Figure 6.1

The court looks to see if it was obvious to the parties that a term was intended to form part of a contract. If something clearly looks like a contractual document, it can be assumed that the party understands that it is to be included and binding, even if the terms have not actually been read. On the other hand, if it is not obvious that a statement is part of a contract, then nothing will be assumed.

Try to find some example of documents or tickets with on them. Are they the kind of documents that you would normally keep? Would you expect to read them before forming a contract?

This arose in the following case regarding a ticket.

Chapelton v Barry UDC (1940)
A receipt for the hire of a deckchair on Barry beach had printing on the back. It was held not to be the type of document that would be regarded as of contractual importance, and the words on it were therefore not incorporated as terms.

A lot of problems regarding notice have arisen out of 'ticket' cases. These are really decisions based on the contractual effect of tickets, often for public transport, but they help to form a general picture of what is need for a term to be incorporated. The Court of Appeal have formulated two questions that need to be considered in considering liability.

• Did the plaintiff read, or was he aware of, the term?
• If not, did the defendant do what was reasonably sufficient to give the plaintiff notice of the term?

Parker v South Eastern Railway (1877)
In this case the plaintiff left a bag at the left-luggage counter and was given a receipt containing a limitation clause. It was held that as this was the kind of receipt which had to be kept and was likely to be read, since it was needed to retrieve the bag. The plaintiff therefore had notice of the term, even though it was on a ticket which she had not read.

The following case shows that if the ticket contains writing which is not legible then the writing will not form part of the contract.

Sugar v LMS Railway (1941)
A passenger was given a ticket which had an instruction on the front to 'see back' for conditions. The words on the back were covered by the

date stamp which the booking-clerk had put there to validate the ticket. It was held that as these words could not be read they could not form part of the contract.

Previous dealings

It can be seen from the above cases that the courts really do try to take a reasonable point of view, and do their utmost to protect the consumer. This does not mean, however, that they will not take an objective stance, and they may consider that sufficient notice has been given if it can be shown that there was a 'course of dealing' between the parties.

Hollier v Rambler Motors (AMC) Ltd (1972)
The plaintiff left his car at the defendant's garage for service, but there was a fire at the garage and the car was destroyed. The defendant claimed exemption from paying damages, relying on a notice inside the garage. However, it was established that the plaintiff only went to the garage infrequently so he had not been regular enough to be deemed to have read the terms.

However, if a term is to be incorporated into a contract through a course of dealing, there must be a consistent pattern of behaviour, as the following case shows.

McCutcheon v David MacBrayne Ltd (1964)
The plaintiff often used the defendant's ferry service, sometimes going into an office for a ticket, sometimes paying outside or on the ferry. On this occasion the ferry sank, and the defendant claimed exemption from liability because of a term in his notice of terms in the office. It was held that the pattern of behaviour was too inconsistent to form a course of dealing, and the defendant was liable for the cost of replacing the car.

How might a ferry operator, or any other person in business, make provision for this kind of event?

If the parties are both involved in the same trade, they may therefore be assumed to have knowledge of the normal trade terms.

> *British Crane Hire Corporation Ltd v Ipswich Plant Hire Ltd* (1975)
> It was common practice in this particular trade that the hirer of equipment should assume responsibility for returning it to the place of hire. This was so even if a crane was stuck in mud since both parties were aware of these terms from the outset.

This seems a reasonable stance to take, since both parties were in the same trade and it was established that both were aware of the normal procedure. It could be argued that if they had been prudent, they would, like anyone else in business, be insured to cover the cost of such events.

The time at which notice of a term is given

It is fairly obvious that a statement can only become a term of a contract if it is given either at the time of making the contract, or before it is made. Afterwards is too late as it would be unfair to impose terms, without any negotiation, on a person who has already made a contract.

> *Olley v Marlborough Court Ltd* (1949)
> Mrs Olley stayed at the defendant's hotel, booking in at reception and paying for the room there. Belongings were later stolen from the room, and Mrs Olley sued the hotel, who tried to rely on an exemption clause on the back of the hotel door. It was held that as the contract had been made when booking in at reception, the terms on the back of the door came too late, and were not part of the agreement.

In *O'Brien v Mirror Group* (2001) the claimant believed that he had won a leading prize in a lottery claim, but through a misprint there was an unusually large number of other winners. The rules which provided for sharing the prize were held to have been properly brought to the attention of the contestants by being printed in the newspaper the previous day. This contrasts with the following case over the issue of sufficient notice.

> *Thornton v Shoe Lane Parking Ltd* (1971)
> Mr Thornton drove into the defendants' car park, paying money into a machine and taking a ticket which activated a barrier to let him in. When Mr Thornton returned for his car there was an accident in which he was injured, partly because of the negligence of the defendants, and Mr Thornton sued for compensation. The defendants tried to rely on a notice which contained a term exempting the defendants from liability for any damage or injury caused. It was held that the term was not part of the contract for two main reasons:

> The notice was sited inside the car park. The contract with Mr
> Thornton was formed at the entrance, so he would not have seen the
> notice until after he formed the contract.
>
> As the exemption clause was very wide, including injury as well as
> damage to property, it was said that it should have been brought to Mr
> Thornton's attention in 'the most explicit way'. In fact, the exemption
> clause was amongst other terms and not likely to be seen.

The term had not in this case been specifically pointed out, and Mr
Thornton was therefore successful in his claim.

> Where could the car park owners have sited the term for it to have
> been incorporated?

Lord Denning pointed out in *Thornton* that the offending clause was in
'regrettably small print', and referred to a statement from *Spurling v
Bradshaw* (1956), where he said that a particularly wide or unusual clause
may need bringing to someone's notice more explicitly, e.g. by being
printed in red ink and with a red hand pointing to it.

> *Interfoto v Stiletto* (1988)
> The defendant borrowed photographic slides from the plaintiff's
> library, but was late returning them. There was a clause in the contract
> requiring £5 per slide per day for overdue slides, and this amounted to
> over £3,700. It was held that as this was a particularly onerous clause
> the plaintiff should have done something positive to point it out to the
> defendant. Here there was clearly some lateness on the part of the
> defendant, so the court ordered payment of £3.50 per slide per week on
> a quantum meruit (as much as was deserved).

Written contracts

The general principle is that if two parties have taken the trouble to put their
contract into writing, they intend that document to be binding and to form
the whole of their agreement, without oral additions or amendments. Two
'rules' have been formed over this, although it will be seen that there are
exceptions to both of them.

The rule in *L'Estrange v Graucob*

This rule is named after the case from which it came, and states that if a person signs a document which forms a contract, then he is bound by that contract, even though he may not have read the terms. This indicates the importance of reading a document thoroughly before signing it.

The parol evidence rule

In the case of *Goss v Lord Nugent* (1833) Lord Denman stated the rule that generally oral or other evidence will not be admitted to contradict or amend a written contract. However, the parol evidence rule is then subject to various exceptions. If the contract was partly written and partly oral, evidence of the remainder of the agreement will then be allowed. Another example is where a collateral contract exists.

Implied terms

It may be that a term has been omitted by mistake, when both parties clearly intended it to apply, or that statute or custom declares that a term must be incorporated. In such circumstances the courts can imply a term into a contract. These circumstances will be considered in turn.

Custom

The common law developed largely by custom, and in the past this played an important part in contract law. It is now less important as statute and case law have defined the boundaries of the law more clearly. Custom still arises, however, in commercial contracts, and we have already seen how a 'course of dealing' can lead to a term being incorporated into an oral contract. In a similar way customary usage within a trade may lead to a term being implied into a written contract. Here it is not necessary to show previous transactions between the parties.

Statute

Where a statute declares that a term shall be included in a particular type of contract, then it will be implied whether the parties intend it or not. Examples are found in such statutes as the Sale of Goods Act 1979 (as amended), Unfair Contract Terms Act 1977, etc. These are in many cases a codification of custom or common law, an example of this being that where goods are sold by sample, this should correspond with the bulk of the goods.

See Chapter 16 for further details.

Terms implied by the courts

The courts also intervene to decide when statutory terms should be implied in uncertain circumstances, and will themselves imply terms if necessary. See, for example, the case below regarding the general implication that goods are fit for the purpose for which they are supplied.

> *Samuels v Davis* (1943)
> A set of false teeth did not fit well and could not be used. It was claimed that they were not fit for the purpose for which they were sold under the Sale of Goods Act 1979, but a defence was raised that they were not 'goods' to be sold, since the fitting of the teeth was a service. It was held that rights established under the Sale of Goods Act 1979 should be applied to this sale by analogy. The teeth were not strictly goods, but there was an item to hand over at the end of the transaction, and the customer was entitled the expect that it would be fit to use.

Terms will be implied in various circumstances. One common example is that in a lease of a furnished house, it is understood that the accommodation will be reasonably fit for habitation at the beginning of the lease period.

The same principle could apply to the hire of a boat which was claimed to be ready for use by the customer, but which did not contain a fire extinguisher; or to a car hired ready for use, but which did not contain a spare wheel.

The readiness to imply terms has been refined somewhat through cases, and there does seem to be a much harsher approach, evident in *Liverpool City Council v Irwin* (see p. 105).

Business efficacy and the intentions of the parties

It should be remembered that the general rule is that parties are presumed to have expressed their intentions fully in a written contract. However, it may be that parties who have formed a written contract have forgotten to include a term, or have failed to allow for a situation which later arises. Generally the court will only intervene in contracts where it is absolutely necessary, following through the idea of freedom to contract. However, the aim of the courts generally is to support contracts, or bargains, where possible, rather than destroy them on technicalities, such as where there is obviously a missing term, so the following principles have been established. The courts will imply a term into a contract:

- to give effect to the clear and obvious intentions of the parties, or
- to give business efficacy to the contract.

The following case is the general authority for the principle that a term may be implied if it is clear that the parties must have intended to include it.

The Moorcock (1889)
The defendants owned a wharf and jetty, and contracted with the plaintiffs to moor and unload the plaintiffs' boat, *The Moorcock*, at the jetty. The water was too shallow at the jetty, so the boat ran aground and was damaged. It was held that in a business contract like this one, where a party invites another to moor at his jetty, there must be a term implied that it is suitable for that purpose, so the defendants were held liable for the damage.

The decision in this case, and the principle outlined, was clearly intended to prevent injustice and give effect to an otherwise workable contract (see also the section in Chapter12 [Mistake] on Rectification). It has been cited many times since as an authority, but it should be used with caution. Clear guidelines are needed on the circumstances when a term may be implied to avoid uncertainty. It is certainly not true that any term which is afterwards thought to be a reasonable one will be implied. A term will only be implied where it is essential to make the contract function, reflecting what the parties must have originally intended. McKinnon J explained this, in words that have come to be known as the officious bystander test, in the following case.

Shirlaw v Southern Foundries (1939)

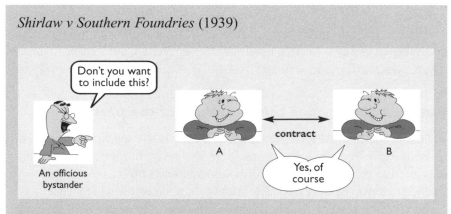

Figure 6.2

Prima facie, that which in any contract is left to be implied and need not be expressed is something so obvious that it goes without saying. Thus if, while the parties were making their bargain, an officious bystander were to suggest some express provision for it in their agreement, they would testily suppress him with a common, 'Yes, of course!'

The following case applied the 'officious bystander' test to an agreement between trade unions.

> *Spring v National Amalgamated Stevedores and Dockers Society* (1956)
> An agreement had been made between unions for the transfer of members from one union to another, known as the Bridlington agreement. The defendant union admitted Mr Spring without including this in their contract. When it was later suggested that it was implied, the officious bystander test was used. If Mr Spring had been asked whether he had intended this agreement to be included in his contract, he would not have known about it, so the answer would have been 'no'.

It is clear from the above case, then, that a term will only be included if both parties would have wanted it. The court will not imply a term involving facts known to one party but not another (as with the Bridlington agreement, above), even if it is a good idea. The principle was applied by Lord Pearson more recently in the next case.

> *Trollope and Colls Ltd v North West Regional Hospital Board* (1973)
> An unexpressed term can be implied if and only if the court finds that the parties must have intended that term to form part of their contract. It is not enough for the court to find that such a term would have been adopted by the parties as reasonable men if it had been suggested to them; it must have been a term that went without saying, a term necessary to give business efficacy to the contract, a term which although tacit, formed part of the contract which the parties made for themselves.
>
> *Wilson v Best Travel* (1993)
> In this case the court used a similar analysis to that in *Trollope and Colls*. A customer claimed that, applying the officious bystander test, a holiday company would have intended to include a term that a hotel would be reasonably safe. The courts did not agree as the standard of the hotel was too remote to be within the knowledge of the operator.

Cheshire and Fifoot claim that *The Moorcock* is still alive. It certainly is, and is a useful measure of whether a term may be implied. It was suggested by Lord Denning in *Liverpool City Council v Irwin* (1976) that a term concerning the maintenance of services to a block of flats should be implied where it was reasonable. This was generally rejected, and it was said that a term should only be implied where the nature of the contract implicitly required it. The cases which follow it help to refine the principles and to ensure that terms are not implied which would not have been included by parties, had they considered them. It is important to realise that the test of this is a subjective one. It is not a matter of what a reasonable man may have included, but what the parties themselves would have agreed. The use of judicial power in this way must reflect the real intention of the parties.

> Why do you think that the courts take such a strict approach to implying terms into a contract?

Collateral contracts

We have already examined collateral contracts, but it will be seen here that they can be used to invoke a representation which may otherwise be outside the scope of the main contract. The use of the collateral contract can be seen in some circumstances as an agreement to make a contract.

> *City and Westminster Properties Ltd v Mudd* (1959)
> The defendant leased a shop from the plaintiffs and was known by the plaintiffs to be in the habit of staying overnight in one room of the premises. When the lease was due for renewal a draft was produced which only allowed the premises to be used for business purposes. The defendant stated that he would sign the lease if the plaintiffs agreed that he could continue to sleep on the premises. They did so, but later sued the defendant for breach. He successfully relied on the collateral contract to which the plaintiffs had agreed before he signed the main lease.

Also relevant is the case of *Esso Petroleum Co Ltd v Commissioners of Customs and Excise* (1976) examined previously, where a collateral contract for the supply of a 'free' coin would be enforceable provided the customer bought a certain quantity of fuel. This approach obviously tempers the apparent harshness of the parol evidence rule, and deals with some of the problems of whether a statement is a term or a mere representation.

Summary

Terms may be written, oral or a mixture. They may also express (clearly expressed by the parties) or implied (incorporated in some other way, for example by statute).

Distinguish between terms and representations

* Special knowledge of the representor – *Dick Bentley Productions Ltd v Harold Smith (Motors) Ltd, Oscar Chess v Williams.*
* Importance placed on a particular issue – *Bannerman v White.*
* Distance in time between statement and contract – *Routledge v McKay.*
* Strength of inducement – *Ecay v Godfrey, Schawel v Reade.*

The importance lies in the different remedies, i.e. damages for breach of contract is the usual remedy for a term which is untrue or not performed, while the usual remedy for an untrue representation is rescission or damages for misrepresentation.

Incorporation of terms into an oral contract

* Degree of notice – *Chapelton v Barry UDC, Parker v South Eastern Railway, Sugar v LMS Railway.*
* Course of dealing – *Hollier v Rambler Motors (AMC) Ltd, McCutcheon v David MacBrayne Ltd, British Crane Hire Corporation Ltd v Ipswich Plant Hire Ltd.*
* Time at which the notice was given – *Olley v Marlborough Court Ltd, Thornton v Shoe Lane Parking Ltd.*

Written contracts

What is agreed on paper normally forms the basis of the contract:

* the rule in *L'Estrange v Graucob,*
* the parol evidence rule – *Goss v Lord Nugent.*

Implied terms

Implied by custom, especially within a trade, as in a 'course of dealing', or in a geographical area.

* Implied by statute, especially in consumer contracts, e.g. Sale of Goods Act 1979 (as amended) sections 12 to 15.
* Implied by the courts: on the facts – *Samuels v Davis*; or via the officious bystander test – *Shirlaw v Southern Foundries, Spring v National Amalgamated Stevedores and Dockers Society, Trollope and Colls Ltd v North West Regional Hospital Board*; or to give business efficacy to an agreement – *The Moorcock, Liverpool City Council v Irwin.*

Collateral contracts

A representation may in some circumstances form part of a collateral contract, where it would not be included in the main agreement – *City and Westminster Properties Ltd v Mudd*.

Questions

1   Smith is talking to Jones one day about motor-cycles, and says that he has a model which is two years old and has done 8,000 miles. Jones decides to buy the cycle and they draw up a written agreement which states their names and addresses, the date, the type of motor-cycle and the price. Jones pays and takes the motor-cycle away. The next day Jones goes on holiday and checks in at the Seaview Hotel. He leaves his belongings in the hotel bedroom, placing some valuables in the safe provided. On his return the safe has been opened and the contents removed. The hotel claims no responsibility because of a term on the back of the bedroom door exempting them from liability for theft of clients' belongings. On his return, a week later, Jones has the motor-cycle serviced, and is informed by the mechanic that the machine is older than he believed.

Advise Jones regarding any claim he may wish to make against Smith regarding the motor-cycle and against Seaview Hotel regarding the valuables which were taken from the safe.

2   There are occasions when terms are implied into contracts which have not been discussed by the parties. Critically consider the circumstances in which this is likely to occur.

OCR 2006

3   'What a man sees and signs is what he has agreed.' To what extent is this an accurate statement of the incorporation of contractual terms?

4   Alex buys a camera from Brillpics Ltd which is described on the packaging as 'ideal for all season general purpose photography.' After using the camera on a ski-ing holiday Alex discovers that his pictures are all very faint. When he returns to Brillpics Ltd the manager says that the camera was not intended for use in low temperature winter conditions, and that he should have bought a more expensive model. Alex also buys a second hand motor cycle from a fellow holiday maker, Callum. Alex purchases this knowing that Callum is an experienced engineer. However, on his first long journey Alex finds that the engine runs erratically and that the motor cycle will only move slowly. Alex now wishes to return the motorcycle to Callum.

Advise Alex of any remedies which may be available to him regarding the camera and the motor cycle.

OCR 2002

7   Types of terms within a contract

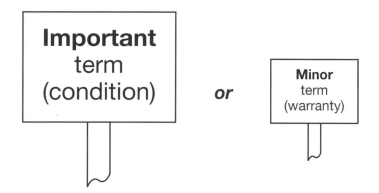

The terms found within a contract are clearly not all of the same importance. For example, in the purchase of a car, if it is found after the sale that a wing-mirror, which was to have been included in the sale, is missing, then the person selling the car is in breach of a term. However, the term is not a major one, and no doubt if the seller were to offer the money to buy a new wing-mirror that arrangement would probably be quite acceptable. On the other hand, if on completing the transaction, the buyer went to drive away the car and discovered that the engine did not work at all, then a far more serious term would be in breach. Money to replace the engine would probably not be satisfactory in this case, and the buyer would probably want to repudiate (or end) the contract altogether.

Conditions and warranties

The more important terms, those which are fundamental to the contract, are called conditions. The less important ones are called warranties. The difference between these two types of terms is illustrated by two cases involving opera singers.

Poussard v Spiers and Pond (1876)
The plaintiff was engaged to sing the female lead part in a new opera. She fell ill and missed the final rehearsals and first four performances. On recovery she tried to take up her place, but the defendant refused to let her. It was held that the defendant was entitled to repudiate as her action amounted to a breach of condition. Blackburn J said, 'Failure on the plaintiff's part went to the root of the matter and discharged the defendant'.

▶

> *Bettini v Gye* (1876)
> The plaintiff was a singer engaged to perform with the defendant's opera company for a fixed period. He should have attended six days of rehearsals but was ill and only able to attend three. He recovered in good time for the performance. It was held that this was a breach of warranty, as the singer was able to perform, so the breach did not go to 'the root of' the contract, and could be settled by damages.

The effect of a breach

As we can see from the above examples, the need to differentiate between terms arises because of the remedies available when a term is breached. The effect in law of a breach of each type of term can be summarised as follows:

* The breach of a warranty only entitles the innocent party to damages.
* The breach of a condition results in a choice for the innocent party:
  (a) he can repudiate, or end, the contract, or
  (b) he can choose to continue with the contract and claim damages instead.

The innocent party can, therefore, choose either to repudiate if a condition is breached, or to affirm (to continue with the contract), and this was confirmed in the case of *Vitol SA v Norelf Ltd* (1995). However, if the innocent decides to affirm, the obligations of that party must be carried out in the normal way. In *Fercometal Sarl v Mediterranean Shipping Co SA* (1988) the original breach may not be used as a reason for the 'innocent' party not to perform further duties.

Condition or warranty?

So how do the courts decide whether a term is a condition or a warranty? There are several approaches:

* The courts can use a traditional approach, looking at the term to decide if it 'goes to the root of the matter' according to the analysis by Blackburn J in *Poussard v Spiers and Pond,* if it is a kind of term which lends itself to this kind of analysis.
* The parties may have labelled the terms at the outset – although this is not necessarily conclusive.
* The terms may be of a kind, usually within a consumer contract, for which provision is made in statute.

- The courts may look at the overall picture presented by the contract and make a decision based on the consequence of the breach.
- There may be a 'course of dealing' between the parties.
- The approach in *Hong Kong Fir* may be used (see p. 113).

Terms specified by the parties

When any dispute arises over a contract the courts do place importance on the original intention of the parties, if this is clear. This is seen in the recent case of *Parham v F Parham Ltd* (2006) where the wording of an employment contract was given its 'ordinary and natural meaning' specified by the parties, even though this involved an increase in salary for an employee from £10,000 to £410,005.88. It could be argued that a similar approach should be taken towards the parties' statements concerning when the terms of a contract are conditions or warranties. This sometimes is the case, and is to be expected, as the contracts will then reflect the original intention of the parties. However, occasionally difficulties may arise over a situation which is apparently straightforward. The following case shows that even if a term is stated to be either a condition or warranty the use of these expressions is not conclusive and does not prevent the court considering the relative importance of the terms.

Schuler v Wickman Machine Tool Sales Ltd (1973)
The plaintiff agreed to give the defendant sole selling rights of certain machinery, provided that the defendant visited the six largest car manufacturers in the United Kingdom at least once every week to solicit orders. Only this clause, out of twenty, was described as a condition of the agreement. The defendant committed significant breaches of this clause during the first eight months. The plaintiff knew of this, and at first overlooked it, but later sought to terminate the contract claiming breach of condition. It was held that the plaintiff was not entitled to repudiate. The use of the word 'condition' was not conclusive, as it was not certain that the parties understood the significance of the expression at the outset, especially since no action had been taken when breaches first arose. If the labelling of a term as a condition was intended to be interpreted strictly, the parties should make that intention clear.

Do you think that the average person realises the distinction between a condition and a warranty when forming a contract?

Reference to statute

Parliament takes a somewhat paternalistic view of consumer protection, largely because the average member of the public is unaware of the need to protect rights until a problem arises. Certain terms are therefore designated conditions within consumer contracts. The Sale of Goods Act (1979, as amended) makes the following provision in section 15:

> s.15 (2) 'In the case of a contract for sale by sample there is an implied condition – that the bulk will correspond with the sample in quality.'

In this case Parliment is stating that such a term, implied into a consumer contract will be a condition rather than a warranty.

This statutory provision is not negotiable, and is not open to dispute according to the wishes of the parties. It is included automatically in a consumer contract if relevant.

Consideration of the terms by the courts

If statute is not applicable, and there is no label placed on the terms by the parties at the outset, then issues are resolved by comparison with other cases.

> *The Mihalis Angelos* (1970)
> A ship was chartered in May 1965 for a journey from North Vietnam to Hamburg. There was a clause in the charterparty (the written document of agreement) that the ship would be ready to load on 1 July 1965. On this date it was in the Pacific and unable to meet the deadline. There was clearly a breach, but of what type? It was held that this was a breach of condition. In a charterparty the ship owner and hirer meet on equal terms. They or their lawyers seek a firm foundation of principle upon which to work, and need definite rules.

Was this remedy satisfactory for the hirer?

To find that the owner had breached a warranty would leave the contract intact and provide damages. This would compensate for loss, but would still leave the hirer at a disadvantage as he would still be without a ship. To find that the owner had breached a condition would allow the hirer to repudiate, or free himself from the agreement, and charter another ship.

'Course of dealing'

Sometimes the courts will find that the parties not only meet on equal terms, but that they have traded with each other before, or within the same trade or professional sphere. In this situation it is likely that the parties themselves know which terms are the more important ones from the outset. This was the finding in the following case.

British Crane Hire Corporation Ltd v Ipswich Plant Hire Ltd(1975)
The normal trade practice for a hirer of this type of equipment was to be responsible for returning it to the place of hire. When a crane was stuck in some marshy ground, the terms involving the return of the equipment were disputed, and it was held that on this occasion the courts could refer to normal trade practice which the parties must have encountered in their previous work.

Can you think of any other trading situations where usual practice may indicate a type of term?

Innominate terms – the *Hong Kong Fir* approach

Generally, more important terms are conditions and less important ones are warranties. Occasions may arise, however, where the importance of a term is not apparent until it is breached. This often applies to a term which is wide in meaning, such as a claim that something is 'in good condition'. This could be breached in a minor way or a very serious way. Where the status of a term is unknown because of its nature, it is usually regarded now as an innominate term.

However, this area of law is still in development, and case law will clarify exactly how the approach is to work in practice. The issue arose in the following leading case.

Hong Kong Fir Shipping Co Ltd v Kawasaki Kisen Kaisha Ltd (1962)
The plaintiff owned a ship which he chartered to the defendant, stating in the agreement that it was 'in every way fitted for ordinary cargo service'. In fact the engines were old and developed trouble, and the staff were incompetent. This resulted in a delay of five weeks on a voyage to Osaka and a further fifteen weeks at Osaka being repaired. The defendant terminated the charterparty and the plaintiff sued for

▶

> wrongful repudiation. The Court of Appeal upheld the plaintiff's claim and would not allow repudiation. It was not simply a question of whether a condition or warranty was breached. The term did not lend itself to traditional analysis. Diplock LJ said that the breach would be considered serious enough to entitle the innocent party to repudiate the contract if the effect of it is to 'deprive the party not in default of substantially the whole benefit which it was intended that he should obtain from the contract'.

This approach is very different from that traditionally taken by the courts. Rather than decide whether a term should be a condition or a warranty, which in turn would indicate the action to be taken, the courts take the approach set out below.

***

The Hong Kong Fir approach
- *Look at the consequences of breach of an innominate term.*
- *Consider how serious the breach is.*
- *Decide whether the term is to be regarded as a condition or as a warranty.*
- *Apply the appropriate remedy, either repudiation or damages.*

***

Note that the courts are only treating the terms *like* a condition or warranty in this situation, not labelling the term. This is necessary because if the contract continues, the same term could later be treated in a different way. In addition, if the courts were merely labelling the terms, the *Hong Kong Fir* approach would not be needed. This new approach is very useful when a term is very wide-reaching and can be breached in many ways with varying degrees of seriousness (for example, if a car was stated to be roadworthy). This is, of course, exactly what happened in the *Hong Kong Fir* case.

The principle was discussed and then applied in the following case.

> *Cehave v Bremer Handelsgesellschaft* (1975) *(The Hansa Nord)*
> A cargo of citrus pellets was under contract to be shipped 'in good condition'. Some of the cargo was damaged but not seriously. It was held by Court of Appeal that the effect of the breach was not serious on this occasion, and that the buyers were not therefore entitled to repudiate the contract. The term was treated as a warranty, with the consequence of damages being payable to compensate for the loss.

The approach was also used in the case of *Reardon Smith Line v Hansen Tangen*.

Reardon Smith Line v Hansen Tangen (1976)
Here the breach was technical and was being used as an excuse to escape from a subsequently unwanted contract. A tanker being built to order was labelled Osaka 354. A subcontractor did some work on it and relabelled it Oskima 004. The buyers tried to reject the vessel, claiming that it did not conform to its original description, a term which could have been breached in a major or minor way. In fact, they really wanted to avoid the contract because the market had slumped.

It was held by the House of Lords that this small technical breach should not allow the buyers to repudiate. A rigid application of rules should not be allowed to lead to injustice. This is an important comment on the *Hong Kong Fir* approach, since it really does aim to bring about justice in the individual case. The problem is that in doing so, it increases uncertainty, as the parties are not sure of the view that will be taken by the court, and do not know of the consequences of any possible breach until after it has occurred.

The debate continues

The commercial standing of the parties and their equality of bargaining power should be taken into account in considering whether the new, less rigid approach should be taken, and the following factors may affect the decision of the court.

- If the term is one which is covered by statute then there it is not open to the courts to discuss its status.
- If a breach of term would 'go to the root' of the contract, then the traditional approach to differentiating between types of terms may be satisfactory.
- If there is a 'course of dealing' it may be clear what type of term has been breached.
- If the parties clearly stated their intentions regarding the status of the terms in the agreement, and understood the significance of their statements, then this may be decisive (but see *Schuler v Wickman*, p. 111).
- If the parties are of equal commercial standing, it may well be justified, in the interests of certainty and consistency, to interpret terms more strictly, to ensure certainty between the parties. This principle will apply particularly in the case of charterparties. The following cases are relevant here.

Awilko v Fulvia SpA di Navigazione (1981) *(The Chikuma)*
A vessel was hired out under a charterparty and a dispute arose over the regularity of payments. The owners claimed that because of this they were entitled to withdraw the ship. The House of Lords held that they were entitled to do so. Although this was harsh, it was felt that in such commercial agreements 'conditions' should be strictly interpreted so that parties know where they stand. In this way, long and expensive litigation would be avoided. So this was really a matter of erring on the side of certainty because of the nature of the transaction.

Bunge Corporation v Tradax (1981)
In a shipping contract, a term requiring notice of readiness to load was breached by a few days. This was held by the House of Lords to be a condition, even though the extent of the breach was small, as a stipulation over time in a shipping contract is of great importance and the outcome needs to be certain.

Lombard North Central v Butterworth (1987)
This case is a recent example of a party stressing the importance of a term being of a specific type. The plaintiff leased a computer to the defendant, with a clause making punctual payment of hire instalments 'of the essence' of the agreement. The defendant was late paying the third, fourth and fifth instalments. When the sixth payment was six weeks overdue the plaintiff terminated the agreement and sought damages for breach. It was held by Court of Appeal that they were entitled to do so, having made their intentions concerning the term quite clear at the outset.

The following is an interesting case which came well before *Hong Kong Fir* but which used a similar approach, showing that the idea behind examining the consequences was not as 'new' as perhaps thought, but merely waiting to be formally introduced via case law.

Aerial Advertising Co v Batchelors Peas (1938)

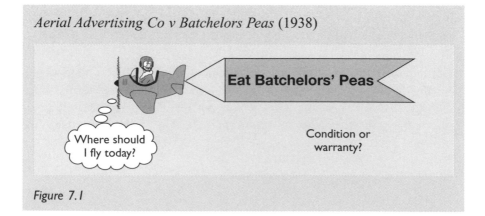

Figure 7.1

The parties agreed that the plaintiff would advertise the defendant company's products by flying over various towns displaying a trailing banner which read 'Eat Batchelors' Peas'. Before starting each day the pilot was to telephone for approval of the location. He did not do this on 11 November 1937, and flew over the main square in Salford during the two minutes' silence which was part of the remembrance day service. Many complaints were received by the defendant company, including threats to avoid buying their products.

The defendant company claimed that it was no longer bound by the contract, and the court upheld this claim. The decision was based not on the original importance of the term, but on the seriousness of the breach.

Summary

The main types of terms

Conditions and warranties – *Poussard v Spiers and Pond, Bettini v Gye*. The effect of a breach of either of these:

* Breach of a warranty: damages.
* Breach of a condition: repudiation or damages – *Vitol SA v Norelf Ltd*; but if affirming, the innocent party must also carry out obligations still due – *Fercometal Sarl v Mediterranean Shipping Co SA*.

Approaches taken by the courts in distinguishing between types of terms

* Traditional approach: examine whether the breach 'goes to the root of the matter' (Blackburn J in *Poussard v Spiers and Pond*).
* The parties may have labelled the terms – *Schuler v Wickman Machine Tool Sales Ltd*.
* Statute may specify the nature of the term (usually within a consumer contract).
* The court may consider the consequence of the breach, for example, the ship in *The Mihalis Angelos* was in the middle of the ocean, so repudiation was needed.
* A 'course of dealing' may exist – *British Crane Hire Corporation Ltd v Ipswich Plant Hire Ltd*.
* The *Hong Kong Fir* approach may be used, where the court examines the effect of the breach and treats the term *like* a condition or a warranty.

Innominate terms

- Examine the approach taken in *Hong Kong Fir Shipping Co Ltd v Kawasaki Kisen Kaisha Ltd*. See also *Cehave v Bremer Handelsgesellschaft* (known as *The Hansa Nord), Reardon Smith Line v Hansen Tangen*.
- Consider the need for certainty between parties of equal commercial standing – *Awilko v Fulvia SpA di Navigazione* (known as *The Chikuma), Bunge Corporation v Tradax, Lombard North Central v Butterworth*. *See also Aerial Advertising Co v Batchelors Peas*.

Questions

1 Discuss whether the increased use of the innominate term means that it is no longer important to differentiate between conditions and warranties.

OCR 4-module specimen paper

2 'The different approaches taken to classifying terms lead to uncertainty.' Discuss the accuracy of this statement.

3 'The intentions of the contracting parties are the main factors in deciding on the relative importance of contractual terms.' Discuss whether this is, in fact, the approach currently taken by the courts.

4 'The different categories of terms found in an agreement are set by the parties and reflect a general freedom to contract.' Is this a reflection of the state of the law regarding the types of terms within a contract?

5 Explain the way in which the courts establish how a particular term should be classified and discuss the importance of this distinction.

OCR 2003

8   Exemption clauses

'What are they trying to avoid?'

An exemption clause in a contract is one which seeks to exclude or limit in some way one party's liability toward the other. Over a period of time these clauses had been used in an oppressive way, where a person in a weak bargaining position had little say in the formation of a fair contract. The courts have therefore limited the use of these clauses through case law, and in addition Parliament has made substantial changes to the common law position through statute.

There are two types of exemption clause:

*   limitation clauses – where a party limits liability in a contract;
*   exclusion clauses – where a party tries to avoid any liability at all in a contract.

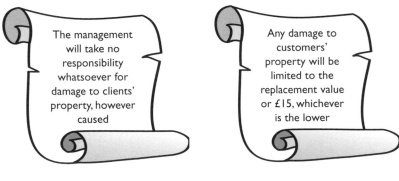

An exclusion clause   A limitation clause

Figure 8.1

Can you distinguish between the limitation and exclusion clauses above?

The courts' approach to both types is similar in the procedure followed, so in this chapter the term 'exemption clauses', where used, refers to both exclusion and limitation clauses.

To examine the validity of an exemption clause there are three steps traditionally taken by the courts. These are seen in the chart below.

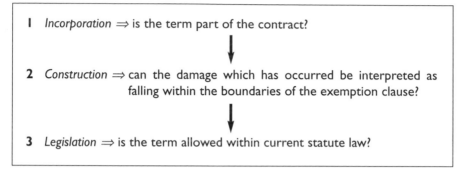

Figure 8.2

If the exemption clause survives the first 'hurdle' and is found to be incorporated, the court then enquires whether the clause can be interpreted to cover the damage. If this is the case, then the relevant statutes will be applied, to see if the clause should stand. This process in logical since, of course, if the term is not incorporated into the contract the other considerations will be irrelevant. In practice, however, the legislation is often the first point of discussion. The traditional route should be followed in analysing problems for examinations, and is pursued in detail here.

Incorporation

The court will ask the question: Is the clause part of the contract? An exemption clause, just like any other term of a contract, must be incorporated into the contract. Incorporation was covered in detail in Chapter 6, but the most relevant issues are that:

• The term must not come too late – *Olley v Marlborough Court* (1949).

• The term must be brought to the attention of the other party in a reasonable way – *Parker v South Eastern Railway* (1877).

For both of the above points in a modern setting, see *Thornton v Shoe Lane Parking Ltd* (1971). In addition, if the term is in a document it should be one which would be regarded as of a contractual nature – see *Chapelton v Barry UDC* (1940), and the writing must not be obscured – see *Sugar v LMS Railway* (1941). Remember also that the parties may have formed a 'course of dealing' – *Hollier v Rambler Motors* (1972).

See Chapter 6, pp. 97–101, for details of the cases mentioned above.

Construction

In this context construction means interpretation. The court will ask the question: Can the exemption clause be construed (or interpreted) to cover the damage which has arisen? Two rules are used to help answer the question: the main purpose rule and the *contra proferentem* rule.

The main purpose rule

The courts will not allow an individual term to defeat the main purpose of the contract. So if an individual term contradicts the very reason for the contract being made, that term will not stand. The following case provides a good example of this.

Glynn v Margetson (1893)
A clause allowed a ship to call at any port in Europe or North Africa. While under a contract to carry oranges from Malaga to Liverpool, the captain relied on this clause to give him the freedom to go into the Mediterranean to pick up extra cargo. While this would not have mattered if he was carrying non-perishable goods and time was not important, in this case it meant that the oranges deteriorated, so were not 'in good condition' as the contract required. The clause would therefore have defeated the purpose of the contract, so was not allowed to stand.

The contra proferentem rule

Any doubt or ambiguity in an exemption clause will be interpreted against the person seeking to rely on it (or proffering it), as seen in *Houghton v Trafalgar Insurance* (1954), where the word 'load' in a car insurance policy was held not to extend to an excess of passengers.

Other common law principles

An overriding oral statement may contradict an exemption clause, as in the following case.

Mendelssohn v Normand (1970)
A garage attendant advised a customer to leave his car unlocked, and items were later stolen from the car. An exclusion clause disclaimed liability for stolen goods, but this was held to be ineffective because of the oral statement of the attendant.

> Can you think of any other circumstances where an oral statement may override what is within a written contract?

Even if a contradictory statement turns out to be untrue, and therefore a misrepresentation, it can have the same effect on an exemption clause as a true statement.

Curtis v Chemical Cleaning and Dyeing Co (1951)
The plaintiff took a wedding dress to be cleaned and was asked to sign a document. On enquiry she was told that it meant that the cleaners would not be liable for damage to sequins and beads. In fact the document contained a clause exempting the cleaners from liability 'for any damage howsoever arising'. The dress was stained by the cleaners and they tried to rely on their exemption clause. It was held that the misrepresentation had overridden the exemption clause, and the cleaners were liable to the plaintiff for the damage.

> Does this place an unfair burden on a sales assistant? What could the assistant do to avoid this? Who would be liable if an untrue statement is made by an assistant?

Legislation

The final step taken by the court is to ask the question: Is there any legislation which affects this clause? The relevant legislation is the Unfair Contract Terms Act 1977 and the Unfair Terms in Consumer Contract Regulations 1999. This legislation has radically changed the idea of freedom to contract, and has given much needed protection to the consumer.

The Unfair Contract Terms Act 1977

This was a major landmark in fairness to consumers, and had the effect of relieving the court of forming principles as each different case is presented to court. The act is largely built upon the principles already established, and states the law clearly, leaving less room for uncertainty, at least as far as exemption from liability for death or personal injury is concerned. As most of the provisions in the Unfair Contract Terms Act 1977 apply to consumer transactions rather than agreements between businesses, two important concepts are:

• Business liability – stated in section 1(3) as 'duties arising (a) from things done or to be done in the course of business ... or (b) from the occupation of premises used for the business purposes of the occupier'.

- A consumer – section 12 defines a consumer as follows: A party to the contract 'deals as a consumer' in relation to another party if:
  - (a) he neither makes the contract in the course of business nor holds himself out as doing so; and
  - (b) the other party does make the contract in the course of a business; and
  - (c) … the goods passing under or in pursuance of the contract are of a type ordinarily supplied for private use or consumption.

Most provisions also apply where one party acts on the standard terms of the other. It is also clear that under the Unfair Contract Terms Act 1977 a person normally in business, or even a company can, in some circumstances, act as a consumer.

> *R and B Customs Brokers Co Ltd v United Dominions Trust Ltd* (1988)
> The plaintiff shipping company bought a car partly for business use and partly for private use by the owners. They did not buy cars regularly and this was not an integral part of their business, but peripheral to it, so they were treated by the Court of Appeal on this occasion as consumers.
>
> *Feldarol v Hermes Leasing* (2004)
> A finance company bought a Lamborghini sports car for its managing director, a sports car enthusiast. As the car was mainly for personal use this was held to be a consumer contract.

The main provisions in the Unfair Contract Terms Act 1977 have had a dramatic effect on exemption clauses in consumer contracts. There is very little scope for exploiting a consumer in this way now, and where exemption clauses in these contracts are allowed, it will only be when the court finds them reasonable. The main provisions are:

- *A contract term cannot now exclude or restrict liability for **death or personal injury** resulting from negligence – section 2(1).*
- *A contract term can only exclude or restrict **other liability** resulting from negligence if it is reasonable to do so – section 2(2).*
- *A further provision is that in a consumer contract, or when dealing on one party's standard business terms, a contract term cannot exclude or restrict liability for **non-performance** or for performance which is substantially different from what was agreed, unless it is reasonable to do so – section 3.*

Reasonableness

The law is quite clear on exemption from liability for death or personal injury in consumer contracts – it is not allowed. However, where an attempt is made to exclude or limit other liability, the court has to decide if this is reasonable. Reasonableness is interpreted to mean fair given the circumstances known to the parties at the time, and, from the case of *Stewart Gill v Horatio Myer Ltd* (1992), takes into account the resources available to meet the liability and the possibility of insurance. Other factors which the court may take into account include:

- the bargaining power of the parties, and whether an alternative source was available
- any inducement to agree to the term, for example, a favourable price
- trade custom and previous dealings
- the difficulty of the task
- whether the goods are adapted to the order of the customer.

Three cases follow which show situations where exemption was held to be unreasonable.

Green v Cade (1978)
A consignment of seed potatoes was supplied to a farmer, with a clause in the contract stating that any rejection or complaint must be reported within three days of delivery. The crop failed because the seed potatoes were found to contain a virus. It was held that this requirement was unreasonable regarding a defect which could not be discovered on inspection at the time of delivery.

George Mitchell v Finney Lock Seeds (1983)
In a contract for the supply of cabbage seed, a clause limited the supplier's liability to the purchase price of about £200. When the cabbage crop failed, this clause was held unreasonable, given that the damage sustained was over £60,000. The courts took the following points into consideration:

- The supplier's admission that *ex gratia* payments were sometimes made in such circumstances (this was seen as an admission that the clause was unreasonable).
- The magnitude of the loss.
- The carelessness of the supplier.
- The availability of insurance to the supplier against such claims.

Smith v Bush and Harris v Wyre Forest (1990)
There are really two separate cases here, but the facts were similar. At Court of Appeal level the decisions differed, but on joint appeal to the House of Lords the outcome was the same in both instances. In each case a surveyor attempted to exclude liability for negligence in valuing a property. In the case of *Smith v Bush* some chimneys had been removed

and the building had not been properly supported, and in the case of *Harris v Wyre Forest* subsidence occurred, costing more than the value of the property in repair. It was held that the surveyor could not rely on the exemption clause, since the house in each case was of a usual kind, and the task of valuation was not difficult. It was the responsibility of the surveyor to carry out the task with professional care, and in any case insurance could be taken out against claims of negligence.

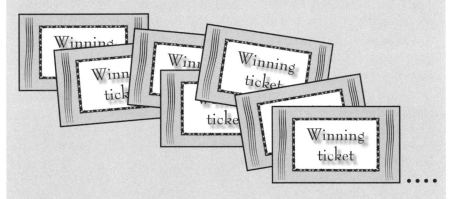

O'Brien v Mirror Group (2001)
A reader of a newspaper held a winning number on a scratch card. However, due to a printing error, a large number of other readers had the same winning number on that occasion. The claimant had not read the terms, in another day's edition of the newspaper, that included a statement that in such a situation winnings would be shared, not paid in full to each winner. Even though the claimant had not actually seen this term, it was held that there had been reasonable opportunity to do so. It was therefore reasonably brought to readers' attention and it was unreasonable to expect such winnings. The court also took into account the fact that the claimant did not have to do very much to 'earn' the winnings. The Mirror Group were therefore held not liable for the large payments.

On the back a packet in which films are sent away for developing the following terms are found, in very very small print, at right angles to the main form which is completed by the customer, 'The company limits any liability for loss or damage to films to twice the cost of the materials.'

Do you think that this is a reasonable term?

Similar clauses are commonly found on such packets, sometimes the 'right' way up, sometimes at right angles, and always in small print (remember Lord Denning in *Thornton* – see Chapter 6, pp. 100 and 101). The following case concerns one of these packets.

Woodman v Photo Trade Processing (1981)
A photographic processor's liability was limited to a replacement film. This was held unreasonable, but it was said that it may be reasonable if it was made clear that a premium service was available, costing more but without the limitation.

Watford Electronics v Sanderson (2001)
The Court of Appeal allowed a computer supplier to limit its liability for computer equipment not being able to carry out the tasks for which it was bought. The decision was largely based on the fact that the two parties were in business and had therefore, presumably, willingly agreed to this limitation.

Granville Oil & Chemicals Ltd v Davies Turner (2003)
The court upheld a nine month limit on reporting problems with goods in transit, again based on the fact that it was reasonable for parties in business to be aware of this limitation.

The Unfair Terms in Consumer Contract Regulations 1999

These regulations were passed following the European Directive on Unfair Terms in Consumer Contracts. The Directive was largely incorporated into English law by the Unfair Terms in Consumer Contract Regulations 1994 and updated in 1999. The kind of terms covered by these regulations are wider than those covered by Unfair Contract Terms Act 1977, in that the regulations apply to unfair terms generally, not just exemption clauses. Examples of the kind of terms envisaged are listed in Schedule 3 to the Regulations, and include

- terms excluding liability for death or personal injury (as before)
- terms which bind the consumer when they had no opportunity to discover the terms before the contract
- terms which allow the seller to alter the contract without a valid reason
- terms which unreasonably exclude the consumer's legal rights

The regulations do not apply the fairness principle to core (central) terms of the contract, providing they are in 'plain intelligible language'. This is in line with the idea that the courts only require consideration to be sufficient rather than adequate (see Chapter 3). So provided the parties do know and understand what they have agreed to (and they are likely to understand the core, central issues) the court will not interfere with fairness in terms of actual value. However there may be difficulty deciding exactly which are the 'core' elements of a contract. When they are known, the task of the court will be to see that all of the other clauses pass the test of fairness according to the regulations. The most recent amendments to the Regulations in 1999 and 2001 give 'qualified bodies' – that is people other than the Office of Fair Trading, such as the Consumers' Association and the weights and measures authorities – the right to apply to the court and to stop an unfair term from being used. This should help to spread the load of policing unfair terms – provided that the rights to supervise in this way is in itself properly controlled.

The consumer

A consumer is defined in a slightly different way under the Regulations, as being 'any natural person who is acting for purposes which are outside his trade, business or profession'. This may exclude a person acting partly within the broad context of his business from being a consumer, as in the case of *R and B Customs Brokers Co Ltd v United Dominions Trust Ltd* (see p. 123). The seller, however, has a wide definition, being 'any person who sells or supplies goods or services, and who in making a contact is acting for purposes related to his business'.

Unfairness in the Regulations

An unfair term in a consumer contract will not be binding, and 'unfairness' is stated in Regulation 5(1) to be 'any term which contrary to the requirement of good faith causes a significant imbalance in the parties' rights and obligations under the contract to the detriment of the consumer'. This is a piece of legislation which is clearly European in flavour, since English law has not in the past recognised the idea of 'good faith' to any extent. The kind of factors which the courts are directed by Schedule 2 to consider in assessing good faith are not unfamiliar, such as:

* the bargaining strength of parties
* any inducement to contract
* special requirements of the customer
* whether the supplier has acted equitably.

It will be seen that these are similar to those applied under the Unfair Contract Terms Act 1977. It is also stated within the Regulations that a seller or supplier should express terms in 'plain intelligible language', and where there is ambiguity, interpretation should favour the consumer. So an unfair clause, in very small print, buried amongst other terms, or in language which a consumer will not readily understand, should not be allowed, whether it be an exemption clause or any other term leading to unfairness toward the consumer. This may well have a serious impact on any honourable pledge clauses still being used in consumer contracts, for example on football pools coupons, should a claim arise (see Chapter 4, Legal intent).

In addition to the specific provisions, the Director-General of Fair Trading has been given the role of supervising unfair contract terms by receiving complaints, asking for injunctions to stop the use of specific unfair terms, and generally publishing information about the Regulations.

How might the judiciary view appraisal of a legal issue by a politician?

The current position

The common law went to great lengths to protect a party with weak bargaining power, whether or not in the position of a consumer, and this is apparent through the decisions and reasoning in cases which have formed the common law rules. The situation with the present extensive consumer law development is that the need to do this has diminished – the courts now assuming a greater role in interpreting the legislation, particularly where a wide-ranging word like 'reasonable' is involved.

One particular effect of legislation in general is to indicate that since consumers and those dealing on standard terms are now very well protected, businesses which negotiate individually may be assumed to know what they are doing when they enter into contracts with each other. This is especially true of limitation clauses, as opposed to exclusion clauses, and here the courts are more willing to agree that it is reasonable for a business to set a limit on what it can afford to pay in the event of a breach, especially bearing in mind the ability to insure. This approach was already seen in two cases involving Securicor, the security firm. In both *Photo Production v Securicor* (1980) and *Ailsa Craig Fishing Co v Malvern Fishing Co and Securicor* (1983) the House of Lords believed that the parties must have made a reasonable assessment of the likely loss in reducing their liability by a limitation clause in each case. The security firm were therefore not liable for the consequences of a fire in the first case and damage to the hull of a ship in the second, while they were on security patrol.

The effect of the legislation in general is to restrict the use of unfair terms, and particularly unfair exemption clauses in consumer contracts. Richard Stone, an academic expert on contract law, is of the view that the effect of the legislation is to cut 'a deep furrow right across the doctrine of freedom of contract.' This echoes the appraisal of Lord Denning in *George Mitchell v Finney Lock Seeds* (see p. 124), where he said of the reform by statute:

> So the idol of 'freedom of contract' was shattered. In cases of personal injury or death, it was not permissible to exclude or restrict liability at all. In consumer contacts any exemption clause was subject to the test of reasonableness … it heralds a revolution in our approach to exemption clauses; not only where they exclude liability altogether and also where they limit liability; not only in the specific categories in the Unfair Contract Terms Act 1977, but in other contracts too.

Further reform

It can be seen that there is a fair amount of overlap between the statutory provisions of the Unfair Contract Terms Act 1977 and the Unfair Terms in Consumer Contract Regulations 1999. Because of this the Law Commission has reviewed the whole package of legislation at the request of the Department of Trade and Industry. Their report entitled *Unfair Terms in Contracts* (2005) made a number of recommendations, including a Draft Bill, but has not yet been implemented. It proposed, among other things, the following:

- One single Act would replace the current legislation, retaining the essence of s. 2(1) on terms purporting to exclude liability for personal injury or death.
- Any other terms apart from 'core' terms, e.g. price, will be subject to a test of reasonableness, with the burden of proof in a consumer contract being on the party trying to rely on the clause.
- A new category of contract would be created, that of Small Business Contract, for those with nine or less employees. These would be given some protection under the new proposals regarding non-negotiated terms.

An interesting aspect of the proposals concerning the assessment of reasonableness is whether the clause is 'transparent', that is clear and understandable.

Conclusion

A consequence of both common law and statutory restrictions on unfair terms is that an inroad *has* been made in the freedom to contract, but also into the freedom to take advantage of others who are under pressure and who may lack bargaining power. To take this to extremes would be paternalistic, of course, but a reasonable amount of protection is surely no more than a developed society has come to expect of the modern law of contract.

Summary

There are two types of exemption clause:

- Limitation clause: limits one party's liability toward the other in a contract.
- Exclusion clause: avoids one party's liability toward the other in a contract.

Incorporation

The exemption clause must:

- not come too late – *Olley v Marlborough Court*.
- be brought to the other party's attention in a reasonable way – *Parker v South Eastern Railway, Thornton v Shoe Lane Parking*.
- be of a contractual nature – *Chapelton v Barry*;
- not be obscured – *Sugar v LMS Railway*.
- not be part of a 'course of dealing' – *Hollier v Rambler Motors*.

Construction

- The main purpose rule – *Glynn v Margetson*.
- The *contra proferentem* rule – *Houghton v Trafalgar Insurance*.
- An overriding oral statement – *Mendelssohn v Normand*.
- An overriding misrepresentation – *Curtis v Chemical Cleaning and Dyeing Co*.

Legislation

The Unfair Contract Terms Act 1977

- Mostly applies to a consumer – section 12.
- A contract term cannot now exclude or restrict liability for **death or personal injury resulting from negligence** – section 2(1).
- A contract term can only exclude or restrict **other liability resulting from negligence** if it is reasonable to do so – section 2(2).
- When dealing on one party's **standard business terms**, a contract term cannot exclude or restrict liability for non-performance or for performance which is substantially different from what was agreed, unless it is reasonable to do so – section 3.

Reasonableness should be based on the position at the time of contract, including resources available and the possibility of insurance – *Stewart Gill v Horatio Myer Ltd*. For examples of reasonableness, see *Green v Cade, George Mitchell v Finney Lock Seeds, Smith v Bush and Harris v Wyre Forest, Woodman v Photo Trade Processing*.

The Unfair Terms in Consumer Contract Regulations 1999

Based on a European directive, and wider than Unfair Contract Terms Act 1977 in scope, covering unfair terms in general, not just exclusion clauses. Includes a requirement of terms to be in plain and intelligible language.

Regulation 5(1) states that a term will be unfair and therefore not binding if it 'contrary to the requirement of good faith causes a significant imbalance in the parties' rights and obligations under the contract to the detriment of the consumer'.

The courts should consider factors such as:

- the bargaining strength of parties,
- any inducement to contract,
- special requirements of the customer,
- whether the supplier has acted equitably.

Note the supervisory role of the Director-General of Fair Trading.

For reasonableness in limitation clauses see *Photo Production v Securicor* and *Ailsa Craig Fishing Co v Malvern Fishing Co* and *Securicor*.

Questions

1   Kelly, a painter, visits NewArt gallery and leaves her coat at a cloakroom where she pays a fee and is given a receipt.

  While Kelly is walking around one of the exhibition rooms an attendant who is moving some paintings accidentally knocks over a ladder which hits Kelly, causing her considerable injury. The attendant apologises to Kelly, but points to a sign at the entrance which states, 'NewArt gallery takes no responsibility for injury to visitors however caused'.

  When Kelly returns to the cloakroom to collect her coat she finds that it has been given to someone else. The cloakroom assistant points out a statement on Kelly's receipt which reads, 'NewArt gallery takes no responsibility for loss or theft of items, however this may arise'.

  Discuss any potential claims that Kelly may have against New Art Gallery.

OCR 2007

2   Alison visits Bestever Theme Park and, wishing to spend some time on rides, leaves her coat at a cloakroom where she pays a fee and is handed a receipt. While Alison is queuing for a ride, a park attendant, Callum, driving a small vehicle collides with her, causing injury to her shoulder and leg. Callum apologises on behalf of the Park, but points to a sign at the entrance which states, 'Bestever Theme Park takes no responsibility for injury to visitors however caused'. Alison decides to leave the Park, but when she returns to collect her coat she finds that it has been given to the wrong person. The assistant, Dana, points out a statement on her receipt which reads, 'All items are left at owner's risk. Bestever Theme Park takes no responsibility for loss or theft of items, however this may arise'. Advise Alison whether she may make a claim against Bestever Theme Park concerning her injury and the loss of her coat.

OCR 4-module specimen paper

3   Critically examine the process by which the court decides whether an exemption clause is valid.

4   'The amount of legislation concerning exemption clauses renders the common law principles of little use.'

  Consider the accuracy of this statement.

5   'Exemption clauses are now outlawed'.

  Discuss whether this claim is accurate.

6   Does the current state of the law on exemption clauses now afford a consumer satisfactory protection against exploitation?

A further 'dilemma' style question on exemption clauses can be found in Part 7 of the book.

9   Privity of contract

The rule of privity

Thinking back to the definition of a contract (see Chapter 2), a contract is essentially an agreement between two parties. The general rule on claiming against a party was stated by Viscount Haldane in *Dunlop Pneumatic Tyre v Selfridge* (1915).

Only a person who is a party to a contract can sue on it.

The reason behind this is easy to see if we consider a situation where a contract is made between two parties, A and B. If the terms of the contract imposed duties on a third party, C, and he failed to perform them, it would be very unfair for A or B to be allowed to sue him as a result. Steyn LJ said, 'Principle certainly requires that a burden should not be imposed on a third party without his consent'. This is easy to accept, as none of us would wish to have some burden placed upon us without agreeing to it. Therefore, by the same principle (but perhaps a little harder to accept) if the contract imposed not duties, but benefits, on C, then he could not sue A or B if they are in breach. This can be seen in the following diagram.

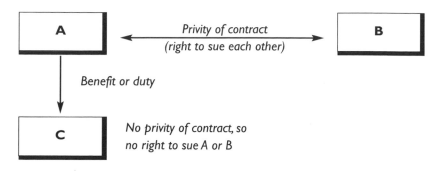

Figure 9.1

We say that there is privity of contract between A and B, but none between A and C, or between B and C. C has not put anything into the contract, and is therefore said to be a 'stranger' to it. This upholds the idea of a contract being a bargain, with something to be gained by both sides. The idea is very closely linked with that of consideration moving from the promisee (see *Tweddle v Atkinson*, p. 149), and was affirmed by the House of Lords in the case of *Dunlop Pneumatic Tyre v Selfridge* (1915).

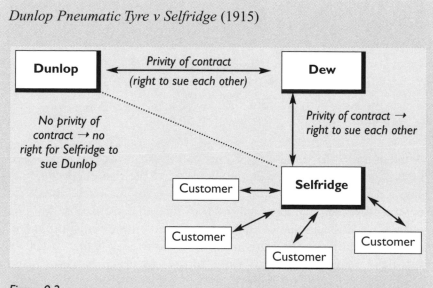

Figure 9.2

Dunlop made Tyres and sold them to Dew, a wholesaler, under a contract where it was stipulated that the tyres must not be resold below a certain price. Dew sold tyres on with the same stipulated to Selfridge, a retailer, who did sell them below that price. Dunlop sued Selfridge, and who therefore had a right to take action, was Dew, and he did not wish to sue.

As we have seen in Chapter 3 (confirmed in *Dunlop v Selfridge*), the principle that consideration must move from the promisee is closely connected to the doctrine of privity, but is still regarded as a separate principle. To enforce a contract, a party must, then, show the following:

• that it is a party to the contract
• that it provided consideration.

The rule seems very reasonable when considering the imposition of a duty on a third party, as nobody would want a duty imposed on them if they had not agreed to it. However, when considering giving a benefit to a third party the rule seems less fair. The following case may be remembered from Chapter 3 (Consideration).

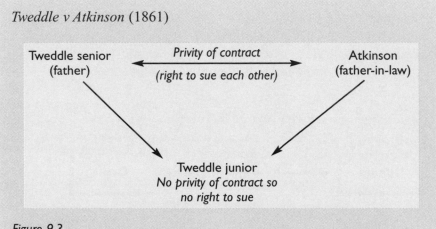

Tweddle v Atkinson (1861)

Figure 9.3

A father and father-in-law agreed between themselves that they would both pay a sum of money on the marriage of their son and daughter. The son was not able to enforce payment due to him, even though the contract between the two fathers was formed specifically for this purpose. It was said that consideration was not given by the promisee, and also that there was no privity between the son and father-in-law. In fact the Contracts (Rights of Third Parties) Act 1999 has now made changes in this area (see below).

Difficulties may arise when the courts try to relieve injustice in particular cases by avoiding, or ignoring, the strict principles of privity. A good example of this is found in the following case.

Jackson v Horizon Holidays Ltd (1975)
Mr Jackson booked a holiday in Sri Lanka, with the defendant holiday company, for himself and his family. The hotel and meals were not as described, and the family were disappointed, so Mr Jackson sued for damages for himself and his family. The Court of Appeal held that damages could be given, despite the fact that the contract for the holiday was between Mr Jackson and the company. According to the strict law of privity he should only have been able to enforce payment for his own disappointment. Lord Denning likened the situation to a host booking a meal in a restaurant for himself and others for a celebratory meal, and finding that the restaurant could not have them. The host would wish to claim return of deposits and compensation for all of the party.

This is sensible law, and brings about justice in principle. The legal theory is more of a problem. Lord Denning's idea was not the actual law at the time, but what he thought the law should be. Predictably, the House of Lords were not too happy about him taking this line, as it was not following precedent, and they took up the debate on this case in the following case.

Woodar Investment Development Ltd v Wimpey Construction UK Ltd (1980)
The House of Lords agreed with the outcome of *Jackson v Horizon* as being just and reasonable in the circumstances, but disagreed with the way in which the decision was reached. They would obviously feel that it was not the role of the Court of Appeal to change the law, but that a special category of cases should be created to deal with situations like this where one person contracts on behalf of a group.

As with *Tweddle v Atkinson*, the law may be different if a similar situation arose today following the introduction of statute. In fact, even before the recent change to the law by statute, there has been a move to allowing claims which were technically within the doctrine of privity, if to disallow them would be unjust. This was so in *Linden Gardens Trust v Lenesta Sludge Disposals* (1994) where the original owners of a building site were able to claim against builders for compensation for breach, when the actual harm suffered was by the later owners of the buildings. Clearly the new owners needed a remedy, and it was just that the original developers should enforce the claim.

Because there were so many problems with the law of privity, a number of exceptions have been established. These have arisen out of obvious need for legislation, and show that the doctrine itself was not totally satisfactory.

Established exceptions to the doctrine of privity of contract

Statutory exceptions

A number of these exist, for example:

* The Married Women's Property Act 1882 allows a spouse or children to obtain the benefit of a contract of life assurance made in their favour. This then gives them the right to enforce a contract to which they are not an original party.
* Under the Law of Property Act 1925 it is possible to assign property rights arising under a contract.
* The Road Traffic Act 1988 makes a person issuing insurance to a driver liable to pay not just the driver in the event of an accident but those covered by the policy, such as a third party whose car the driver damages.

This last exception is obviously essential, as the contracts of insurance would be pointless if they were not enforceable, and, regarding the Road Traffic Act, innocent members of the public would be left unprotected from traffic in a busy environment.

Agency

Agency is a common law exception to the doctrine of privity, and is where one person acts as the representative of another (often for commercial convenience). The principal (person A) appoints someone else, the agent (person B), to act on his behalf with a third party (person C). Generally, the principal may sue the third party. In fact, the principal and his agent, A and B, are treated as one person, and form contracts as one of the parties, the other being the third party, C.

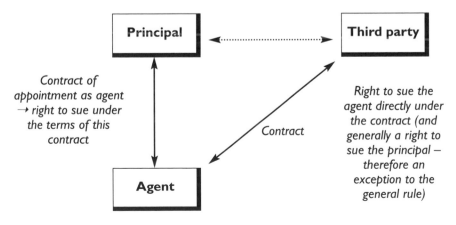

Figure 9.4

NZ Shipping Co v Satterthwaite Co Ltd (1974) *(The Eurymedon)*
A contract was made between the plaintiffs and the defendant carriers
to ship a cargo from Liverpool to New Zealand, the bill of lading
containing various exemption clauses, including one which said that a
servant or agent of the carrier would not be liable for damage to the
cargo due to negligence in carrying out the work. The carriers then
contracted with stevedores to unload the cargo, and they damaged it
while unloading it. The plaintiffs argued that the stevedores could not
rely on the exemptions in the bill of lading because they were not party
to the contract, but it was held that the carriers were acting as agents
for the stevedores, so were treated as one party to the contract with the
plaintiffs.

Collateral contracts

These are not strictly exceptions to privity, but have been used to circumvent
the privity rule.

Shanklin Pier Ltd v Detel Products Ltd (1951)
The plaintiffs, who owned Shanklin pier on the Isle of Wight,
contracted with painters to paint the pier. The plaintiffs required
assurance over the quality of the paint, so the painters agreed with
Detel that they would buy Detel paint if Detel gave a warranty to the
plaintiffs that it would last for seven to ten years. The painting went
ahead on this basis, but the paint only lasted for three months. A
problem of privity arose in that Detel had given assurance to the
plaintiffs, but it was the painters who had made the contract to buy the
paint. It was held that the pier owners could sue the paint manufacturers on a collateral contract, thus providing a remedy but avoiding
the issue of privity.

Covenants which run with the land

A principle of land law provides another exception to the doctrine of
privity. In certain circumstances, covenants (or promises to do something)
imposed on land may 'run with the land'. This means that the promises
attach themselves to the land, and go with it when it is sold to someone else.
The covenants are then enforceable against subsequent owners.

> *Smith & Snipes Hall Farm v River Douglas Catchment Board* (1949)
> A number of properties backed on to a river, and agreed to maintain the
> river banks. This duty was passed on with the land and was enforceable
> against subsequent owners who had not realised that they had this duty.

Similarly, this approach was applied to restrictive covenants, which may
also run with the land, in the following case.

> *Tulk v Moxhay* (1848)
> The garden area in the centre of Leicester Square, London, was sold by
> Tulk to Elms, the contract containing a covenant not to build on the
> garden, but to keep it for all time for the enjoyment of the residents in
> the square. Elms sold the land and Moxhay eventually became the
> owner, and although he knew of the covenant, he had the intention to
> build on the land.
>
> Tulk succeeded in obtaining an injunction to prevent this, despite not
> having contracted with Moxhay. This particular case was based on the
> fact that Moxhay did know of the restriction, but later cases followed,
> basing their argument on the outcome of this case, even when there was
> no knowledge of a restrictive covenant. This is obviously contrary to
> the rule of privity, but a necessary exception to bring about a just
> solution.

Should one person be able to prevent another from doing whatever they
wish with land which they have bought? Why do you think that the courts
allow this?

Attempts to avoid privity of contract (other than the established exceptions)

Attempting to apply land law to chattels (goods other than land)

It can be seen from *Dunlop v Selfridge* that difficulties arise when a
supplier tries to control the price at which goods are subsequently resold. A
similar situation arose in the following case concerning the price of
tobacco, and the manufacturer tried to apply the rule in *Tulk v Moxhay* to
goods other than land (known as chattels).

Taddy v Sterious (1904)
The plaintiff tobacco manufacturers sold a quantity of tobacco to wholesalers, with a term included to prevent them from reselling it below a stipulated price. The wholesalers resold the tobacco to the defendant retailers with the same restriction. The defendant nevertheless sold the tobacco at a lower price, and the plaintiff sued, claiming that the term concerning price 'ran with' the tobacco, in the same way as a covenant 'ran with' the land in *Tulk v Moxhay*. The court would not allow this, holding that the original seller had no claim against the eventual retailer.

If allowed, this would mean that almost any restriction on the use of an item could be enforced against a subsequent owner who is not a party to the original contract. The idea arose in the following Privy Council case.

Lord Strathcona Steamship Co v Dominion Coal Co (1926)
Dominion had chartered a ship to use for a number of years on the St Lawrence river. The ship was later sold to the Lord Strathcona Steamship Co, who knew of the charter to Dominion, but refused to honour it. Applying the rule in *Tulk v Moxhay*, Dominion argued that rights 'ran with' the ship, and succeeded in obtaining an injunction against the new owner, despite not having a contract with the company, to prevent them from acting inconsistently with the contract between Dominion and the original owners.

It was probably important in the *Strathcona* case that the new owners were well aware of the charter to Dominion. Even so, the case has been criticised, especially by Lord Wright MR in the case of *Clore v Theatrical Properties Ltd* (1936), where the Court of Appeal said that the decision in *Strathcona* should be confined to the circumstances of that charterparty. In the later case of *Port Line Ltd v Ben Line Steamers Ltd* (1958) Diplock J stated bluntly that the decision in *Strathcona* was wrong. No further development took place in this area for a number of years, leading Davies to suggest that 'the *Strathcona* case has now descended into the limbo of lost causes'. However, the idea did raise its head again briefly in the case of *Swiss Bank Corporation v Lloyds Bank Ltd* (1979) concerning the sale of shares, but that appears to be an isolated case.

Implying a trust

Another attempt to evade the strict application of privity is to show that one of the parties to a contract holds contractual rights on trust for a third party.

This could arise, for example, where A contracts with B to do something for the benefit of C. If B were to be considered as holding the benefit on trust for C, then C could be in a position to claim in trust law against A in his position as beneficiary of a trust. Implying a trust in this way can be traced back some time, but the leading case on the point is *Les Affreteurs Reunis SA v Walford*.

> *Les Affreteurs Reunis SA v Walford* (1919)
> Walford was a broker who arranged the chartering of ships between the owners and the hirers. Within the charter was a clause stating that the owners would pay him 3 per cent commission for his work. When this was not paid he claimed that the money was held on trust by the owners, and sued them successfully to obtain payment.

The courts have been wary of using one area of law to avoid another, so through cases the scope of the doctrine has been narrowed. Evidence of a trust does not come from a particular form of wording, but it is necessary to find an intention. Had this been widely developed, the doctrine of privity would have eventually been of little significance. However, the courts are reluctant to imply a trust where none was really envisaged. Whether they do so in future depends on the readiness of the court to construe a trust out of a contract. The general trend seems to be against implying a trust, as the following two cases illustrate.

> *Re Schebsman* (1943)
> Schebsman was due to receive money after working for a company, so entered into an agreement where he would be paid, or if he died, his wife and daughter were to receive the money. He did die, and no money was paid to his family. They sued, but were not successful, the courts not wanting to create a trust where none had ever been intended by the parties.
>
> *Beswick v Beswick* (1968)
> Mr Beswick sold his business to his nephew and in return was to receive a sum of money each week, or, on his death, £5 per week to his widow. After he died she only received one payment, so sued in the following alternative ways:
>
> • on the basis of a trust
> • under the Law of Property Act 1925 (see below)
> • in her personal capacity as administratrix of her husband's estate.
>
> The court rejected the first two arguments, but allowed her to succeed as she was administering the estate. It could be argued that it was

fortunate that she was, as otherwise she would have received nothing, despite this arrangement clearly being made so as to support her if she became widowed.

So this method of creating a trust is not likely to operate generally as a method of evading the rules of privity. It should be noted that even if successful, it is only really an apparent exception to the common law rules, as the rights of a beneficiary are equitable.

The Law of Property Act 1925 s.56

This Act contains in s.56(1) a provision that a person who is not named as a party to the 'conveyance or other agreement' can still benefit under the agreement. This appears to contradict the rule of privity, and some have attempted to use the section to acquire rights where they would otherwise be stopped by privity.

If the sections were to be interpreted freely according to the plain meaning of the words, then 'other property' could include contractual rights. This would clearly provide a way to evade the doctrine of privity of contract, taking the law back to the position before *Tweddle v Atkinson* (1861).

In fact, such a liberal interpretation has not found favour in the courts, as can be seen in the case of *Beswick v Beswick* (above), as the Act was intended to be interpreted in the context of land law, and to use it in this way would be to abuse it.

The law of tort

Although an injured party may not be able to obtain a satisfactory remedy in contract law, it should always be remembered that a remedy may exist in another area of law. This particularly arises with the close relationship of the law of contract with the law of tort.

The Contracts (Rights of Third Parties) Act 1999

There have been many calls for reform of the strict doctrine of privity, to allow a person to enforce the handing over of a benefit due under a contract. The most recent report was that of the Law Commission in 1996, *Privity of Contract: Rights of Third Parties*, Law Com No. 242. This formed the basis of the bill which led to the Contracts (Rights of Third Parties) Act 1999, now in force, and long overdue. The main principle of the Act is that where a contract is made specifically for the benefit of a third party, and that party is clearly identified, they may enforce the contract, even though they are not a party to the contract.

The relevant sections of the act read as follows:

1 (1) Subject to the provisions of the Act, a person who is not a party to a contract (a 'third party') may in his own right enforce a term of the contract if:
(a) the contract expressly provides that he may, or
(b) subject to subsection (2), the term purports to confer a benefit on him.
(2) Subsection (1)(b) does not apply if on a proper construction of the contract it appears that the parties did not intend the term to be enforceable by the third party.
(3) The third party must be expressly identified in the contract by name, as a member of a class or as answering a particular description but need not be in existence when the contract is entered into.

So the Act allows a third party to enforce a benefit, but lays down the following conditions:

• The contract must either actually say that the benefit is intended for this person, or it must be clear that this is what the contract meant (it 'purports' to confer a benefit).

• The parties must have intended the benefit to be enforceable by the third party.

• The third party must be identified in the contract by name, or description, or as a member of a group.

So what is left of privity? Would it have been better to simply abolish the doctrine?

The Contracts (Rights of Third Parties) Act 1999 has certainly brought about the changes recommended by many, including the Law Commission, over a long period of time. The act should prevent injustice in individual circumstances, such as Beswick. It should also avoid attempts to get around the difficulties of privity and the need to stretch other legal principles, such as trusts and collateral contracts, to their limits, in an attempt to avoid its constraints. It should remove the need to 'find' exceptions to the doctrine. If Mr Jackson (*Jackson v Horizon*) were to book a similar holiday today, with his wife and family named on the booking form, they would clearly be intended to benefit from the contract, so would satisfy section 1(1)(b), and would be identified within it, so would satisfy section 1(3). They would then be able to enforce the benefit and claim damages if the contract was breached.

The change will bring English law into line with that of many other countries. Most other EU countries, including Scotland, do not have such a restraint, and neither do many American states. However, the passing of the act clearly does not do away with the whole of the law of privity. The common law rules that we have examined, which have developed through case law, still stand. This is justified, as it would be unfair to remove the law of privity if it meant that a duty could then be imposed on a person under a contract to which that person had not agreed. The rule is also needed to prevent a benefit claimed by a third party, where one was not originally intended.

Welcome as the statute is, though, it will need refining through interpretation. Not every third party claim will – or necessarily should – succeed.

- It must be clear that a benefit was intended by the original parties to the contract. Until cases are considered by the courts we will not know how clearly and precisely this intention needs to be expressed.

- The third party who is to receive the benefit must be identified in the contract – either by name or by their role or capacity. Again – how precise does this need to be?

- In *Nisshin Shipping v Cleaves* (2004) importance was placed on what the original contracting parties would have considered to be an appropriate interpretation at the time of forming the contract.

It is largely these potential problems that have caused some concern since the passing of the statute, and they arise particularly in the construction industry, where a mistake in the use of the statute could have extensive and long-term consequences. The act has been viewed, therefore, as potentially beneficial, but until it has become more refined it is said, in an article by Donald Bishop in *Construction Law*, to be a 'trap for the unwary'. Until the interpretation of the act becomes clearer by case law, those in commerce and industry, and particularly the construction industry, may choose to make their intentions regarding the act precise by stating expressly whether they intend to pass any benefit to a third party.

The doctrine is now, then, in the state that has been recommended so many times by law reform bodies and individuals, although it will need some fine-tuning. The doctrine of privity has relaxed enough to ensure that justice is achieved but remains unshaken as a foundation of the law of contract.

Summary

The rule of privity according to common law:

* Only a person who is a party to a contract can sue on it – *Dunlop v Selfridge*.
* At common law this applies to both burdens and benefits – *Tweddle v Atkinson, Jackson v Horizon Holidays Ltd, Linden Gardens Trust v Lenesta Sludge Disposals*; but also see the Contracts (Rights of Third Parties) Act 1999.

Established exceptions

* Statutory provision, for example the Married Women's Property Act 1882, the Law of Property Act 1925, the Road Traffic Act 1988.
* Agency – *NZ Shipping Co v Satterthwaite Co Ltd (The Eurymedon)*.
* Collateral contracts – *Shanklin Pier Ltd v Detel Products Ltd*.
* Covenants which run with the land – *Smith & Snipes Hall Farm v River Douglas Catchment Board, Tulk v Moxhay*.

Attempts to avoid privity of contract

* Attempting to apply land law to chattels (goods other than land) – *Taddy v Sterious, Lord Strathcona Steamship Co v Dominion Coal Co, Clore v Theatrical Properties Ltd, Port Line Ltd v Ben Line Steamers Ltd, Swiss Bank Corporation v Lloyds Bank Ltd*.
* Implying a Trust – *Les Affreteurs Reunis SA v Walford, Re Schebsman, Beswick v Beswick*.
* The Law of Property Act 1925 s.56(1) – *Beswick v Beswick*.

The Contracts (Rights of Third Parties) Act 1999

This changes the rule of privity regarding the enforcement of *benefits* by a third party, but not of duties. The main provisions are:

* A third party may enforce a right under a contract if (a) the contract expressly provides that he may, or (b) the term purports to confer a benefit on him.

- Part (b) does not apply if on a proper construction of the contract it appears that the parties did not intend the term to be enforceable by the third party.
- The third party must be expressly identified in the contract by name, as a member of a class or as answering a particular description but need not be in existence when the contract is entered into.

Remember that if a remedy is not available under the law of contract, one may be available in a different way, for example under the law of tort.

Questions

1 Ursula's neighbour, Victor, regularly cleans her windows, for which she pays him £10. On one occasion whilst he is doing the work, Ursula mentions that she is worried about her garden which is in need of maintenance. Victor replied that he will do some work on it when he has the time. Two weeks later Ursula arrives home to find that Victor has mowed the lawns, planted new trees in the garden and cleaned her windows. She is very pleased and promises to pay him £70 for the work on the garden and the usual £10 for cleaning the windows.

Ursula also receives a telephone call from Yolanda who supplied Victor with the trees for Ursula's garden. Yolanda requires payment of £30.

Advise Ursula whether she must pay Victor and Yolanda.

2 Critically evaluate the recent reform to the doctrine of privity.

3 'The third party rule prevents effect being given to the intentions of the contracting parties, and can not be justified.' Discuss this view of the doctrine of privity of contract and consider how it has been reformed.

4 Critically evaluate the effect on the doctrine of privity of the Contracts (Rights of Third Parties) Act 1999.

5 'The aim of recent legislation was to remedy the injustice of the third party rule.' Explain and discuss the development of the rules of privity of contract.

OCR 2002

Part 3

Vitiating factors

RULES OF FAIR PLAY

No duress
No undue influence
No misrepresentation
No important mistakes
No illegality

That's not fair – I was pushed into the agreement!

We have seen from Part 1 of the book that provided that there is offer and acceptance, consideration, legal intent and capacity, a contract will have been formed, as these are the strict formation requirements. However, the very nature of a contract is *agreement* which means that there should be true exercise of a person's free will. If someone stands in front of another, gun in hand, threatening to shoot unless a contract is signed, then that can hardly be called true agreement! In fact, we would say that the contract is signed under duress, and it would not be binding. Duress is one of several factors which could jeopardise an otherwise well-formed contract, and lead the court to decide that it was not formed in a fair way. In the years ahead there is likely to be a much greater emphasis on contracts being formed 'in good faith', in light of decisions relating to European law.

So, the following factors will be considered here:

Duress – threats which leave no alternative

Duress is where unfair pressure of the kind mentioned above is used in forming a contract. It is hopefully not too common to find someone forming a contract under the threat of a gun, but the doctrine has now been widened to include economic duress, which is a very relevant problem in a developed and fast moving economy.

Undue influence – plain unfair pressure

Undue influence is any other unfair pressure placed on one party by another to enter into a contract, which does not amount to physical violence.

Misrepresentation – they lied to me!

A misrepresentation is where one party has lied in the forming of a contract. It could be some time before the contract is formed, but if one party enters into the contract on the basis of lies, this again cannot be regarded as true agreement.

Mistake – we got it wrong

Sometimes one or both parties form a contract and then afterwards find that they have done so on the basis of some false assumption. This is not necessarily a situation of deceit, it could be that parties were genuinely mistaken. An example would be if a contract was formed to buy six cakes from a bakery, but unknown to both parties they had already been bought and taken away by another customer. Here, even though the contract was correctly formed, there would be no subject matter, or goods to be bought and sold, so the court would declare the contract void.

Illegality – a contract to break the law

Again, this could arise where there is a well formed contract, but what if the agreement involved something unlawful? An example may be a contract to pay someone to break into an office and steal something. It would make a nonsense of the law if it supported such a contract, and indeed the contract would again be void.

These reasons for unfairness are known as vitiating factors, as they vitiate, or deny the existence of, a binding agreement. They are obviously very important in ensuring fair play in a business environment, but also of importance to a consumer. If a brochure gives misleading information, or a seller makes false claims about a product (either knowingly or innocently), it is not fair that the buyer of the service or product should be bound by the agreement with no remedy. This essential unfairness in forming a contract is the subject of this part of the book.

10   Duress and undue influence

If a contract is formed correctly, containing all the necessary elements to make it valid, but is formed under unfair pressure, then it cannot in reality be a genuine agreement, which is the essence of the law of contract. Common law has recognised for a long time that a party may have been coerced, or forcibly persuaded against their will, into making a contract. The courts deal with this by setting the contract aside under the common law doctrine of duress and the equitable doctrine of undue influence.

Duress

This doctrine was developed by common law. It was once very narrow and limited to situations where a contract was induced by unlawful physical violence to the person, or the threat of it, or the unlawful constraint of the other party or someone close to the other party. The following are examples of the operation of the common law doctrine of duress:

Cumming v Ince (1847)
A threat was made to confine an elderly lady to a mental hospital (when it was not necessary) if she did not make an agreement to transfer property. The agreement was held to have been made under duress, and was therefore void. This is an example of threat of unlawful constraint.

Kauffman v Gerson (1904)
Threats were made to have Mrs Gerson's husband prosecuted if she did not make an agreement to pay of his debts. The agreement was held to be made under duress.

The following case is a more recent example of threats to the person, and it is clear that this particular threat need not be the only incentive to enter the contract for duress to be claimed successfully.

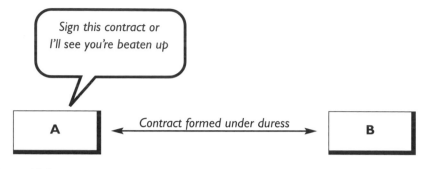

Figure 10.1

> *Barton v Armstrong* (1976)
> (On appeal to the Privy Council from Australia.)
> The plaintiff contracted to buy some shares from the defendant under various threats which included statements such as, 'The city is not as safe as you may think between office and home. You will see what I can do against you and you will regret the day when you decided not to work with me.' P also received telephone calls in the night, usually containing heavy breathing, but on one occasion also containing a death threat. It was held that the contract was made under duress and was invalid.

Threats to property

As the definition arising from common law is a strict one, the doctrine of duress does not normally apply to threats to property, as seen in *Skeate v Beale* (1840), where threats of distraint property (to take it to set against debts) were held not to amount to duress.

> Are threats to property always less important than threats to the person?

More recent cases show that in some circumstances courts are prepared to take a more flexible approach towards threats to property. For example, in *The Siboen and the Sibotre* (1976) it was said that threats to property could in some circumstances amount to duress, and suggestions were made of likely situations, such as the threat to burn down a house, or to slash a valuable painting.

This seems reasonable, since some very serious threats to property could, on occasions, be more coercive than minor threats to the person. However, the problem is knowing how far the courts would go in accepting threats to property. For example, would threats to wealth amount to duress, and if so, what about threats to breach a contract which would damage a person's wealth? In fact, the cases which have followed *The Siboen and the Sibotre* show that the courts have indeed accepted the idea that such threats could amount to duress, developing the idea of economic duress, providing that they are substantial. Most of the cases involved in this development have arisen concerning shipping cases, since these are very valuable contracts.

North Ocean Shipping Co Ltd v Hyundai Construction Co Ltd (1979) *(The Atlantic Baron)*
The defendant shipbuilders agreed to build a supertanker for the plaintiff company. They later threatened to breach the contract unless 10 per cent more was paid. The plaintiff company agreed to pay the extra amount in order not to lose a valuable charter, but after delivery of the ship attempted to recover the extra payment. It was held that the threat of breach of such a valuable contract would have been economic duress, but the length of time taken in bringing a claim to court tended to indicate affirmation.

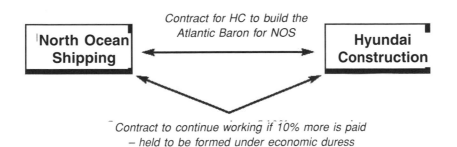

Figure 10.2

This was the first time that the court really acknowledged that economic duress could have a vitiating effect on a contract. As the concept is still being developed, the courts are no doubt anxious not to widen the scope of the doctrine too freely. The following case shows that the mere threat of a breach of contract alone would not amount to economic duress, and in the case of *Pao On v Lau Yiu Long* the Privy Council took the opportunity of laying down some guidelines.

Pao On v Lau Yiu Long (1980)
It was said that to amount to economic duress, a threat to breach a contract must be more than normal commercial pressure. The sum must be substantial to the injured party, possibly involving a threat of loss of livelihood. Four possible factors were identified by Lord Scarman to decide if a party had entered a contract under duress:

* Did the person protest?
* Was there an alternative?
* Was independent advice taken?
* Were steps taken to avoid the contract after entering into it?

These factors were repeated in the recent case of *DSND Subsea Ltd v Petroleum Geo Services ASA* (2000). Nevertheless, where the threat is real the courts are in some cases willing to recognise economic duress, if the consequences of carrying out the threat are sufficiently serious, as is seen in the following House of Lords case.

Universe Tankships of Monrovia v International Transport Workers Federation (1982) *(The Universe Sentinel)*
A ship was 'blacked' by unions, so prevented from loading, etc., unless the company agreed to make certain payments. It was held that the agreement was made under economic duress, since there had been no practical alternative but to make the payments. So here the court acknowledged that the threat to breach a contract, coupled with a substantial loss, did amount to economic duress.

Consider the following situations:

* If a travel agent is told by a holiday company that if he agrees to sell 20 holidays to Spain he will receive a free holiday to Greece, is this economic duress or normal commercial pressure?
* If an estate agent has a contract to sell the houses produced by a large building company, and is told that if he does not sell a group of new houses by the end of the month the building company will end the contract under which he sells their houses. Is this economic duress?

The following recent cases provide further guidelines as to when the courts may recognise economic duress, and provide a distinction between substantial duress and normal commercial pressure.

Williams v Roffey (1990)

The full facts of this case are in Chapter 3 (p. 54). The defendant building firm had offered to pay the plaintiff carpenters extra money to complete work, but had later refused to pay them. When sued, amongst other things they claimed economic duress. However, there was no evidence of economic duress, merely the normal commercial pressure evident in the building trade at that time. The courts were clearly prepared to consider economic duress, but none was found in this particular instance.

Atlas Express v Kafco (1989)

Kafco was a small firm of basketware manufacturers who had agreed to supply Woolworths with a large quantity of goods for their seasonal trade. As Kafco did not have enough of their own transport, they contracted with the Atlas Express to transport the goods for an agreed price. Atlas Express, however, found later that they had underestimated their costs, and found more lucrative work elsewhere. They told Kafco that they would not deliver any more unless Kafco paid nearly twice the amount originally asked. Kafco wanted to maintain their contract with Woolworths, and had taken on extra workers and had increased their working capacity to produce the required quantity, so had no practical alternative, but to agree, under pressure, to pay Atlas Express. Kafco later refused to pay the extra money to Atlas Express, claiming economic duress. It was held that the agreement for the extra money was made under duress and was not therefore binding.

This shows that it is the scale of operation, rather than the actual amount at stake, which is significant, as Kafco was a small company who would have been ruined financially had the larger company, Atlas Express, been able to insist on the extra payment. The courts found economic duress to exist in the recent case of *Carillion Construction Ltd v Felix (UK) Ltd* (2000) when Carillion were found to have agreed to pay an excessive amount to Felix in order to avoid a liquidated damages clause.

> Can you think of any other situations where a person or company may be very badly affected financially by a threat to breach a contract?

The legal effect of common law duress being proved is that the contract is void. However, economic duress has been developed under the equitable powers of the courts, and the courts normally say that any contract made in such circumstances is 'set aside'. This really means that the contract is voidable, rather than void, which means that, for example, third-party rights may arise, and affirmation or lapse of time may be a problem.

There is also a problem now of exactly what will amount to economic duress. With the strict doctrine of common law duress there was not really a problem, since the limits were reasonably clearly defined. However, the more flexible approach now taken by the courts, taking account of a society heavily dependant on commerce, and allowing economic duress to vitiate a contract, results in a higher degree of uncertainty than was previously the case. We therefore await cases to come before the courts to provide greater definition of the boundaries of the doctrine.

Undue influence

Because the common law doctrine of duress was so narrow in scope, there developed, in equity, the doctrine of undue influence. This provided a remedy in cases where there was clearly improper pressure on one of the parties to the contract, but where it fell short of duress at common law. Undue influence is a good example of the law placing a restriction on the parties' initial freedom to contract, in order to prevent blatant unfairness. The cases coming before the courts can be divided into two broad categories:

- where there is no special relationship between the parties
- where there is a fiduciary relationship (either because of the very nature of the parties' relationship, or because on a particular occasion one party relied heavily on the other).

Where there is no special relationship

Here it is clear from such cases as *Williams v Bayley* (1866) that the burden is on the person pressed into the contract to prove undue influence on the particular facts. The person alleging undue influence therefore has the burden of showing that that there was no exercise of independent free will. Where the existence of undue influence is proved, the court will assume that it was actually exerted, unless proved to the contrary.

Where there is a fiduciary relationship

There is a rebuttable presumption of undue influence where the parties to a contract are in such a position that one is able to exploit a fiduciary (or confidential) relationship with the other. This presumption arises where the relationship is such that one party would normally expect to rely on the confidence of the other (often where one party is dominant, or in a position of trust). The law does not say that one person necessarily *has* taken advantage of the other, or has exploited the relationship, but that it *could* have arisen, and that it is up to the party who could have stood to gain to prove that they did not do so. The presumption could arise from:

- the situation being one of a list where case law states that there is a fiduciary relationship, or
- it could be that on this particular occasion the court decides that the relationship is on where one party was in a position to advantage of the other. Some examples of such a relationship are:
  solicitor – client
  parent – child
  doctor – patient
  trustee – beneficiary
  guardian – ward spiritual/religious
  adviser – person being advised.

This is not a definitive list of possible fiduciary relationships, but a group of relationships which have been considered by the courts in cases. It is not a closed list, in that should other situations be presented to the courts, they may well be decided in a similar way.

Can you think of other relationships which the courts may add to this list, if a suitable case should arise?

Note that husband and wife are not included in the list, although it will be seen that many of the more recent cases concern this relationship. Another point is that where the presumption is shown to apply, it may continue for a short while after the relationship ceases to exist. This is shown in the following case concerning a mother superior and a nun, which, of course, comes within the last category on the above list.

Allcard v Skinner (1887)

A nun joined a convent, taking vows which were normal to the order of poverty, chastity and obedience, and as a consequence she handed over her savings. She later decided to change to a different order, and some time afterwards was advised that she could ask for what remained of her money to be handed back, to take with her to the next order. It was held that because the mother superior was in a position of authority regarding the nun, there was a presumption of undue influence, which would have allowed the money to be returned if the nun hadacted sooner. A short time after leaving would have be staisfactory, but in the circumstances it was too late. This is an example of lapse of time (see below).

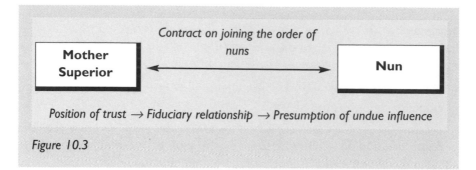

Figure 10.3

Rebutting the presumption

When a fiduciary relationship is found to exist, undue influence is presumed to have arisen. In order to rebut this presumption (or deny it), a declaration (or a verbal denial) is not enough. There must be clear evidence to show that there has been free exercise of independent will. Suggestions were made in the following case as to how this could be accomplished.

Re Brocklehurst (1978)
Lord Hailsham LC suggested that free exercise of 'independent will' can be shown by proving that:

- Independent advice had been sought. This is a point much laboured by the courts in the recent line of banking cases (see below), as if an independent advisor is heeded this is likely to override the influence of the other party. It is similar to the situation where a person is not influenced by a misrepresentation where they have relied on their own expert survey.

- A full declaration had been made of the possible outcome of the transaction. Provided that evidence of the declaration is available, this is also powerful evidence of honest intention.

- Consideration given was adequate. The general position is that consideration need only be sufficient, so if a party goes out of the way to ensure that it is adequate, for example, that it was good value for money, then again this is evidence of good intention.

- Any gift given was spontaneous. This is not likely to arise often, but could do so where a person is given a valuable gift as an incentive. Spontaneity may be evidence of honesty in such situations.

The effect of a finding of undue influence

As the doctrine of undue influence in equitable in nature, the usual principles of equity apply. The remedy where undue influence is found to exist is therefore discretionary, so any contract formed is voidable, not void, which means that it *may* be set aside. The right to rescission may be barred by:

- affirmation
- restitution impossible (although precise restitution may not be necessary)
- lapse of time
- third-party rights.

An example of the operation of the presumption of undue influence is found in the following case.

> *Inche Noriah v Shaik Ali Bin Omar* (1928)
> Here a nephew formed an agreement with an older relative to hand over property, and it was presumed that he had used undue influence. He was unable to rebut the presumption.

The banking cases

The relationship between a banker and his client needs special mention. This was not on the list of situations where a fiduciary relationship automatically exists, and this is because the nature of the relationship between a particular banker and client will vary. The normal transactions which take place every day between a client and a banker, such as paying in or withdrawing money and changing currency, would not give rise to a fiduciary relationship. However, where particular transactions call for expert advice, for example an interview with the bank manager to investigate the possibility of a loan to finance a new business venture, a bank may go beyond its normal everyday banking duties. In this case a fiduciary relationship could exist. Obviously there is point at which this kind of relationship begins and this was identified and explained in the following case.

Lloyds Bank v Bundy (1975)

Sir Eric Sachs said in this case that there comes a point in the relationship between the banker and client when the bank may 'be crossing the line into the area of confidentiality, so that the court may then have to examine all the facts including, of course, the history leading up to the transaction.'

In this case a bank manager had been in the habit of visiting an elderly farmer both socially and to advise on his financial arrangements. The farmer had requested a loan to finance his son's business, and the manager had agreed that the bank could arrange this, using the farm as security. When the son's business failed, the bank recalled the loan. When the farm was to be taken in repayment, Mr Bundy claimed undue influence. It was held that as Mr Bundy trusted the manager and relied on his advice, the bank in this situation was in a fiduciary relationship with Mr Bundy, and this raised a presumption of undue influence. The bank had not rebutted this presumption, so the loan was set aside. It was said that the bank could have rebutted the presumption of undue influence by ensuring that Mr Bundy had received independent advice concerning the loan.

This case obviously worried banks generally, as a large part of their business involves loans such as this. Further advice was therefore welcomed when the following case was considered by the House of Lords.

National Westminster Bank v Morgan (1985)

Mr and Mrs Morgan wished to borrow money from the bank to settle other loans and to support a failing business. Against the bank's advice they went ahead with the loan, using their house as security. As in Mr Bundy's case, when the business failed, the bank tried to recall the loan, and wished to sell the house to settle the unpaid amount. The Morgans claimed undue influence, relying on *Lloyds Bank v Bundy*, but on this occasion the court held that the couple had not 'crossed the line' into a fiduciary relationship. It was said that Mr and Mrs Morgan were independent people who could well make their own decisions, and were not influenced by the bank in obtaining the loan. If anything, they went against the advice of the manager.

The House of Lords took the opportunity of stating two elements which they felt must be present for a presumption of undue influence to be established in these cases:

- there must be a fiduciary relationship where one party exercises dominance

- the transaction must be actually disadvantageous to the weaker party (this was a new requirement).

Here the Morgans had asked for help and had received it. This was not seen as a disadvantage to them. Had their business been successful, presumably they would have been grateful for the help.

The case of *Midland Bank v Shephard* (1988) followed in the courts, and confirmed the approach taken in *National Westminster Bank v Morgan.* There then followed a series of cases, refining the doctrine and raising particular issues. Consider the particular facts of the following cases.

BCCI v Aboody (1990)

Mrs Aboody was a young Saudi Arabian wife who was totally dominated by her older husband in financial matters. There was no manifest disadvantage, but there *could* have been undue influence between husband and wife, even if unintentional. This case was a landmark in the light of the reluctance of the courts to find such a relationship between husband and wife.

CIBC v Pitt (1993) then confirmed that in cases of proved undue influence (undue influence which arises on this particular occasion) manifest disadvantage need not be shown. However, the following case is now seen as a key authority, giving the courts the opportunity to restate the law in this area.

Barclays v O'Brien (1993)

This case went to court as a claim by Mrs O'Brien of undue influence. Mr O'Brien had told her that he needed to borrow £60,000 from the bank for a short period to support his business, and on that basis Mrs O'Brien signed papers presented to her by Mr O'Brien after he had visited the bank. In fact the loan grew to reach £135,000 and was repayable over a much longer period. When it was not repaid the bank sought possession of the family house which had been used as security. Mrs O'Brien claimed undue influence, and at the Court of Appeal it was held that the loan was only repayable up to the amount that Mrs O'Brien originally expected to borrow. On appeal, however, to the House of Lords it was held that the whole loan could be set aside. However, the findings were somewhat unexpected. The court found that Mrs O'Brien was an intelligent and independent-minded woman, so there was no undue influence. But, it was held that there was a misrepresentation between husband and wife, and banks in these cases should be 'put on enquiry' (alerted, or informed) that if a spouse or cohabitee was involved in a loan, they may be at some disadvantage. The doctrine of notice applies, so that the bank should be aware of the

▶

rights of the weaker party (here Mrs O'Brien) unless adequate steps have been taken to ensure that she received independent advice. In such circumstances the banks have a duty to ensure that there is no misrepresentation or undue influence, which they did not carry out on this occasion, so the House of Lords set aside the whole of the loan.

Why do you think that the House of Lords allowed the whole of the loan to be set aside, changing the Court of Appeal decision?

Following this case, some questions remain open. For example, just how far must a bank go in ensuring that independent advice is received, in order to discharge its responsibilities? Some indication comes from the cases which follow *O'Brien*, and these cases will help to clarify both the legal position and the duty of the banks. However, to some extent at least, the recent cases also cause further confusion, certainly regarding the precedent set by *O'Brien*, as although the cases immediately following it appeared to confirm the decision, the more recent ones tend to move away from support for the borrower.

- The case of *TSB v Camfield* (1994) followed the decision of the House of Lords in O'Brien that the effect of the misrepresentation in this particular case was to set aside the whole transaction. Similarly, in the case of *TSB v Camfield* the whole loan was set aside. Various reasons could be suggested for this. Firstly, there is the theoretical problem of contract law not having a 'halfway measure' as in tort. The idea of contributory negligence in tort does not exist in contract law, and a party is wholly liable or not liable. To decide otherwise is to create a whole new concept of contributory fault (this has been suggested by the Law Commission). Secondly, if Mrs O'Brien had been liable for part of the debt, she would still have had to sell the house, and in part, at least, the aim of the court was to prevent that.

- Some cases have stressed that banks will probably only be obliged to take reasonable steps to ensure that independent advice is received (see *Banco Exterior v Mann* (1994) where the husband and wife used the same solicitor, and *Midland Bank v Serter* (1994) where the wife used the bank's solicitor). However the case of *Royal Bank of Scotland v Etridge* has now provided the House of Lords an opportunity for review of the area in a set of eight appeals over similar issues, each with their own facts.

Royal Bank of Scotland v Etridge (2001)
The wife owned property in her own name, her husband handling the transfer of ownership and dealing with the bank. Amongst the documents

signed by the wife were two mortgages in favour of the plaintiff bank. They sought to enforce these, and the wife claimed that the bank had constructive notice of undue influence or misrepresentation, following *O'Brien*. The Court of Appeal rejected this claim, and found unanimously for the bank. The House of Lords confirmed the Court of Appeal decision, and found for the bank. In doing so they laid down guidance. They confirmed the approach to these cases established in *O'Brien*, in asking: Did the wife enter the transaction under the influence of her husband? If so, was the lender put on enquiry? Did the lender take reasonable steps to be satisfied that there was no undue influence? Of course, the wife factually must have provided the security because of the undue influence – which denies the existence of free will.

• Banks should, then, take certain steps to ensure that the wife is fully in the picture. They should not just advise her to obtain legal advice, but either see her independently from her husband and advise her of the situation, or ask her for a named solicitor and a written confirmation that she has received advice. They should also co-operate with the solicitor in passing on information. The aim of the law is to balance the protection needed for a wife (or any other person in a surety position) with the needs for banks to be able to lend money with security. This balance was expressed by Lord Bingham as follows,

"It is important that lenders should feel able to advance money, in run-of-the-mill cases with no abnormal features, on the security of the wife's interest in the matrimonial home in reasonable confidence that, if appropriate procedures have been followed in obtaining the security, it will be enforceable if the need for enforcement arises. The law must afford both parties a measure of protection. It cannot prescribe a code which will be proof against error, misunderstanding or mishap. But it can indicate minimum requirements which, if met, will reduce the risk of error, misunderstanding or mishap to an acceptable level. The paramount need in this important field is that these minimum requirements should be clear, simple and practically operable."

- The problem of sharing loss where neither party had acted with any devious intention arose in *Cheese v Thomas* (1993) where it was said that if an investment was made which became worth less in value, the two parties would share the effect of the loss.

This whole area is still developing, but it is clear that the courts will still look for free exercise of independent will, which is the essence of contract law.

Inequality of bargaining power

It has been said, notably by Lord Denning in *Lloyds Bank v Bundy*, that all of these cases could be settled by examining whether the parties are of equal bargaining power, and setting aside the contract where it was 'unconscionable', or against the court's conscience. Support for this approach was found in *Watkin v Watson-Smith* (1986). However, in *National Westminster Bank v Morgan*, the House of Lords had rejected Lord Denning's wider view, taking a traditional approach. The courts will not, they said, protect persons against what they regard as mistakes, merely because of inequality of bargaining power. Nevertheless, Lord Denning's approach, although his personal view, does have merit, perhaps ahead of its time. We await developments.

Summary

Duress

Definition

Unfair pressure which persuaded a party to contract, arising from physical violence or unlawful constraint, or the threat of it, to the party or someone close. Originally a common law doctrine, therefore strict adherence to the doctrine – *Cumming v Ince, Kauffman v Gerson*. Effect: the contract is void.

Development of economic duress

- Threats to property did not amount to duress at common law – *Skeate v Beale*.
- Slight relaxation (a very serious threat may amount to duress) – *The Siboen and The Sibotre*.
- Recognition that threat to breach a contract causing financial loss could be economic duress – *The Atlantic Baron*.
- Economic duress found in a shipping case – *The Universe Sentinel*.

- A threat to breach contract must be more than commercial pressure and the sum will normally be substantial, e.g. loss of livelihood – *Pao On v Lau Yiu Long.*

Four possible factors identified:

- Did the person protest?
- Was there an alternative?
- Was independent advice taken?
- Were steps taken to avoid the contract after entering into it?

The value of the contract is considered in relation to the scale of operation of the parties – *Atlas Express v Kafco.* Contrast this with legitimate commercial pressure – *Williams v Roffey* Effect: the court sets the contract aside (makes it voidable).

Undue influence

Definition

Unfair pressure on a party when forming a contract, which does not amount to common law duress. An equitable doctrine, developed to provide relief in cases of injustice.
Effect: the contract is voidable, therefore the bars to rescission apply – lapse of time, third-party rights, restitution impossible, affirmation.

Where there is no special relationship between the parties

Undue influence must simply be proved by the injured party (as with duress) – *Williams v Bayley*

Where a fiduciary relationship exists

This may be:

- where a relationship is one of a recognised group – *Allcard v Skinner*
- where a particular relationship on this occasion was a special one – *BCCI v Aboody.*

In either situation, the stronger party is *presumed* to have exercised undue influence, unless it can be *rebutted* according to the suggestions in *Re Brocklehurst*:

- Was independent advice sought?
- Was full disclosure made?
- Was the consideration adequate?
- Was any gift spontaneous?

Banking cases

These are situations where there is not normally a special or fiduciary relationship, but there *may* be in particular circumstances.

- Has the client 'crossed the line' into an area of confidentiality? – If so, undue influence would be presumed – *Lloyds Bank v Bundy*.

- Has the weaker party suffered manifest disadvantage? *National Westminster v Morgan*.

- Was there a relationship of trust in the particular circumstances of the case? – *BCCI v Aboody*.

- In cases of proved undue influence (i.e. undue influence which arises on this particular occasion) manifest disadvantage need not be shown – *CIBC v Pitt*.

- For an appraisal of the current situation, see *Barclays v O'Brien* concerning a claim of undue influence. The court found that (a) there was a misrepresentation between husband and wife, and (b) the banks in these cases should be 'put on enquiry' (alerted, or informed). The whole loan was set aside.

- Regarding the extent of the banks' responsibility, see *Banco Exterior v Mann, Midland Bank v Massey, TSB v Camfield, Royal Bank of Scotland v Etridge, Bank of Scotland v Bennett*.

Questions

1 Jake is a lecturer in economics. Kevin is one of Jake's students who has frequently sought his advice over finance. Jake advises Kevin to invest his student loan and savings, amounting to £3000, in a local company, Leeways Ltd, in which Jake is a director. During the next year Leeways Ltd has operating difficulties, and the value of its shares falls dramatically, so that Kevin's investment is now worth £500. Kevin was planning to use the money to start a business of his own, and is now unable to do this. He claims that he was greatly influenced by the advice given by Jake, and feels that Jake should have known of the difficulties of Leeways Ltd, which have caused him to lose a lot of his investment.

    Advise Kevin of his remedies, if any, in the law of contract.

2 'The grounds upon which economic duress may be claimed are vague, the doctrine itself suffering from a lack of definition.' How far do you agree with this statement?

3 Critically examine the recent line of 'banking cases' which have been the subject of claims of undue influence.

4 True agreement cannot really be said to exist if unfair pressure is placed upon one of the parties. How do the doctrines of duress and undue influence deal with such situations?

5 'The law relating to undue influence has now developed to the extent that banks should be well aware of the steps needed to ensure that a loan will be repaid.' Does this assertion represent the current state of the law?

6 Evaluate the circumstances in which a claim of economic duress may allow a person to escape their contractual liabilities.

11 Misrepresentation

A contract may be well formed, containing all the necessary elements to make it valid, but could still be unfair because of something in its formation. What if, for example, a person was encouraged into a contract because someone lied before it was made? A person who has been misled by this may well have bought items which are not satisfactory, just as they would have done had there been a misleading term within the contract, so a remedy for this situation may be just as important to the injured party as a remedy for breach of contract.

Representations and terms

It was seen when examining incorporation of terms (Chapter 6) that statements made prior to or during contractual negotiations are representations. Some of these may later become terms of the contract, whilst others remain mere representations. There are obviously remedies available for breach of a term (see Chapter 7 on types of terms and Chapter 15 on remedies), but this chapter will examine the situation where someone has been misled into making a contract by representations.

Where representations of facts prove to be untrue, and mislead a person into entering into a contract, there may be a situation of misrepresentation.

Definition

A misrepresentation is an untrue statement of fact, made by one party to a contract to another, which is not a term of the contract, has an inducing effect on it.

An untrue statement of fact

To be actionable, a misrepresentation must be a mis-statement of an existing fact. It must not be:

- a mere commendation
- a statement of opinion
- a statement of future intentions
- a statement of law.

Mere commendation

It may be difficult to distinguish between a permissible commendation of an advertising nature and an actionable false statement. Obviously there is a difference between an advertisement stating, for instance, that 'Camay soap will make you a little lovelier every day' and one stating that if a product does not perform as specified, money will be refunded.

> *Dimmock v Hallett* (1866)
> An estate agent's description of land as 'fertile and improvable' was held to be a mere commendation and not actionable.

Statement of opinion

Opinion is NOT a misrepresentation

Figure 11.1

A statement may at first sight appear to be more factual that a mere commendation, but yet be hedged around with qualifications, such as 'I think' or 'I believe'. Generally, such a view or opinion on a matter, which is unable to be proved, cannot result in an action for misrepresentation.

> *Bisset v Wilkinson* (1927)
> A seller of a sheep farm in New Zealand was said to be able to support about 2000 sheep. This was found to be untrue, but held not to be a

misrepresentation because the buyer knew that the seller had never farmed sheep in New Zealand, and was only voicing an opinion.

So, usually, a statement of opinion will not give rise to a claim in misrepresentation. However, what seems to be a statement of opinion may by implication involve a statement of fact; for example, a person may represent that he holds an opinion when it is found as a fact that he did not believe what he said. Obviously this will depend on reasonable evidence being available.

A statement of opinion may be regarded as a statement of fact in a situation where one party possesses greater skill or knowledge than the other, and represents by implication that he knows facts which support or justify the opinion.

Smith v Land & House Property (1884)

A seller described the occupier of the property as 'a most desirable tenant'. It was subsequently found that he had only paid rent erratically and under pressure. This was held to be a misrepresentation because the seller was the only person who could have known this information, so he had an extra duty to take care over his statements as his opinion would be regarded as authoritative.

A more recent illustration of this point came in the interesting case of *Esso v Mardon* (1976).

Esso v Mardon (1976)

The defendant was thinking of opening a petrol station, and sought the advice of a specialist from Esso as to what would be the likely throughput of petrol (and therefore the likely profit). On the basis of these figures the defendant decided to go ahead with the purchase of the business. Between the initial negotiations and the eventual purchase the local authority insisted on the resiting of the petrol pumps, to the back of the site, with access off a side road. This meant that the trade was not as expected, and the throughput and takings were about half of those expected. The defendant decided that he could no longer carry on, and when Esso sued for repossession of the property, he made a counterclaim for misrepresentation. It was held that there was a misrepresentation by Esso for several reasons:

• the Esso expert possessed greater skill, and therefore responsibility, than the defendant, and was in possession of more material facts

- there was a relationship between the two where the Esso expert owed a duty to take greater care than the average person over his statements (see page 168 for more on this)

- there was a change in circumstances (of which Esso were aware) which meant that Esso should have revised the forecast throughput of petrol before the purchase of the business took place (again, see later for more on this).

Inntrepreneur v Hollard (2000)
A wrong statement of the takings of a pub was held to be a misrepresentation because it was made by a person who, it was felt, should know the accurate takings. This is moving a long way from the usual principles of contract law where the court looks for external evidence rather than trying to 'read' the minds of the parties.

British Gas v Nelson (2002)
British Gas made forecasts of sales to Nelson before forming a contract under which Nelson would install appliances on basis of the estimated number of clients. The figures were badly inaccurate and Nelson sued British Gas for misrepresentation as they did not have the quantity of work envisaged. British Gas were seen to be the party who held the accurate knowledge (or should have done) and were led liable.

Sykes v Taylor-Rose (2004)
This case contrasts with those above. It was held that the sellers of a house did not have a duty to tell the buyers that the house had once been the setting for a murder, even though this meant that, as a consequence, the buyers then resold the house at a loss of £25,000.

Statements of future intentions

These are not generally actionable as misrepresentations. However, if it can be proved that the representor never intended to do the promised act at the time of making the statement, then the claim may be regarded as a statement of fact, that is to say a mis-statement of the state of the representor's mind. Again, this raises problems of evidence, but if sufficient proof is available, then there is no reason why this should not be actionable.

Edgington v Fitzmaurice (1885)
Shares in a business venture were sold, the publicity stating that the aim was to expand and improve the business. However, in letters to other people there was written evidence that the company planned to use the money raised by shares to pay off existing debts. These statements of

future intentions were held to be misrepresentations. In such circumstances, where there is clear proof of what a person intends to do, Bowen LJ said that 'the state of a man's mind is as much a fact as the state of his digestion'.

Statements of law

These have traditionally not been actionable, as they are not regarded as statements of fact. Also, people are generally taken to be as equals before the law and to have equal access to it (although this is obviously an ideal, rather than reality). However, some points should be noted.

- A lawyer (or similar person) mis-stating the law will not be absolved from liability for breach of professional duty of care on this basis. This is quite logical, given his professional expertise.
- A wilful misrepresentation of law may be actionable as a statement of opinion not actually held.

Difficulties may arise in deciding whether a statement is one of law or fact, and it may be a mixture of the two. For example, a statement that the Sale of Goods Act 1979 s.13 requires goods sold to correspond with their description is clearly one of law. If a shopper complains to a friend that the packet of biscuits she bought as custard creams were found inside to be ginger snaps, she is obviously making a statement of fact. However, if her friend then advises her that the item should be exchanged because the biscuits inside did not correspond to the description on the packet, this is a mixture of fact and law.

More recently, there has been some move away from the traditional position regarding wrong statements of law, as seen in the following case.

Pankhania v Hackney London Borough Council (2002)
This case concerned a £4 million purchase of commercial property and the wrong statement concerned whether the property was legally subject to a licence or a tenancy. The decision heralds a change in stance in this area of law. There is now liability for a mistake over the law (see *Kleinwort Benson v Lincoln City Council* in Chapter 12), and in the case of *Pankhania v Hackney* the High Court judge held that a similar shift in attitude should apply to misrepresentation. He said that to maintain the traditional position would be 'no more than a quixotic anachronism'.

Silence and misrepresentation

The general rule is that silence does not amount to misrepresentation. There is no liability for failing to disclose relevant facts to the other party, even if those facts might have influenced the other party, and even if it is obvious that the other has a wrong impression that could be remedied by disclosure. In this situation, the initial presumption, at least, is that the principle of *caveat emptor* applies. Translated literally this means 'let the buyer beware', or, in other words, do not rely on the statements of a seller, but use your own judgement. The following case is the usual authority for this.

Fletcher v Krell (1873)
A governess was appointed to a post, and when it was later found that she had previously been married, a claim of misrepresentation was made against her for not disclosing this (it was not desirable at that time to have a governess who was married, let alone separated). However, it was held that merely keeping quiet about something about which no questions had been asked was not a misrepresentation, and the claim failed.

Is there a difference between remaining silent over a matter of personal life in an interview and remaining silent over an item which is being sold?

Misrepresentation, then, does not arise normally out of mere silence. This was stated by Lord Campbell in *Walters v Morgan* (1861), when he said that 'simple reticence does not amount to legal fraud, however it may be viewed by moralists'. However, he went on to point out that there were circumstances where this general rule does not apply.

• Conduct may amount to misrepresentation. Lord Campbell said that this may be in the form of 'a nod, a wink, a shake of the head or a smile', but is not difficult to imagine other situations where a prospective buyer, for example, may be misled by the conduct of the seller. Equally a photograph or image may mislead, as in the following recent case.

St Marylebone Property v Payne (1994)
A misleading photograph of land which was for for sale by auction gave sale. This was held to be a misrepresentation, overriding an exemption clause concerning errors, and resulting in the bidders rescinding the contract and obtaining the return of their deposit.

Spice Girls v Aprilia World Service (2000)
The Spice Girls group all took part in filming an advertisement for Aprilia's motor scooters. This action was held to be a misrepresentation of the fact that they knew that they would not be remaining together as a complete group, even though nothing was actually said about this.

- If a seller of goods does some positive act to deliberately conceal defects in goods, this may amount to misrepresentation. In *Schneider v Heath* (1813) a boat which was being sold was partly submerged by the seller to conceal a rotten hold.

- A half-true statement which is accurate as far as it goes, but which conveys a misleading impression by being incomplete may give rise to misrepresentation. In *Dimmock v Hallett* (1866) a seller of land stated that all the farms on an estate were let to tenants, but omitted to say add that the tenants had all given notice to leave.

- Changed circumstances may imply a duty to disclose facts, which would not be misrepresentations at all if nothing had been said originally about the matter. If a representor knows of a change in circumstances, and thereby knows that his originally true statement is now false, this may amount to a misrepresentation. This arose in *With v O'Flanagan* (1936) when a doctor wanted to sell his practice. He told a prospective buyer the current income, and then became ill. By the time the sale eventually took place, many of the clients had transferred to another practice, and the income was much less than originally stated. As the doctor did not revise his original statement it was held to be a misrepresentation. A similar situation arose in *Esso v Mardon* (see above) where the Esso representative did not revise his sales forecasts in light of the new siting of the petrol pumps.

- A fiduciary relationship may indicate that there is a duty to disclose facts. All of the situations above involve people meeting on relatively equal terms. In these situations there is only a duty to tell the truth, but no general duty to disclose. So if something *is* said, it must be true, but there is not a general duty to say anything at all. If a person sells a stereo system to another, they can simply make no claims at all about it, letting the buyer form their own opinion of whether it is good value. In some circumstances, however, where one party is in a position of responsibility towards the other, the law may consider there to be a fiduciary relationship between the two. Some examples are: parent and child, solicitor and client, trustee and beneficiary. In these situations there is a greater duty to disclose relevant facts than in ordinary relationships between average people. A failure to disclose relevant facts in these circumstances may lead to misrepresentation. An example of a fiduciary relationship is found in the following case, which, although it failed on a technicality, shows how a misrepresentation could arise. You may remember that in *Esso v Mardon* (page 168) the court found that the Esso expert owed a duty of care to Mr. Mardon, therefore finding that there had been a negligent misrepresentation.

Hedley Byrne and Co v Heller & Partners Ltd (1964)
Heller bankers gave assurances of creditworthiness to Hedley Byrne concerning a mutual client, Easipower. The bank were the only people

who held this information, so they were deemed to be in a position of trust. When Easipower defaulted on payments a claim of misrepresentation was made against Heller. This would have succeeded, because of the relationship, had it not been for a technical clause in the letter of assurance (it was given 'without responsibility'). So the principle of law from *Hedley Byrne* is *obiter* (not technically binding), but is respected as the current legal position.

- Contracts *uberrimae fidei* (of utmost good faith) go a step beyond fiduciary relationships, and impose an absolute duty to disclose all material facts to the other party. In certain contracts, where only one party possesses full knowledge of all the material, or relevant, facts, the law requires that party to show *uberrima fides* (utmost good faith). The main example of this is in contracts of insurance, especially now when the contract is often made over the telephone, and the insurer has no idea whether the customer is telling the truth. Material facts (those which must be disclosed) were said in the Marine Insurance Act 1906 to be those likely to influence the prudent insurer in setting the premium (the payment) or in deciding whether to take the risk at all. This applies to all forms of insurance (motor, life, fire, theft, accident, etc.). The penalty for non-disclosure is usually that the insurance company will claim that the contract is rescinded (ended – see p. 179), and they can either decide not to pay at all when a claim is made, or they may decide to make a reduced payment as a gesture of goodwill. The following case is an early example of non-disclosure.

Seaman v Fonereau (1743)
A ship was sited in difficulties when out at sea, but it recovered from them. When it was later captured by Spaniards, the insurers refused to pay for it, since the previous difficulties had not been reported. It was held that they were entitled to do so, as this was a contract of *uberrima fides* which imposed a duty to report all material facts, and the ship being in difficulties was one such fact.

In *Bufe v Turner* (1815) an insurance company refused to pay when a house owner did not report the circumstances of a fire in an adjoining property. In *Lambert v Co-operative Insurance Society* (1975) a lady was not entitled to recover the cost of her stolen jewellery because she had not informed the insurers of her husband's conviction for conspiracy to steal.

Can you think of any facts which may affect an insurer in deciding whether to insure a person to drive a car, or in deciding how much to charge for the insurance cover?

Misrepresentation passed on via a third party

Once an untrue statement has been made from one party to another, it is usually considered 'spent', so it is no longer a misrepresentation if the second party passes it on to a third. However, if the first party knows that the wrong information is likely to be passed on, then an actionable misrepresentation may arise. This was so in *Pilmore v Hood* (1838) when the seller of a pub wrongly stated the takings, knowing that the information was likely to be passed on to another person who bought the business.

Inducement

In the definition of misrepresentation, we saw that the untrue statement must have induced the representee to contract. If the other party had not read or heard the representation, or had not placed any reliance on it at all, then they have no claim against the representor.

> *Attwood v Small* (1838)
> The buyers of a mine claimed misrepresentation when the amount of minerals in it were found to be less than that stated by the seller. However, it was held that they had relied on the results of their own private survey rather than the statements of the seller (of course, the buyer may have had a claim in negligence against the surveyor, had the case arisen more recently).

So, if a person with reasonable skill makes enquiries of their own (for example, if a mechanic examines a car thoroughly), it is likely that they will be held to have relied on those enquiries rather than the ones made by the seller. If the representee tests for accuracy, but fails to discover the truth, the case of *Redgrave v Hurd* (1881) suggests that they may still be regarded as having relied on the representor's untrue statement.

The case of *Barton v County NatWest* (2002) found that there is a rebuttable presumption that a claimant relied on an inducing statement if a reasonable person would have done so.

Remedies

Where a misrepresentation is found to exist, the innocent party will need a remedy. Two main remedies exist: rescission and damages. Rescission is where the parties are restored to their original position by handing back whatever they have acquired under the contract. So if a contract had been made to buy a car, rescission would mean that the buyer hands back the car and the seller hands back the money paid. Damages is the award of money as compensation for the misrepresentation, and is often the amount needed to put right a defect, plus an amount for inconvenience. These remedies are both explained in more detail below.

The innocent party makes a decision as to which is appropriate, and today has a genuine choice, although that was not always the situation, as the remedy at one time depended greatly on the type of misrepresentation which had occurred. As it is often difficult to prove fraud, a party who has suffered from a misrepresentation often now sues as if the misrepresentation had not been fraudulent, just to make the process simpler. However, the choice of action is still available in theory, as will be seen.

The distinction between those misrepresentations which are fraudulent and those which are not is therefore less important that it once was, but it is still significant in making a claim. Obviously the difference depends on the state of mind of the representor (like the requirement of mens rea in many crimes).

Fraudulent misrepresentation

The classic definition of fraudulent misrepresentation comes from the House of Lords case, *Derry v Peek* (1889), in which it was said that a fraudulent misrepresentation was a false statement made 'knowing, without belief in its truth, or recklessly as to whether it be true or false'. Really a fraudulent statement could be summed up as one which the maker does not honestly believe to be true.

The courts regard fraud seriously, and will therefore look for more than mere negligence or carelessness, and since the proof concerns a state of mind, fraud is very difficult to prove in most cases. In fact it was confirmed in the case *Ahmed v Addy* (2004) that the standard of proof should be the criminal standard (beyond reasonable doubt). If fraudulent misrepresentation is proved, two remedies are available:

- The plaintiff may claim damages. Damages for fraud are based on the tort of deceit, rather than on a strictly contractual remedy, and are therefore calculated in a slightly different way given for breach of contract. Whereas damages in contract aim to put the plaintiff in the position that he would have been in if the contract had been fully performed, the damages in tort try to restore the plaintiff to the position in which he would have found himself if the tort (here, the fraud) had not been practised. The plaintiff may also apply for an order to have any property handed over to be restored to him.

- The contract may be rescinded (see below). This means handing back any property (including money) passed over during the contract, and going back to the original position. As the remedy of rescission is an equitable one, in certain circumstances where unfairness would arise it is not allowed (see bars to rescission later). Note that a fraudulent misrepresentation can be used as a defence if the innocent party is sued for rescission. They can refuse to hand over goods or benefits obtained through the contract. This may arise, for instance, where a party has obtained insurance cover by fraudulent misrepresentations (remember these contracts are *uberrimae fidei*). If the contract is rescinded, the insurance company is entitled to keep any premiums paid.

Non-fraudulent misrepresentation

Before 1964 there was only a remedy of rescission for non-fraudulent misrepresentation, and damages were not available unless fraud was proved (see above). Any non-fraudulent misrepresentations were regarded as 'innocent', and therefore without a monetary remedy.

In 1963, the House of Lords changed this position by stating, *obiter*, that in certain circumstances, where a negligent mis-statement resulted in financial loss, damages may be recovered in tort. For this liability to arise, there had to be a duty of care, arising from a 'special relationship' between the parties. In the case of *Hedley Byrne and Co Ltd v Heller and Partners Ltd* (1964) (see p. 172), the banker, Heller, was seen to have been negligent, rather than deliberately fraudulent. Had it not been for a technical matter, the court would have been willing to make an award of damages, even though fraud was not proved. Another example is seen in *Esso v Mardon* (p. 168) which despite going to court in 1976 actually took place before the Misrepresentation Act was passed in 1967.

Although it is not certain exactly what the term 'special relationship' means, some guidelines do exist. Firstly, the principle of liability is based on the duty of care in tort.

Donoghue v Stevenson (1932)
When a partly decomposed snail was found in a bottle of ginger beer, it was held that the manufacturer of the drink owed a duty of care to the eventual consumer, and was therefore liable for her inconvenience and illness. This is known as the 'neighbour' principle (where it is foreseeable that a person will be affected by actions, then a duty of care is owed to that person).

Secondly, from *Esso v Mardon* (see above, p. 168) it is likely that such a relationship will be considered to exist where the representor possesses relevant knowledge or skill, and would expect the other party to rely on this.

The Misrepresentation Act 1967

The Misrepresentation Act 1967 provided, for the first time, a remedy of damages for non-fraudulent misrepresentation. The remedy is available where the person *would* have had a remedy, if the misrepresentation had been fraudulent. This provision is found in s.2(1), and is as follows:

> Where a person has entered into a contract after a misrepresentation has been made to him by another party thereto and as a result thereof he has suffered loss, then, if the person making the misrepresentation would be liable to damages in respect thereof had the misrepresentation been made fraudulently, that person shall be so liable notwithstanding that the misrepresentation was not made fraudulently, unless he proves that he had reasonable ground to believe and did believe up to the time the contract was made that the facts represented were true.

This section of the Act places a burden on the defendant to prove that it was both reasonable to believe, and that he did in fact believe, in the truth of his statements. Note that in this way, unlike the common law requirement to prove liability, the burden of proof shifts to the maker of the statement to disprove negligence, once misrepresentation has been alleged. This burden is a heavy one to discharge, as seen in the following case.

Howard Marine v Ogden (1978)
The hirer of some barges were told their carrying capacity by the owners, who looked up the information in Lloyds register (the established authority on this issue). In fact, on this occasion (and very unusually) the register was wrong, and the hirers were given wrong information, causing them inconvenience. On investigation the correct information was found on the owner's records at their main office. The owners had done what most people would have regarded as a reasonable practice, but since they owned the information, and made false statements, what they said was held to be a misrepresentation, albeit not a deliberately deceitful one. This shows that the burden of disproving misrepresentation is a very heavy one indeed.

Applying the above case, if a person selling a house is asked if the woodwork is sound, and replies that it is, and later some woodworm is found in the corner of the roof, he would be liable for misrepresentation, as he owns the house. What could he do to avoid such a situation?

Once it is decided that damages should be awarded, then the issue arises as to the basis on which they should be assessed. Traditionally they are assessed in contract on an expectation basis, that is what the party would have expected to receive had the contract been carried out correctly. This would, of course, take into account lost profit. On the other hand, in tort damages are assessed on a reliance basis, that is where the aim is to put parties back to the position at the outset, which they would have been in before the wrong happened. So, in the case of a sale, it takes parties back to the starting-point, but does not replace lost profit. Because in fraud damages are assessed on a tort basis, it has been decided, in the case of *Royscott v Rogerson* (1991), that damages under the Misrepresentation Act 1967 should also be awarded on this basis. However, this has been taken a step further by the case of *East v Maurer* (1991) where it was said that in certain circumstances lost profits may also be recovered.

A further provision is made in s.2(2) that where misrepresentation is found to exist, the court 'may declare the contract subsisting and award damages in lieu of rescission, if of opinion that it would be equitable to do so, having regard to the nature of the misrepresentation and the loss that would be caused by it if the contract were upheld , as well as the loss that rescission would cause to the other party. Damages are then given in lieu – see Zanzibar v British Aerospace (2000). When used, this is a statutory bar to rescission (see page 180).

Indemnity

In its aim to restore the parties to their original position, the court may order an indemnity to accompany an order of rescission. This is a money payment in respect of obligations necessarily created by the contract, and should be distinguished from damages. The difference can be seen clearly in the following case.

Whittington v Seale-Hayne (1900)
The buyer of a farm enquired particularly about the water supply, drains and sewage system, and was told that they were all in order. He subsequently bought the farm and installed his prize poultry. However, the water system and drains were found not to be satisfactory, the manager becoming ill and many of the poultry dying as a result. The court allowed rescission, but as the misrepresentation was not fraudulent, and this was before the Misrepresentation Act 1967, damages were not payable. This took the buyer back to the original position as far as the farm went, and an indemnity was ordered which

repaid the costs necessarily incurred in buying the farm, such as rates and other legal requirements. However, it did not replace the cost of the poultry, as it was said that the buyer did not have to put these on the farm, but chose to do so.

The position may have been different if the case had arisen today, as damages may have been recoverable instead of an indemnity. An indemnity may still be awarded, even since the Misrepresentation Act 1967, but will not apply where damages are given. However, it is a useful remedy where a contract is rescinded for a wholly innocent misrepresentation.

Rescission

To rescind is to set the contract aside. The aim is to put the parties back into the position that they were in before the contract existed (i.e. to terminate it *ab initio*, or from the outset). A contract may be rescinded whether the misrepresentation is fraudulent or non-fraudulent, even if wholly innocent.

Is it right that a person who makes a misrepresentation totally innocently may have the contract rescinded? Think about this from the point of view of both the misrepresentor and the misrepresentee.

When a misrepresentation occurs, the contract is voidable rather than void. This means that it remains in force unless the person to whom the misrepresentation has been made chooses to set it aside. The injured party must indicate his intention to rescind either:

- by notifying the other party directly, or
- by some other act which clearly shows that he does not intend to be bound by the contract.

An example of the second situation arose in the Court of Appeal case of *Car and Universal Finance Co Ltd v Caldwell* (1965), where it was held that notifying the police and other appropriate authorities would be evidence of the wish to rescind.

Bars to rescission

It is clear that there is a general right to rescind where misrepresentation is proved. However, as rescission is based in equity it means that the contract is voidable, rather than void, and on some occasions ending the contract may be deemed by the court to be unfair, and therefore barred. The following are circumstances when this arises.

1 Statutory bar

Under the Misrepresentation Act 1967 s.2(2) the court has a right to award damages in lieu of rescission (see above). This arose in the recent case of *Zanzibar v British Aerospace* (2000).

2 Lapse of time

If a person discovers a misrepresentation but waits too long before making a claim, the right to do so may be barred. This arose in *Leaf v International Galleries* (1950) where a painting thought to be a Constable was found to be a copy five years after the sale, but it was too late to rescind. It should be noted that lapse of time is slightly different according to whether the misrepresentation is fraudulent or non-fraudulent.

For fraudulent misrepresentation the time in which a claim can be made begins at the point of discovery of the misrepresentation, so lapse of time is rarely an issue.

For non-fraudulent misrepresentation the time is measured from the point of contract, as in *Leaf v International Galleries*, so it is very important that the misrepresentation is discovered quickly.

3 Affirmation

Affirmation is indication that the misrepresentee is willing to continue with the contract (and possibly claim damages). This arose in *Long v Lloyd* (1958) where a lorry-driver bought a lorry about which the seller had made claims. When these were found to be untrue and the lorry developed problems, the buyer telephoned the seller and agreed to share the cost of repair. The buyer took the lorry on another journey and it again broke down. He then tried to claim rescission, but it was held that his willingness to share costs and use the lorry indicated affirmation and he had barred the right to rescind.

4 Restitution impossible

When claiming rescission items must be handed back in their original condition. The courts recognise that absolute restitution is not always possible, since some things must be used for the misrepresentation to be discovered. However, it should be as near to complete as possible. In *Vigers v Pike* (1842) restitution of a mine was not possible because considerable extraction had taken place.

5 Supervening third-party rights

If someone else, a third party, now has the goods, rescission cannot take place. This arose in *White v Garden* (1851) where iron bars had been delivered but rescission was barred because the bars had already been sold on to a third party.

Remedies for misrepresentation

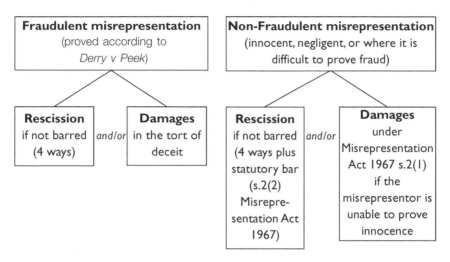

Figure 11.2

Comparison with remedies for breach of contract

When a contract is breached the remedy is damages, or if the term breached is serious, the right to repudiate. With misrepresentation the right to rescind is wider, but subject to various bars.

When damages are awarded for breach it is on an expectation basis, and when awarded for misrepresentation it is on a tortious, or reliant, basis. This would have meant that someone claiming misrepresentation would not have been compensated for lost profits, but now that these may also be given the two remedies are very similar.

Summary

Definition

A misrepresentation is an untrue statement of fact, made by one party to a contract to another, which, while not forming a term of a contract, has an inducing effect on it.

What will form a misrepresentation?

Must *not* be:
* A mere commendation – *Dimmock v Hallett*.
* A statement of opinion – *Bisset v Wilkinson*.
* A statement of future intentions – *Edgington v Fitzmaurice*.
* A statement of law.

Silence

Generally not a misrepresentation – *Fletcher v Krell*.
Exceptions:
* Conduct may amount to a misrepresentation – *Schneider v Heath*.
* A half-true statement may be a misrepresentation – *Dimmock v Hallett*.
* A change of circumstances may be a misrepresentation – *With v O'Flanagan*.
* Where one party is in a position of skill *v* responsibility – *Esso v Mardon*.
* A fiduciary relationship may impose a duty to disclose – *Hedley Byrne v Heller*.
* Contracts *uberrimae fidei* – *Seaman v Fonnereau*.

Inducement

The untrue statement must persuade, or induce, the other party into the contract – *Attwood v Small*.

Types of misrepresentation

May be fraudulent, according to *Derry v Peek* (deliberately dishonest), negligent or wholly innocent. For cases pre-1966, courts were only really interested in whether misrepresentation was fraudulent or not. Now full remedies exist for non-fraudulent misrepresentation.

Remedies

Rescission

An equitable remedy which restores the parties to original position unless barred by:

* Affirmation – *Long v Lloyd*.
* Third-party rights – *White v Garden*.
* Restitution impossible – *Vigers v Pike*.
* Lapse of time – *Leaf v International Galleries*.

- Statute – s.2(2) Misrepresentation Act 1967 – damages may be awarded in lieu – *Zanzibar v British Aerospace*.

Damages

- If fraudulent misrepresentation is proved: damages via the tort of deceit – *Derry v Peek*.
- If fraud cannot be proved, damages available under if a 'special' relationship exists – *Hedley Byrne v Heller*.
- Damages under the Misrepresentation Act 1967 s.2(1).

Points arising:

- The Misrepresentation Act 1967 is now the normal route to a remedy, and the most widely used.
- The burden of proof shifts to the misrepresentor to prove innocence.
- This is a heavy burden and it is difficult to avoid liability – *Howard Marine v Ogden*.
- Damages are assessed on a tort basis putting the injured party into the position which they would have been in had the wrong not happened – *Royscott v Rogerson*.
- Loss of profits may also be recoverable in some circumstances – *East v Maurer*.

The remedies for non-fraudulent misrepresentation are now more or less equivalent to those for breach of contract or fraudulent misrepresentation.

Questions

1   Bill describes his car to his friends. 'It's a good little runner,' he says. 'It has been serviced regularly, and is very reliable. It had a complete overhaul only recently, and has had a new clutch fitted.'

Ben was involved in this conversation, and a few weeks later hears that Bill is now wanting to sell his car. Ben is thinking of running a taxi service to earn some extra money during the summer holiday season, and, remembering his previous conversation with Bill, decides to buy the car. A week after the sale, Ben finds several problems with the car, including the need to fit a new clutch.

He also discovers that the service and overhaul have been undertaken by Bill himself. Ben uses the car for another week as he has clients relying on his taxi service, but now wishes to claim against Bill. Advise Ben.

2   Bill is a student at a local college. He was advised that he should have a computer to help him with his studies. He visited a nearby specialist computer shop, 'AB Computers' and explained that he wanted a computer 'for college work only'. Bill asked advice of the assistant, Conn, over which model to buy and was told that he needed a Supremo, the most expensive model in the store, as this was the only computer compatible with

those used by the college. Conn knew that this was not true, as virtually any computer would be compatible as long as it used the correct software. Bill knew nothing about computers and accepted that Conn, as an expert, must be correct. He agreed to buy the computer, paid a deposit and said he would collect and pay the remainder of the cost later in the week.

Later, when returning home, Bill was unfortunately knocked over by a car and suffered such serious injuries that he could not complete his college course and no longer needed the computer.

(a) What effect will the statements made by Conn have on any contract that has been formed?

(b) Discuss the effect on the contract between AB Computers and Bill of Bill's accident and departure from his college course.

(c) Consider whether the remedies available to the innocent party when there has been a breach of contract are satisfactory.

3 There are some untrue statements which induce a contract which will give rise to no remedy in misrepresentation.'

Consider the validity of this argument.

4 Critically assess whether the remedies which are available to a person who has been induced into a contract by misrepresentation are satisfactory.

5 It could be argued that the remedies for misrepresentation can now be equated with the remedies for breach of contract. How far can this argument be justified?

6 The remedies available to a person suffering from a misrepresentation are now not very different from those for breach of contract.'

Discuss the accuracy of this claim.

A further 'dilemma' style question on misrepresentation can be found in Part 7 of the book.

12 Mistake

A contract which is well formed, but where one or both parties have made some fundamental false assumption in forming it, is said to be made under a mistake. This is not necessarily a situation where one party has gone out of the way to mislead the other, but where a false assumption about the goods or the situation is genuine.

A mistake may be made by either party during the formation of a contract which is inconvenient but which in law does not affect the validity of contract. However, other mistakes could be much more fundamental, and could make the contract void. The cases where mistake has arisen can be categorised in various ways, since the doctrine of mistake is a developing one. Cheshire and Fifoot divide the cases into three main groups, and that is the way they will be discussed here, with a fourth category added concerning mistakes made which particularly relate to documents. The categories are:

- common mistake – where both parties are labouring under the same false assumption
- mutual mistake – sometimes known as shared mistake, where the parties are at cross purposes
- unilateral mistake – where only one party is mistaken and the other is aware of this
- mistake over documents.

Common mistake

Common mistake is where the parties are in agreement, but make the same false assumption in forming a contract, so their contract is based on a situation which is false.

Two main groups of cases have arisen in this way:

* cases where the mistake is over the existence of the subject matter
* cases where the mistake is over the quality of the subject matter.

(Note: by subject matter, we mean whatever is being bargained for within the contract – the goods, services, etc.)

Where the subject matter is non-existent

Where the mistake is over existence of the subject matter of the contract, the situation is known as *res extincta* (the thing is destroyed). Here the contract has been formed over something which is not available, so the mistake is so fundamental that the contract is held void. Examples of this are found in the following cases which concern a non-existent cargo of corn, a non-existent marriage and a non-existent person!

Couturier v Hastie (1856)
A ship was carrying corn to the United Kingdom, and while it was still in transit a sale was agreed over the corn. However, the corn had begun to deteriorate, so, unknown to the parties it had been sold at Tunis to prevent total loss of the cargo. The subject matter (the corn) did not therefore exist to form the basis of a sale, and the contract formed was held void.

Galloway v Galloway (1914)
A separation agreement was made between a husband and wife, but it was then found that they had not been legally married. The separation agreement was therefore held to be void.

Scott v Coulson (1903)
A contract of insurance was made on the life of a person, ironically called Mr Death, who had unfortunately already died at the time that the contract was made. It was held void as the subject matter was clearly not in existence.

This common law situation is now confirmed by statute in the Sale of Goods Act 1979 s.6, which states, 'Where there is a contract for the sale of specific goods, and the goods without the knowledge of the seller have perished at the time when the contract is made, the contract is void'.

It may be, because of the wording of a contract, and bearing in mind the very nature of the contract, that although the situation appears to be one of *res extincta*, the courts decide that one party has warranted (or assured the other party of) the existence of the subject matter. This arose in the following case.

McRae v Commonwealth Disposals Commission (1951)
The plaintiff paid the defendants for the right to salvage an oil tanker which was said by the defendants to be laying off the journal Reef. The plaintiff spent money on equipment and an expedition to salvage the tanker, but it was found that there was no tanker in the area and the reef did not exist. It was held that the defendants had warranted the existence of the tanker in selling into the plaintiff, and the court ordered damages to be paid.

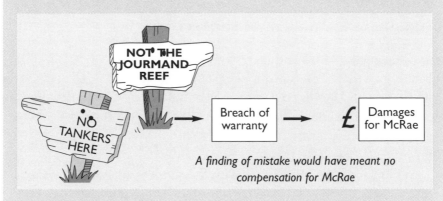

A finding of mistake would have meant no compensation for McRae

Figure 12.1

It is interesting that if mistake had been found, the remedy for McRae would have not been at all satisfactory, since the contract would have merely been declared void. In the event, the payment of damages for breach of warranty compensated him for the expense of setting up the expedition, and is a a fair remedy in this case. However, on the facts the situation does not seem to be very different from that in *Couturier v Hastie*, except that in *McRae* the tanker may never have existed.

It should also be noted that the doctrine is closely connected to the discharge of a contract by frustration. If a conference building is examined by a potential hirer, but before the contract is concluded, and unknown to both parties, it is destroyed by fire, then the contract would be void for common mistake. If however the contract was formed, but the fire occurred between then and the day of hire, the contract would be frustrated. The distinction between the two, then, depends solely on the point in time at which the disaster strikes.

Mistake over title

An extension of the principle of *res extincta* is that of *res sua* (literally, the thing is his own). It will rarely arise, but in the case of *Cooper v Phibbs*

(1867) a lease was drawn up to transfer a fishery, and unknown to both parties at the time, the buyer was already the owner. It was held that the contract was void for mistake, but that the party who thought that he had been the owner should have a lien on the property (a legal right over it) until he had received a sum of money to compensate for what he had spent on repairs and maintenance. This is a good example of the courts using their equitable powers to bring about a suitable remedy, when the common law remedy would not be satisfactory.

Mistake over quality of subject matter

The general position is that where the mistake of the parties merely results in a bad bargain for one of them, the contract will not be void. This is consistent with the principle that the law only requires sufficiency of consideration, not the normal market value. This arose in the following leading case.

Bell v Lever Bros (1932)
Lever Bros wanted to dispense with the services of Bell, who was a senior member of staff, managing one of their enterprises abroad. They thought that they were obliged to make a large settlement to persuade him to leave – a 'golden handshake' – and in fact gave him £30,000. They then found out that the payment need not have been made, because some time before he had behaved in such a way that they could have ended his contract anyway. Lever Bros argued that they had formed the contract to pay the golden handshake under a mistake which was fundamental. However, the House of Lords disagreed, although it was by a majority of 3 to 2, saying that the contract was to terminate the employment, and that was what had been achieved. It was only the cost which would have been different. The contract was therefore not impossible to perform, just a bad bargain for Lever Bros.

Lord Atkin stated in the case the principles on which the court would judge whether a mistake was over existence or quality of subject matter. He said,

> In such a case a mistake will not affect assent unless it is the mistake of both parties, and is as to the existence of some quality which makes the thing without the quality essentially different from the thing as it was believed to be.

So the court is looking for a fundamental quality which makes the contract essentially different from what was expected, but decided in the case of *Bell v Lever Bros* that the giving away of £30,000 did not come into that category. Given that the case was heard in 1932, it must be concluded that there is a very strict approach here, as this would, even for a company, have been a large amount of money to lose.

The point is perhaps more easily seen in the following case.

Leaf v International Galleries (1950)
A painting was sold which was believed by both the buyer and seller to be painted by Constable. In fact it was proved, some years later, to be a good copy. The court held that the contract would not be void for mistake, as the painting itself was the subject of the contract, and it did exist. The mistake was merely over its value, or quality. The reasoning seems quite logical, if it is considered what would happen if the situation was reversed and the value had increased. However, applying the criteria of Lord Atkin (above), it could also be argued that a copy of a painting is not at all the same thing as the original, and that if this fact been known at the time of sale, the contract would not have been formed at all.

The criteria have been restated in the following more recent case.

Associated Japanese Bank Ltd v Credit du Nord (1988)
A guarantee was given over some gaming machines. The gaming machines were found not to exist, so the guarantee was worthless and was held void. This was not really *res extincta*, since the contract was over the guarantee (which did exist, but was of no use), not over the gaming machines (which did not exist). Lord Steyn said that the guarantee concerning non-existent machines was 'essentially different' from a guarantee concerning machines which both parties believed to exist.

The same test was used in *William Sindall v Cambridgeshire County Council* (1994) where land was found to be worth less than its purchase price and to contain sewers originally thought not to be there. The contract was said not to be 'essentially and radically different' from the original, but just worth less.

If a person buys an item of old furniture in a street market which turns out to be a valuable antique, should they return it to the seller? Should this be the same if they pay a lot for what appears to be a Roman coin at a historical site, and the coin is later proved to be a copy?

Great Peace Shipping v Tsavliris Salvage (2002)

Solle v Butcher had extended the test in *Bell v Lever Bros* (a mistake must be over 'some quality which makes the thing without the quality essentially different from the thing as it was believed to be'). The test was now whether the mistake was 'fundamental' – much more an equitable decision of a judge on grounds of fairness or equity. Great Peace said that there should not be this distinction. The test in *Bell* is to stand until such time as legislation changes the doctrine.

There must be (according to Lord Phillips):

- a common assumption over a state of affairs
- no warranty by either party that the state of affairs exists
- non-existence of the state of affairs must not be the fault of either party
- non-existence of state of affairs makes performance impossible.

A state of affairs may be the existence of, or a vital attribute of, consideration.

In situations of common mistake it cannot really be said that there is ever any true agreement between the parties. There is no *consensus ad idem* – meeting of minds – and it could be argued that the contract had not therefore been correctly formed. This is certainly true where the mistake is over existence of the subject matter, which is why the courts find the contract void. However, in cases involving mistake over quality it could be argued that the main terms of the contract are clear, and it is only the intrinsic value that is under dispute, leaving the contract itself intact.

Mutual mistake

In mutual mistake, the parties are not really in agreement right from the outset, as they make different assumptions in forming the contract.

In such cases if there is total ambiguity the contract is held void, as in the following case.

Raffles v Wichelhaus (1864)

An agreement was made to buy a cargo of cotton, on a ship named *Peerless*, sailing from Bombay to England. There were actually two ships of the same name, both loaded with cotton, one of which left Bombay in October, and one in December. As the parties were completely at cross-purposes it could not be decided which ship had been intended to be the subject of the contract, so the court held it too ambiguous to enforce.

Where there is some 'extra' factor the contract may be allowed to continue, as in the following case.

Wood v Scarth (1858)
A lease was drawn up concerning a pub, and after a conversation with the seller's clerk the buyer accepted, believing the only payment to be the rental of £63. The seller had also intended a premium of £500 to be paid. Here the contract was upheld on the buyer's terms, because of the 'extra' evidence of the statements of the clerk which had misled the buyer.

Unilateral mistake

Unilateral mistake is where only one party has contracted on the basis of a false assumption. The other party will normally know of this mistake, and in some cases will have encouraged it, or even planned it.

Mistake over quality of subject matter

The courts again take the view that merely being mistaken over the quality or value of the goods is not fundamental enough to avoid the contract. This was one argument raised in *Smith v Hughes* (see Chapter 1, p. 2) where the court said that even if the seller knew that the buyer was mistaken over the quality of the oats which he bought, this would not make the contract void. On the other hand, in *Scriven v Hindley* (1913) the court held void a contract where a buyer at an auction had paid a very high price for a consignment of a fibre called tow, believing it to be hemp, which was more valuable.

Taking this a step further, some mistakes may be so fundamental and obvious that one party will be taken to have known about the mistake of the other. In *Hartog v Colin and Shields* (1939) a mistake over the price of hare skins was found to be so obvious and fundamental to a buyer who was familiar with the market that he was deemed to have been aware of it, the contract being held void.

Mistake as to identity

This is an aspect of unilateral mistake, and in many cases has occurred when one person has posed as someone else in order to persuade a seller to part with goods on credit. The issue before the courts is whether the case is genuinely one of identity or creditworthiness. The cases fall into two groups:

- *Inter absentes* – where the parties are not in each other's presence, but deal 'at arm's length'.
- *Inter praesentes* – where the parties meet face to face.

The following case is an example of *inter absentes*, where the parties communicated by post.

Cundy v Lindsay (1878)
Cundy supplied a quantity of handkerchiefs to another firm called Blenkarn, operating from Wood Street. Cundy was under the mistaken impression that he was dealing with a reputable firm called Blenkiron, who also operated from Wood Street. In fact a person had fraudulently posed as this firm to mislead Cundy, even in the way in which he produced stationery and signed his name. The goods were supplied and sold on to Lindsay, an innocent third party. Cundy was found to have been fundamentally mistaken in dealing with a rogue posing as someone else, so the House of Lords held that the contract between Cundy and Blenkarn was void for mistake. The consequence was that the contract between Blenkarn and Lindsay was also void, obliging Lindsay to return the goods.

The following sequence of *inter praesentes* cases have been the subject of some debate.

Phillips v Brooks (1919)
A rogue posed as Sir George Bullough, giving a reputable address, in order to obtain various valuable items of jewellery. When presented with a cheque the seller, Phillips, was at first dubious, but checked the details given by the buyer, and then allowed him to take away a ring. The cheque was dishonoured but by the time Phillips discovered this the jewellery had been sold for cash to Brooks, an innocent third party, and the rogue had disappeared. The court held that the mistake was not crucial enough to avoid the contract, since it was not really one of identity, but creditworthiness. The seller was taken to have contracted with the person before him, whoever that may be, and Brooks was therefore allowed to keep the ring.

Apart from the mistake issues, there was a fraudulent misrepresentation in presenting the cheque, but rescission was barred as a third party had now bought the goods.

Ingram v Little (1961)
This involved similar facts to the case above, except that this time three elderly ladies were selling a car. A rogue introduced himself as Mr P. G. M. Hutchinson of a certain address, and wanted to buy the car. The ladies were happy until the point where he produced a cheque. A telephone directory was consulted to check the details given, and then the sale was concluded. The cheque was dishonoured and the car sold on to Little for cash, the rogue again disappearing. This time the court held that the identity was crucial, and the contract was therefore void for mistake, the car being returned to the ladies.

Can you think of any reason for the different decisions in the two cases above?

Lewis v Averay (1971)
A similar situation arose again, but this time a postgraduate student sold a car to a person claiming to be Richard Greene, the actor, well known at the time, who played Robin Hood in a television series. He produced a pass to Pinewood studios, and thus persuaded Lewis to part with the car for a cheque. The cheque was dishonoured, but by then the car had been sold to Avery for cash, the rogue again disappearing.

Lord Denning took the opportunity to examine the two previous cases, and felt that the legal principles in *Phillips v Brooks* were to be preferred. Where parties are *inter praesentes* they intend to deal with the person before them, identified by sight, hearing, etc., and their contracts are therefore binding on that basis. It is not a matter of identity, but creditworthiness.

There is in practice very little difference between the cases apart from the plaintiffs in *Ingram v Little* being elderly ladies and the seller in *Phillips v Brooks* being in business. It could also be argued that the seller who

Sir Richard Bullough

Is identity or creditworthiness important?

Figure 12.2

begins the negotiations assumes responsibility for the risks involved. Lord Devlin, suggested in *Ingram v Little* that the court should apportion the loss in some way between two innocent parties, but although his views have merit they have not so far been acted upon.

The following recent case combines a number of the points raised above.

Shogun v Hudson (2003)

A rogue obtained the driving licence of Mr Durlabh Patel of an address in Leicester and went to buy a Shogun car saying he was Mr Patel. A loan was obtained from Shogun Finance using Mr Patel's identity for a credit check. The rogue paid the deposit partly in cash and partly in a cheque (which bounced) and drove it away. Later he sold the car to Hudson for cash, and then vanished.

It was held by the House of Lords that there was no contract. Even though the parties were in each other's presence they only looked at the details of Mr Patel. Identity materials were now 'essential to the checking of credit rating'. The court found that the 'intention was to accept an offer made by the real Mr Patel and no one else'. Although Shogun appears to be *inter praesentes* – face to face – in reality the contract was actually between Shogun Finance and the rogue – therefore it was *inter absentes*. The waters are muddied, however, by the fact that the transaction was given approval by the motor dealer in the showroom.

The court in Shogun disapproved of the policy approach of Lord Denning in *Lewis v Avery*, in which he asked 'Which is the better law?' Lord Phillips said that the innocent party 'will have in mind, when considering with whom he is contracting, both the person with whom he is in contact and the third party whom he imagines that person to be'.

The court confirmed the outcome of *Lewis v Avery*, saying that there should be a 'strong presumption' that each party intends to contract with the other in situations where parties are in each other's presence. This could, on rare occasions, be rebutted, e.g. in a case of impersonation, where the parties are known to each other.

Mistake over the law

Until recently a mistake over the law would not have led to a contract being set aside, based on the argument that ignorance of the law was not an excuse. However, in an increasingly complex legal environment it is reasonable that if a contract is formed based on a mistaken understanding of the law it is not really a true agreement. This view was taken by the House of Lords in *Kleinwort Benson v Lincoln City Council* (1999) and followed by the Court of Appeal in *Brennan v Bolt Burdon* (2005).

Mistake relating to documents

The general rule is that if parties sign a written document they are bound by it (see *L'Estrange v Graucob* in Chapter 6). However, if a party has been induced to sign under a misrepresentation or some unfair pressure, then the contract will be voidable. In addition, two measures exist which may help where a written contract is not in accordance with the parties' original intentions

* the plea of *non est factum*,
* rectification.

Non est factum

In very limited circumstances the plea of *non est factum* may be available, which literally means 'not my deed'. It was proved successfully in the following cases.

> *Foster v Mackinnon* (1869)
> An elderly man with poor eyesight was induced into signing a document, being told that it was a guarantee. When it was found to be a bill of exchange in favour of the plaintiff the court allowed the defendant's plea of *non est factum*.
>
> *Lloyds Bank v Waterhouse* (1990)
> A father who could not read or write signed an agreement as guarantor for his son, thinking that it was for the purchase of a farm. In fact it was also an agreement to be responsible for all of the son's previous debts. It was established that the father would not have signed the agreement if he had known the true nature of it, and he had taken steps to ask the bank for information. The plea of *non est factum* was upheld by the Court of Appeal on this occasion.

The second case is unusual, being recent, as the plea is not used a great deal now. It is not allowed too easily, lest it be used as an excuse to escape an unwanted contract, as was the fear in the following example.

> *Saunders v Anglia Building Society* (1971)
> (also known as *Gallie v Lee*)
> Mrs Gallie, an elderly widow, was unsuccessful in her claim, as the document which she signed was not very different from what she intended to sign. Having broken her reading glasses, she was misled by her nephew into signing a document which assigned the lease of her house to someone else, whereas she thought she was giving it to her nephew as a gift. However, the court did not think that what she had done was different enough from her original intentions to amount to *non est factum*.

Rectification

Rectification is a measure used by the courts to amend a written contract so that it reflects more accurately the parties' previous oral agreement. This will be an exception to the general principle of the parol evidence rule (see Chapter 6) and is available where both parties are mistaken, as in common mistake, or where one party has let the other continue under a mistake, as in unilateral mistake. As will be seen in the following cases, the courts will need clear evidence of the previous oral agreement.

Joscelyne v Nissen (1970)
An agreement was formed between a father and daughter whereby he handed over the business in return for her paying certain bills. A dispute arose when some bills were not paid, and on investigation the written agreement was found not to contain any reference to payment of the bills. However, it was rectified because of the evidence of regular payments having been made so far by the daughter.

The doctrine of mistake in general

The idea of a doctrine of mistake is still developing and has not met with universal approval. In many cases it could be argued that it is not really needed, since the cases could be raised in other areas of contract law, certainly if these were developed a little. In some instances, as in the cases of mutual mistake, there is no real agreement. In others, the consideration does not exist, or a precondition has failed. Yet others could be argued on the basis of the terms of the contract, as was the situation in *McRae*.

The case of *Sheik v Oschner* (1957) is a good example of this overlap between doctrines, as the parties had contracted over a certain quantity of a crop, and it was found that it was impossible for the land to produce this quantity. The contract was found void for mistake, but it could well have been argued that the contract lacked consideration or that it was frustrated. The distinction between a claim under the doctrine of frustration and a claim in mistake often depends solely on the identification of the moment of contract. This was so in the case of *Amalgamated Investment and Property Co Ltd v John Walker and Sons Ltd* (1976), where a purchaser of a building was mistaken over the value of a building because the building was 'listed' and therefore subject to restrictions. Had the 'listing' taken place before the contract the claim may have succeeded in mistake, but in fact the 'listing' occurred after the point of contract.

Summary

Definition

A 'mistake' is a false assumption made by one or both parties in the formation of a contract.

Common mistake

Where both parties are labouring under the same false assumption.

* Mistake over existence of the subject matter (i.e. whether the goods exist) will generally render the contract void – *Couturier v Hastie, Galloway v Galloway, Scott v Coulson.* See for comparison with breach of warranty – *McRae v Commonwealth Disposals Commission.*
* Mistake over title may invoke an equitable remedy – *Cooper v Phibbs.*
* Mistake over the quality of the subject matter (i.e. the value of the bargain) will leave the contract intact if the mistake is not 'fundamental' – *Bell v Lever Bros, Leaf v International Galleries, Associated Japanese Bank Ltd v Credit du Nord, William Sindall v Cambridgeshire County Council.*

Mutual mistake

Sometimes known as shared mistake, where the parties are at crosspurposes.

* Where there is total ambiguity, the contract is void – *Raffles v Wichelhaus.*
* Where some 'extra' factor exists, the contract may be upheld – *Wood v Scarth.*

Unilateral mistake

Where only one party is mistaken and the other is aware of this (and may have deliberately planned the situation).

* Mistake over quality will generally leave the contract intact – *Smith v Hughes, Scriven v Hindley, Hartog v Colin and Shields.*
* Mistake over identity *inter absentes* (not in each other's presence) may render the contract void – *Cundy v Lindsay.*
* Mistake over identity *inter praesentes* (in each other's presence) may be seen as one of creditworthiness and will often leave the contract intact – *Phillips v Brooks, Ingram v Little, Lewis v Averay.*

Mistake over documents

Generally parties are bound by written documents – *L'Estrange v Graucob*. Where a written contract is genuinely not in accordance with a parties' intentions, the following may apply:

* *Non est factum* ('this is not my deed') – *Foster v Mackinnon, Lloyds Bank v Waterhouse, Saunders v Anglia Building Society* (also known as *Gallie v Lee*).
* Rectification (amending a written contract to reflect more accurately the parties' previous oral agreement) – *Joscelyne v Nissen*.

The relationship between mistake and frustration

Mistake occurs before or at the point of contract, but frustration occurs during the lifetime of a contract – *Sheik v Oschner, Property Co Ltd v John Walker and Sons Ltd*.

Questions

1 Faridah wishes to sell her valuable violin, so advertises it for sale. Germaine visits Faridah, explaining that she would like to buy the violin, and they agree on a price. Germaine produces a cheque book, but Faridah hesitates, saying that she would prefer cash. Germaine then replies, 'Look, you can see who I am', and produces various items of identity, bearing the same surname as a famous musician. Faridah is embarrassed and agrees to take the cheque, handing over the violin to Germaine.

    A few days later Faridah is contacted by her bank, who informs her that the cheque from Germaine is worthless, and that Germaine cannot be traced. Faridah is upset at this, but to her surprise a few days later to see 'her' violin for sale in the window of a musical instrument supplier, Humbuskers. She tries to recover the violin from Humbuskers, but they claim that they paid a good price for it from someone going abroad, and would certainly not be prepared to just give it back to her.

    Advise Faridah.

    OCR 2001/2 specimen

2 Adrian enjoys visiting art galleries and has a small collection of quite valuable paintings. He decides to buy a painting from the Artefactus gallery, which both he and the gallery believe to be by the well known contemporary painter Brush. Adrian pays £5000 for the painting and hangs it in his gallery.

    He decides to refurbish the gallery and buys a collection of second-hand furniture from a London street market, including some reproduction eighteenth-century chairs.

    Two months later Adrian has the contents of the gallery valued for insurance purposes, and discovers that the painting is only a copy of the original by Brush, and probably worth no more than £15, but that one of the chairs is original and worth £3000.

    Adrian seeks your advice.

3 Nazir advertises her car for sale in the local newspaper. A woman calling herself Pauline Smith arrives to see the car. She says that she likes the car, but as she knows little about cars, would like to take the car to a mechanic friend for inspection. Pauline persuades Nazir to let her take both the car and the registration document. Although Nazir has doubts, Pauline produces a local authority identity pass, which has a photograph. Nazir telephones the council offices to check the identity card. She is told that there is a Pauline Smith on the staff of the council and takes a cheque as security.

One week later Pauline has not returned the car and so Nazir banks the cheque. Three days later Nazir is notified by her bank that the cheque is a worthless forgery. In the meantime Pauline has sold the car to John.

Discuss whether Nazir can recover the car and what action she might take against Pauline if she can be found.

OCR 4-module specimen paper

4 Discuss the criteria applied by the courts when deciding whether a contract is is rendered void for mistake.

5 'A buyer who pays a large sum for what turns out be of little value must be satisfied with his purchase.' How far does the law support this view of common mistake?

6 'In practice there is little difference between identity and creditworthiness, when it concerns a customer paying for goods.' Discuss this view of unilateral mistake.

7 'The law relating to common mistake fails those relying on it in not allowing a contract to automatically end when the parties do not get what they bargained for.'

Critically discuss this view of the doctrine.

13 Illegality

Even though a contract is well formed it may contain some element which is considered unlawful in its very nature, such as a contract to break into premises to steal. The courts will clearly be against the idea of enforcing such an agreement, but in addition there is an area of activity which is not in the interests of society to enforce, and is said to be against public policy.

> Can you think of any other examples of contracts which are likely to be illegal because of the nature of the activity within them?

The nature of illegality

Some contracts are illegal in their very nature when they are formed, and as seen below, this is not always because of obvious criminal activity.

> *Re Mahmoud and Ispahani* (1921)
> A quantity of linseed oil was sold to a dealer without a licence, contrary to statute. Because of the lack of licence, this contract could not be carried out in a legal manner.

Other contracts begin in the normal way, but become illegal in the way in which they are performed.

Anderson v Daniel (1924)
The labelling on a consignment of manure did not conform to legal requirements for this type of manure. There was nothing illegal in general in forming a contract to supply this manure, but it became illegal in the way in which the manure was delivered with the wrong labelling.

Sometimes it is statute which causes a contract to be illegal. This was the case in *Re Mahmoud and Ispahani* (above). On other occasions a contract is illegal because of common law. This was so in the following case.

Everet v Williams (1725)
An agreement was formed between two highwaymen to rob a coach and share the swag. After the robbery one went away with all the proceeds, and the other sued. The contract was (predictably) held to be illegal.

A contract that is definitely illegal will be void. A contract which is not actually illegal, but prejudicial to the state, preventing the administration of justice, promoting sexual immorality, defrauding the revenue or promoting corruption in public life will not be legally binding and therefore unenforceable in court.

Parkinson v College of Ambulance (1925)
Here an agreement was made to obtain a knighthood in exchange for a generous donation to charity. This is not actually criminal but is not in the interests of society, given the nature of a knighthood and of donations to charity.

Contracts which are not actually illegal may be allowed to stand but are held to be unenforceable, such as wagering agreements, contracts prejudicial to marriage, and those in restraint of trade.

Restraint of trade

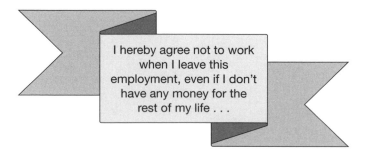

If a contract restricts a person's freedom to trade or to work it is seen as a starting point to be against public policy and therefore void, unless it can be justified in some way. It is quite common to find this kind of restraint in a contract of employment or in the contract by which a person buys or sells a business.

To persuade the court that a term which restrains trade, and prevents a person working, should not be void the party wishing to include it must show the court that it is a reasonable term, both between the parties, and in the public interest.

What valid reasons may exist to persuade a court that one person has has a right to stop competition?

Various factors may affect reasonableness and these in turn may depend to some extent on their own particular set of circumstances.

Protection of trade secrets

Where an employee knows the secret ingredients of a product, or the secrets of the operation of a business, it would be sometimes be unfair if that employee were to leave and then use that knowledge in working for a competitor.

Forster v Suggett (1918)
A restriction on a manager's freedom to work in the manufacturer of glass, for five years after the end of a particular employment, was held valid, given that the manufacture involved secret processes.

Protection of a range of clientele

Often when a person leaves employment a restriction is imposed on their freedom to work for an immediate competitor in order to avoid the clients of the first business transferring their business to the competitor and making it impossible for the first business to have a reasonable chance of continuing. In the case of *Lansing Linde v Kerr* (1991) the Court of Appeal said *obiter* that the phrase could cover customers' names as easily as chemical formulae. A restriction could be in terms of geographical location or length of time. Compare the following cases. In the first case the restriction was held to be too wide, whereas in the following three cases restraints were allowed because of the nature of the work and the need to protect the employer's ability to continue trading without losing custom. The last case shows that too great a restraint will lead to doom!

Mason v Provident Clothing (1913)
A trade canvasser who sold clothes to trade outlets was restrained from working in a similar capacity within a 25 mile radius of London. This was held to be too wide, given the nature and dense population of the area.

Fitch v Dewes (1921)
A solicitor's clerk was prevented from working within a 7 mile radius of Tamworth town hall. This was held to be reasonable given the nature of the practice and the number of potential clients.

Home Counties Dairies v Skilton (1970)
The court upheld a restraint on a milkman not to sell milk to any former customers of his former employer for sixth months.

White v Francis (1972)
A restriction was placed on a hairdresser leaving employment not to work for 12 months within ½ mile radius of her place of employment.

Office Angels v Rainer-Thomas (1991)
This case shows that the moral is not to be too greedy. A modest restraint, for a reason which can be justified, will be upheld, but an over wide restraint will be held void. A restraint was placed on the defendant who worked for an employment agency not to try to solicit custom from anyone who had obtained work through this agency for a period of six months after leaving her post. The company was a large one, with 34 branches, and must have had a very large database of workers and placements. The restraint was held void, and the court said (*obiter*) that if it had just concerned the limited number of clients with whom the defendant had worked, a restraint may have been reasonable, but to cover the whole of London was too wide.

The need to serve the public

Where a business is sold, and there is a need for the public to be served by such businesses, the court may allow a restriction that would otherwise be void. This may be considered according to the state and breadth of the market.

Nordenfelt v Maxim Nordenfelt (1894)
A world-wide restraint for 25 years was upheld, given the nature of the business of manufacturing guns and ammunitions, and the limited number of clients. This case reached the House of Lords, where they took the opportunity to lay down the following guidelines:

▶

- The starting point is to view a restraint of trade clause as void, and then to place the burden on to the party seeking to enforce it to show that it is valid.
- In order to show this there must be evidence that the restraint is reasonable in two ways: (a) between the parties and (b) regarding the public interest (the general good of the public). Cases will vary according to their own facts in showing this.
- The courts will uphold a restraint if it protects a legitimate interest.

Inducement

An employee may have knowingly and willingly accepted a restraint in order to take on the post, and may have agreed to accept a financial incentive in return for the restraint. If this takes place with an employee who is not especially vulnerable, and therefore freely negotiated, the court will uphold the restraint.

Allied Dunbar v Weisinger (1988)
An employee agreed not to work in the field of insurance for two years following his current employment and in return received two years' additional salary by way of compensation. The court upheld this restraint.

Exclusive dealing arrangements

If an exclusive dealing arrangements exist, for example where an employee or a contractor forms an agreement only to work for one particular person, or to supply or take supplies from one business (sometimes known as solus arrangements), this arrangement must be shown to be reasonable.

Schroeder Music v Macaulay (1974)
A wide restraint on a songwriter, which was formed when the writer was new to the business, young and unknown, and therefore in a vulnerable position with little bargaining power, was held to be unreasonable in still restricting freedom when the writer was more established and successful.

Aylesbury FC v Watford AFC (1977)
Lee Cook, a 17 year old footballer, was contracted to Aylesbury but allowed to treat the contract as not binding on him so that he could form a new contract to play for Watford. A restraint of trade clause in his original contract was held to be too onerous on a young, vulnerable and relatively new player.

Esso v Harper's Garage (1968)
In two cases involving the same parties and various restrictions including the agreement to only sell one brand of fuel, a restriction for 4 years was held valid, but another on a separate property for 21 years was held to be unreasonable. Under European law the guideline is now that a restriction for up to ten years would be reasonable.

The effect of a clause in restraint of trade

If a restraint of trade is found to be unreasonable, then it will be void as far as it is against public policy. So this does not necessarily mean that the whole contract is void. Severance may be possible, if the offending clause can be removed without altering the essential meaning of the contract. The court may be willing to strike out offending words, retaining the general nature of the contract. This is known as the 'blue pencil test' – the court takes a blue pencil and deletes part of the agreement that is found to be unfair, leaving the rest intact and therefore enforceable. The courts traditionally will not rewrite the contract in any way, but there is an apparent slight relaxation of this strict approach, by interpretation of the offending clause in a way that makes it reasonable – see *Littlewoods v Harris* (1978).

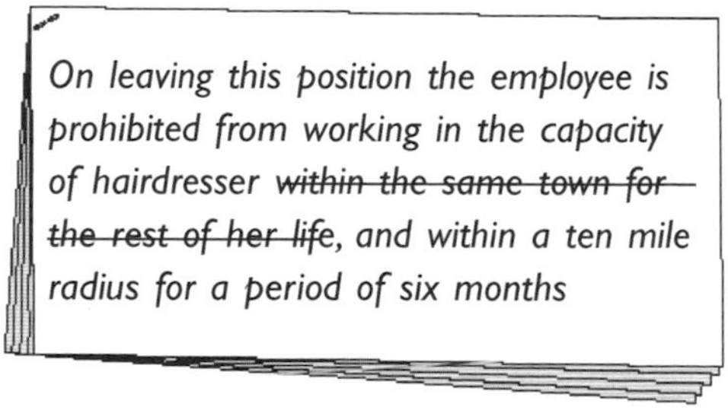

On leaving this position the employee is prohibited from working in the capacity of hairdresser ~~within the same town for the rest of her life~~, and within a ten mile radius for a period of six months

An unfair restriction may be deleted by the court if the rest of the contract can stand and make sense.

Figure 13.1

The effect of European law

It should be noted that European law has had a great impact on this area, as it involves the principles of free competition and free movement within the European Union. The Treaty of Rome makes void any practices that adversely affect competition within the European Union.

Summary

Illegal when formed or performed

A contract may be illegal in either of the following situations:

* when it is formed – *Re Mahmoud and Ispahani*
* when it is performed – *Anderson v Daniel*.

Cause of illegality

A further division arises between cause of the illegality:

* statute – *Re Mahmoud and Ispahani*
* common law – *Everet v Williams*.

Illegal or void

Yet another division arises over the undesirable nature of contracts. They may be:

* illegal in the criminal sense, as in *Everet v Williams*
* not in the interest of society, and therefore unenforceable, as in *Parkinson v College of Ambulance*.

Restraint of trade

A contract which restricts a person's freedom to trade or earn a living is against public policy and therefore void, unless justified by:

* Protection of a trade secret – *Forster v Suggett.*
* Protection of a range of clientele – *Mason v Provident Clothing, Fitch v Dewes.*
* Need to enable business to be carried on – *Nordenfelt v Maxim Nordenfelt.*
* Showing reasonableness in exclusive dealing arrangements – *Schroeder Music v Macaulay, Esso v Harper's Garage.*

The effect of a restraint of trade clause:

* The clause itself is void, or unenforceable, if against public policy and not proved reasonable.
* The whole contract is not necessarily void, and severance may be possible.
* The court may strike out offending words leaving the rest intact.
* A slightly more relaxed approach may now interpret the clause in a way that makes it reasonable – *Littlewoods v Harris*.

The effect of European law:

* Article 85 of the Treaty of Rome makes void any practices which adversely affect competition within the European Union.

Questions

1 Fred orders some garden plants and seeds from Gardenwell, to be delivered in one month's time. He pays for these at the time of ordering. He also orders a quantity of fireworks from the same firm, to be supplied in time for his 30th birthday party. George is to pay for these on delivery. When the plants and seeds are delivered they do not have the correct labelling, required by law, and by this time Fred has decided that he does not want the plants anyway, as he can obtain them from another, less expensive, source.

   Gardenwell supply the fireworks, but the delivery person does not ask for the money. George enjoys his birthday party, during which someone informs him that Gardenwell supplies fireworks without the required licence. George then remembers that he has not paid Gardenwell, and decides not to do so.

   Advise Gardenwell.

2 Critically consider the difference between a contract being found illegal and one being void for policy reasons.

3 Analyse the circumstances in which the courts will uphold a contract in restraint of trade.

Part 4

Discharge and remedies

Ending the agreement

In forming a true agreement, as described in the first part of the book, the two parties involved have a clear picture of exactly what is expected under their contract. When all of this, as agreed, has been performed, then the contract is said to be discharged. Sometimes, however, the performance of the contract is not complete, or exactly as specified. So how close does it have to be to the agreement? In theory, performance should be total, but in practice, in a real world, this is not always possible, and to avoid extensive litigation over minor issues, there is a certain amount of compromise. Some of this forms the basis of the material in this part of the book on performance.

I'll agree to take less if you reduce the price

Quite often, in reality, people cannot perform their obligations, and make an agreement with the other party to compromise on their original positions. In this case the contract is discharged, really by forming a further contract to end the original one! This also is discussed as a method of ending the agreement.

Sorry, I just can't do it

Sometimes a person or organisation just cannot meet their obligations, for one reason or another. It may be a deliberate decision not to do something, but could have a relatively 'innocent' explanation. Both of these still leave one party responsible for the loss to another, and this is known as breach. It is certainly a method of ending a contract, but not a pleasant or satisfactory one, so it leads into a further area of what can be done to rectify the situation, i.e. remedies (see below).

Nobody's fault

If a contract is breached, one party is to blame for the loss to the other. Sometimes, however, something arises which prevents performance, which really is nobody's fault. An example could be a flash-flood preventing the holding of an outdoor event, such as a barbecue. Clearly neither party can control the extremes of weather, and the contract would be said to be frustrated, rather than breached. The role of the court would then be to apportion any loss in a fair way.

Remedies

If a party has suffered from a breach, whether the other intended it or not, there is a right to a remedy. A common remedy for breach of contract is compensation in money, known as damages, and this is intended to put right the defect. Sometimes, however, that is not satisfactory, and so in some circumstances the contract can be completely ended, or repudiated. This will be examined in this part of the book, as the sequel to ending the contract.

14   Discharge of a contract

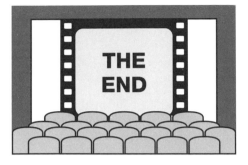

The ending of a contract should normally be very straightforward, since all that is required is that the parties carry out the tasks agreed according to the terms in the contract. In fact, the total performance required by law has given rise to some problems, and when a party has thought that performance has been undertaken, the actions have been found to be a breach. The following ways of ending a contract will be examined in turn:

- performance
- agreement
- breach
- frustration.

Performance

For performance to be total, the courts expect it to be exact and complete. In expecting exact performance, the courts mean that performance must match contractual obligations.

> *Re Moore and Landauer* (1921)
> Tins of fruit were supplied to a retailer as requested, packed in the wrong size cases. Although all of the goods had been supplied, the obligations did not match those specified in the agreement, and the buyer could therefore reject the whole consignment.

In requiring a contract to be complete the court is merely saying that any work undertaken must be carried out to the end of the obligations.

Cutter v Powell (1795)

A sailor died during a voyage. His widow's claim for payment for the part of the journey completed was unsuccessful, because although the sailor may have carried out his tasks exactly according to the agreement, the obligations would not be complete until the end of the voyage.

Substantial performance

This is where work agreed is almost finished and the court then orders that money must be paid, but deducts the amount needed to correct a minor defect. This would only arise where the defect would amount to a breach of warranty, because if there was a breach of condition the innocent party would be able to repudiate. The idea of substantial performance is to take into account the reality of a situation where it is impractical to insist on absolute completion, and in order to see a contract fulfilled a small compromise is accepted. The origins of substantial performance are said to lie in the somewhat condescending case of *Boone v Eyre* (1779), where a plantation was sold, complete with slaves, but on transfer of ownership it was found that the slaves had gone. The performance was said to have substantially taken place because the main subject matter of the contract was there.

Hoenig v Isaacs (1952)

A flat was to be decorated and furnished for £750. When the work was over the customer only paid £400 saying that the work was not yet complete. It was found, however, that although there were defects, the cost of putting them right was far less than the amount deducted. It was held that there was substantial performance, and the full amount was payable less £55 to remedy the defects.

An example of performance could be seen if a new kitchen was to be fitted in a house. Imagine that the work was complete except for one wall cupboard, and the fitter requested payment. It would be unfair to have to pay the whole price if the work was defective, but if the fitter was clearly not going to fit the remaining cupboard for some reason, it would be better to settle the account and get a new fitter to complete the work. In this case the court would order the agreed amount to be paid, but deduct the amount that would be needed to pay another fitter to install the remaining cupboard.

What if several cupboards were missing, or half of the kitchen was still in pieces in packing crates? How much would need to be completed to be 'substantial'?

Partial performance

Partial performance is where some work has been done, but where the degree to which the obligations have been fulfilled is less than what would be required for substantial performance. However, the difference between substantial and partial performance is sometimes difficult to determine. There are two important differences which should be noted:

- Partial performance must be accepted by the other party – in other words the innocent party really agrees not to sue for breach, but instead agrees to pay a lesser amount for the quantity of work done.

- Payment is made on a different basis from that for substantial performance. It is made on a *quantum meruit*, which is literally as much as is deserved. So, for example, if half of the work was completed, half of the money would be payable.

In *Christy v Row* (1808) this arrangement for payment was said to be based on the theory that the parties have really discharged the contract by agreement, in stating that if only a certain proportion of work is done then only a certain proportion of payment will be made. The party not at fault must have a genuine choice over whether to accept partial performance. In *Sumpter v Hedges* (1898), for example, a builder did half of the work towards building houses and stables, and then left. With a job half-done, the defendant had no choice but to finish the work. When sued for the full price the court held that partial performance had not been accepted, so the contract had been breached.

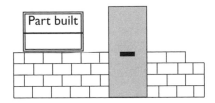

For a finding of partial performance, there must be a genuine choice over whether to accept

Figure 14.1

Time of performance

If time is crucial to one or both parties, it may be seen to be 'of the essence'. The obligations then *must* be performed within the time expected, and this will be considered as a term of the contract. However, the time limit must be clear to both parties, and this is where difficulties are likely to arise. Sometimes this will be obvious; for example, if perishable goods are to be delivered it is obvious that the delivery should be complete within a very short time. There are situations where it is not apparent that time is of the essence, but it becomes clear during the course of the contract. For example, if I ask someone in June to paint my house, 'during the summer', and by the end of August the painter has not done the work, I would probably want to introduce a term that if the work was not undertaken by the end of September then the contract would be breached. Time would then have become 'of the essence'.

Vicarious performance

What if one person carries out the duties of another under a contract? Performance by a third party is known as vicarious performance, and is allowed in certain circumstances. If the task is not of a personal nature, for example the supply of an item which is easily obtainable, then it is not important who actually delivers it. In that case, providing that the main terms are fulfilled, so that the item is exactly as expected, the price is correct, etc., then vicarious performance would be acceptable in place of performance by the original party. If, however, the task is of a personal nature, for example the painting of a portrait, then vicarious performance is unlikely to be acceptable.

Edwards v Newland (1950) concerned the storage of furniture in a warehouse, and it was said that the personal skill and care of the warehouseman is 'of the essence' of such a contract. It was held that passing the property on to another party to store was not acceptable, and the obligations had not therefore been performed vicariously. The court said that care was taken in choosing a firm to store goods, and a particular firm may be chosen to carry out tasks because of their skill. The transfer of this work to another would not in such cases be allowed as performance. This seems reasonable in some circumstances, for example if a storage firm had been chosen because it had storage available at a certain temperature, or because its employees were experienced in transporting musical instruments. However, in other circumstances vicarious performance is a practical option, and is often used with coach hire, another firm supplying a coach of similar specification for an outing, enabling further and possibly more valuable bookings to be taken.

What if a luxury coach which had 50 reclining seats, a video player and drink-making facilities was booked for a two-day trip to France, and at the starting time a coach arrived, but an older model with 45 fixed seats, no video player and no drink-making facilities?

Agreement

In the example above, if the party booking the coach decided to continue on the trip using the coach supplied, and then on return agreed with the original coach company to pay less, as the coach was of a lower specification than intended, they would have discharged their contract by agreement. Discharge by agreement arises when a contract is abandoned, or the terms within it are changed, and both parties are in agreement over this. Really both parties have provided consideration for a new contract to end or to vary the old one. Where there are special formalities, such as where written evidence is required in a contract of sale of land, there is likely to be a similar requirement to vary the contract.

Breach

Where one party fails to perform their contractual obligations, or performance is defective, or a lie is found within a contract, the party at fault is said to have breached the contract. Breach of contract leads to two main remedies.

> If, in the above example of coach hire, the coach does not turn up at all, what would be a suitable remedy?

Returning to the example of the coach hire above, the trip begins in working hours and another coach is readily available, the innocent party may wish to end the contract and use the money to obtain a coach from another firm. This is repudiation, or ending the agreement. If, on the other hand, the trip begins during the night, and another coach is not readily available, the hirer may wish to continue, but seek compensation for inconvenience. This is obtaining damages. Whether an innocent party is allowed to end the contract or not depends on the type of term breached (see Chapter 7). The following remedies are generally available:

- For breach of a condition, a major term, the innocent party can either repudiate, or claim damages.
- For breach of a warranty, a minor term, the innocent party can only claim damages.

(See *Bettini v Guy* and *Poussard v Spiers and Pond,* p. 109, on these issues.)

Similarly, where one party has lied within a contract, the remedy will depend on whether the lie amounts to a breach of condition or warranty. There is a fine dividing line, however, between a lie within a contract, leading to breach, and a lie before a contract, which may lead to misrepresentation.

Breach may be actual or anticipatory, which means that it may have already happened, or it may be about to happen. If a supplier of goods does not deliver on the agreed date, this is actual breach of contract, and the injured party would then be able to sue the supplier. If some time before the due date the supplier informs the buyer that they are definitely unable to supply, this would be anticipatory breach, and the buyer could sue immediately to recover any costs and find another source for his goods. Anticipatory breach arose in the following case.

Hochster v De La Tour (1853)
A contract of employment was formed for a courier for a summer holiday season. The courier was informed that he would not be needed before the date on which he was due to begin work. He sued before the starting date, and recovered damages, which were needed to support him during the time when he would have been employed.

Frustration

Frustration arises when some event occurs, during the lifetime of a contract, at the fault of neither party, which makes the contract impossible, illegal, or radically different from that originally undertaken. It typically occurs where some natural disaster outside the control of the parties means that one party is unable to fulfil obligations under the contract, and is then claimed as an alternative to a claim of breach.

At one time obligations within a contract were viewed as absolute, so a party was responsible for total performance or was held in breach, whatever the circumstances. This strict approach is seen in the following seventeenth-century case.

Paradine v Jane (1647)
Enemies of the king prevented a tenant from entering property, but rent was nevertheless payable on the property despite not being able to use it.

Courts later began to take a less harsh view of contractual obligations, bearing in mind the reality commercial transactions, and in the leading classic case of *Taylor v Caldwell* frustration was held as a fairer solution than a finding of breach.

Taylor v Caldwell (1863)
A music hall and gardens were hired for a concert, but the hall caught fire and burnt down before the performance. The contract was held to be frustrated, as it was now impossible to carry it out, but this was through the fault of neither party.

Frustration can then arise, from the definition given above, through:

- impossibility
- illegality
- radical difference between the original agreement and the present situation.

Impossibility

A contract could become impossible because the subject matter of the contract (whatever is being hired or sold) is destroyed, or because it is now unavailable. *Taylor v Caldwell* is a good example of impossibility because of destruction (here by fire). The following case is an example of unavailability.

> *Morgan v Manser* (1948)
> The music hall compere Charlie Chester was called away for war service. Since it was unknown how long the war would continue, his contract was held to be impossible to perform through unavailability, and therefore frustrated.

Similarly where there is genuine incapacity through illness a contract may be held frustrated, as in the case of *Condor v Barron Knights* (1966), where a member of the Barron Knights pop group was ill and unable to perform.

Illegality

A contract which begins legitimately but then becomes illegal may be held to be frustrated, if this is at the fault of neither party. A typical situation is where a new statute is passed or where war breaks out and a contract to supply goods, perhaps to an enemy country, then becomes illegal, or where property is requisitioned, as in *Metropolitan Water Board v Dick Kerr* (1918). However, this situation is in peaceful times less common than claims of impossibility or radical change.

Radical change in circumstances

This is where a contract began well but for some reason has now become pointless. A group of such contracts found their way to court in 1903 as a result of the postponement of the coronation of King Edward VII through illness. Note that this is not a case of unavailability through illness, since the king was not a party to the contracts, but the event which was central to many contracts was cancelled, the parties themselves not being at fault. Many of the contracts were then said to be radically different from what was expected, and this change amounted to frustration.

Krell v Henry (1903)
A room was hired overlooking the coronation procession route, to provide a good view of the procession. Since this was the only purpose for hiring the room, it was no longer required when the procession was cancelled. An empty room overlooking a street in London was so radically different from one overlooking the route of the coronation procession that the contract was held to be frustrated.

However, if there is still some point to the contract, the court may hold that it should continue. This was the finding in another coronation case.

Herne Bay Steam Boat Co v Hutton (1903)
A boat was hired to watch the naval review which was to take place as part of the coronation celebrations, and then for a trip around the bay. It was found that the pleasure trip could still be enjoyed, even though the King's review of the fleet was cancelled. Because there was still something to be gained from the contract, it was not totally different from the original agreement, and the contract was therefore held not to be frustrated.

The question could be raised as to what proportion of the contract must be pointless. What if the naval review was scheduled to take three hours, and a pleasure trip around the bay lasted for ten minutes?

Limits to frustration

Because frustration is often used as a kind of defence to breach, and can result in a beneficial sharing of loss, there could be attempts to claim frustration where there is not a genuine basis for it. Similarly, if the doctrine was allowed too easily, the number of instances could be huge (the so-called 'floodgates' argument). The courts are therefore wary of allowing a claim too easily, and have shown through case law that there are defined limits within which the doctrine may be claimed. So, for example, a person claiming inability to perform through illness would have to show that the illness was substantial and genuine, and a person claiming radical change would have to show that the contract was now futile, not just less than expected (see *Herne Bay v Hutton*, above).

Where a contract is merely more onerous, that is more difficult, more expensive, or takes longer to perform, then it will not be frustrated. This means that in many cases the courts feel that parties should take more care in planning contracts. This may well be true with hindsight, but can be harsh where circumstances are genuinely unforeseen.

Tsakiroglou v Noblee Thorl (1962)
The closure of the Suez Canal in 1956 meant that a ship had to take a longer, more difficult and more expensive journey to deliver a cargo of goods. The contract to carry the goods was held not to be frustrated, since the carrier could have planned for the consequences of having to take a longer route. A clause providing for the eventuality of having to take a longer route is now usually built into a contract to carry goods by ship.

Davis Builders v Fareham UDC (1956)
The builders agreed to build a certain number of houses by a particular date at a fixed price. Having tendered as low as possible in order to obtain the contract, they were unable to complete the agreed number of houses on time because of lack of labour and materials. The contract was held not to be frustrated, since it could have been completed if more money had been spent on obtaining materials from another source and on employing more people.

Thames Valley Power v Total Gas (2005)
Total Gas were unsuccessful in claiming that their contract to supply gas to Thames Valley Power was frustrated, since the basis was a rise in gas prices. This was merely a less lucrative contract for Total Gas (in fact it meant that they would lose about £9 million). It is not unlike the two cases above, but more recent, and therefore the loss seems greater.

Where a party has some control over the event which is claimed to frustrate a contract, it is said to be self-induced, and this will not be allowed as frustration.

Maritime National Fish v Ocean Trawlers (1935)
The owner of five trawlers arranged contracts of hire on the boats, before obtaining the required licences to use them. They were then only granted three licences, and had to decide on which of the five trawlers to place the licences. As they had a free choice over whhich ones to licence, the court held that the contracts on the other two were breached rather than frustrated. A way of avoiding this would have been to obtain the licences before forming the contracts. The decision was confirmed in *The Super Servant Two* (1990).

▶

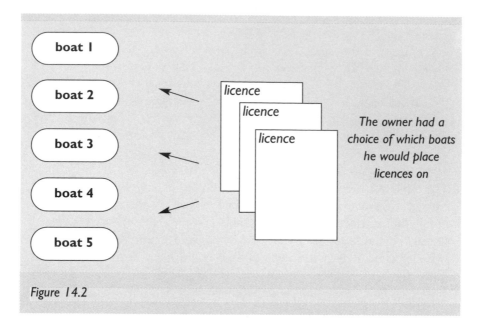

Figure 14.2

These facts could be applied to a person who wishes to buy a house because it is a suitable property on which to build an extension for private or business use. Assuming that planning permission must be obtained from the local authority before building, what should he do to ensure that the buyer is not in a similar position to the above case?

Legal effects of frustration

At one time when a contract was found to be frustrated it was said that 'the loss lay where it fell'. This meant that all duties ended at the point of frustration, any money paid remaining paid and any money due remaining due. This was fair where only a small deposit, or no deposit at all, had been paid, the rest being due on completion of the contract, but could be harsh where money had been paid in advance, as this would not be recoverable. The *Fibrosa Case* (1942) changed this position a little, holding that where there was a complete lack of consideration, and nothing at all had been done under the contract except the paying of money, the money should be recoverable. But this was still unfair in many cases. What if the work had just begun before the frustrating event, but all of the money had been paid?

Reform came in 1943 in the form of the Law Reform (Frustrated Contracts) Act 1943 and this remains the basis of the doctrine of frustration today. The following provisions were made under the act:

- Money paid is recoverable – s.1(2).
- Money due is no longer due – s.1(2).
- Where expenses have been incurred, the court may order a just sum to be paid – s.1(2).
- Where a valuable benefit is obtained, the court may order a just sum to be paid – s.1(3).

Figure 14.3

A point to note is that in *BP v Hunt* (1982) it was suggested that if goods were obtained under a contract which was frustrated, and the goods themselves were destroyed, for example by fire, then there would be no valuable benefit, possibly leaving the other party out of pocket. However, the responsibility of insuring the goods destroyed may be taken into account by the court in deciding this point, should it arise.

The statutory provision is welcome as an appropriate supplement to the case law forming the original doctrine of frustration. It means that all money now moves back to the original position, and the courts can then decide whether either party needs to be reimbursed for expenses, or to pay for the value of goods or services already obtained under the contract. In effect Parliament has given the courts the power to apportion loss fairly between parties, in a similar way to the apportioning of loss under the concept of contributory negligence in tort. This hopefully provides a fair solution to a situation where no one party is to blame for the ending of a contract.

| **A comparison between frustration and breach** ||
Frustration	**Breach**
• Arises when a contract cannot be performed as expected.	• Arises where a contract cannot be performed as expected.
• Arises where neither party is at fault.	• Also arises where an untrue statement is found within a contract.
• Money is returned to where it came from.	• All of the blame or fault lies with one party.
• An order for expenses incurred may be made.	• Full damages are normally available for the innocent party.
• An order for benefits received *may* be made.	• The burden of loss is wholly on the party at fault.
• The burden of loss is shared.	

Figure 14.4

Summary

Performance

Total performance must be *exact* and *complete*:

- Exact, must match contractual obligations – *Re Moore and Landauer.*
- Complete, must be carried out to the end – *Cutter v Powell.*

Performance which is not exact and complete may be:

- Substantial performance, nearly complete, money must be paid less the amount needed to correct minor defect – *Hoenig v Isaacs.*
- Partial performance, less than substantial, must be accepted by the other party, payment made on a *quantum meruit* – *Sumpter v Hedge.*
- Time of performance – if important may be 'of the essence'.
- Vicarious performance – performance by a third party. Allowed if not of a personal nature – *Edwards v Newland.*

Agreement

Where both parties are in accord over the amendment or ending of a contract. Really both parties have provided consideration to either change the contract, or to end it and begin a new one.

Breach

Where one party fails to perform their contractual obligations. Also arises where one party has lied in a contract.

- May be actual or anticipatory (yet to happen) – *Hochster v De La Tour.*
- The type of term is important to determine whether the breach is repudiatory – *Bettini v Guy, Poussard v Spiers and Pond.*
- Where the contract is breached, damages are payable by the injured party.

Frustration

Definition

Frustration arises when an event occurs, during the lifetime of a contract, at the fault of neither party, which makes the contract impossible, illegal, or radically different from that originally undertaken.

At one time obligations were absolute – *Paradine v Jane.*

A contract may be frustrated through:

- Impossibility – *Taylor v Caldwell*.
- Unavailability or incapacity – *Morgan v Manser, Condor v Barron Knights*.
- Illegality – *Metropolitan Water Board v Dick Kerr*.
- Radically changed in circumstances – *Krell v Henry*.

Limits to frustration

- There may still be some point to the contract – *Herne Bay Steam Boat Co v Hutton*.
- Where a contract is merely more onerous it will not be frustrated – *Tsakiroglou v Noblee Thorl, Davis Builders v Fareham UDC*.
- Self-induced frustration (may be a choice of action or control over the circumstances) – *Maritime National Fish v Ocean Trawlers*.

Legal effects of frustration

The Law Reform (Frustrated Contracts) Act (1943). The main provisions:

- Money paid is recoverable.
- Money due is no longer due.
- Where expenses have been incurred, the court may order a just sum to be paid.
- Where a valuable benefit is obtained, the court may order a just sum to be paid.

Questions

I Fern books a room, for one day, in the Grove hotel so that she and her friends can watch the Notting Mount festival activities to take place one Saturday in May. Fern pays a deposit of £20 on making the booking in March, the remaining £100 to be paid on the day of the festival. The festival is unexpectedly cancelled on the Friday before the festival, due to storm damage in the area.

Fern has also ordered a new dress for the festival from Harriet's boutique. It is a particularly unusual dress, and is being made to order, to be ready in time for the festival. One week before the delivery date, Fern tells Harriet that she will not need the dress, as her aunt has given her a similar one.

Fern also orders a luxury taxi from Kardeals for a dance on the evening of the festival. When the taxi arrives Fern is told that Kardeals are busy with other customers, so Jellicabs are to take her instead. The small taxi supplied is cold, noisy and dirty, and breaks down on the way to the dance, so that Fern and her friends arrive late.

Advise Fern concerning her agreements with the Grove Hotel, Harriet's boutique and Kardeals.

2 Andrew owns the Hotel Splendid. In May Bruce reserves and pays for accommodation in the hotel, including a very large meeting-room. This is for himself and for some business colleagues for a conference in July. In June Andrew informs Bruce that a fire has damaged most of the hotel, but that the group could have rooms in a nearby guest house which Andrew also owns. However, the facilities are inferior and there are no conference rooms. Bruce wishes to cancel the booking, but Andrew insists that the payment can not be refunded.

Advise Bruce as to how his contracts with Andrew and the members of the group may be discharged.

3 Critically discuss the ways in which a contract may be discharged.

4 'The general rule is that performance, to be effective, must be exact and complete.' Discuss whether the strict application of this rule leads to injustice.

OCR 4-module specimen paper

5 How have the courts attempted to place limits on the doctrine of frustration, and why should they wish to do so?

6 To what extent does the doctrine of frustration give the courts the opportunity to apportion loss between two relatively innocent parties?

7 'Sometimes it is convenient for one party to claim that a contract has been frustrated rather than breached.'
  (a) When is a contract frustrated?
  (b) Critically discus the effect that frustration will have on the contract.

8 An English manufacturing company signs a contract on 1st January to manufacture machine parts for a Ruritanian company. Both companies know that an export licence will be required. The contract, worth £80,000 in total, states that the goods will be delivered in three instalments with payments of £20,000 on signing, and £20,000 after each instalment, payment within 30 days and a final delivery on 1st September. The English company receives only £10,000 on signing but decides to send the instalment when ready and claim £30,000. They apply for an export licence but are only granted one for the first instalment on 1st April. The government department issuing the licences states that each instalment requires a separate licence. The English company finds that its prices fail to cover the costs of production because of a fall in the value of the pound after the first instalment is despatched. On 15th May the government department refuses to issue any further export licences in accordance with a United Nations resolution passed on 1st May introducing trade sanctions against Ruritania which makes the machine parts prohibited goods, and the three remaining instalments thus impossible.

Discuss the liability of the English company.

OCR 2002

A further 'dilemma' style question on frustration can be found in Part 7 of the book.

15 Remedies

Clearly, if a problem arises with a contract a remedy is needed for the innocent party. We have seen some remedies in operation throughout this book, when considering aspects of the law of contract, such as remedies for misrepresentation.

The usual remedy for a party to seek as a result of a breach of contract is damages, and this may be claimed as a right at common law. There are instances, however, when this does not provide a reasonable solution, so repudiation (ending the contract) is allowed in some circumstances, and alternative remedies are available, many based in equity, to suit the needs of the situations which arise.

Repudiation is where a contract is brought to an end. If goods have been bought they are usually returned and money is handed back. This is only possible if a breach is of a condition, rather than a warranty, or if breach of an innominate term is treated as a breach of condition under the *Hong Kong Fir* approach (see Chapter 7 on types of terms).

> Under what circumstances might a party want to repudiate rather than claim damages?

Damages

Damages is the word used in law for money obtained as compensation. Damages can be:

- liquidated, where the amount awarded has been decided by the parties, as a genuine pre-estimate
- unliquidated, where no fixed amount has been decided, and the court makes an assessment.

Liquidated damages should be distinguished from penalty clauses. Liquidated damages are a reasonable estimate of the amount which would be needed to put right a defect, and are agreed by the parties. These have some merit in that they save time if a breach arises, they enable parties to make an informed decision whether to continue or to breach, and they help parties to make insurance estimates. A penalty clause is seen as a kind of threat within a contract and will not be upheld by the court.

Dunlop Pneumatic Tyres v New Garage (1915)
Some principles emerged from this case, perhaps the most important being that:

- the use of the words 'penalty clause' or 'liquidated damages' is not conclusive, as it is for the courts to decide within which of these categories a terms falls
- an obligation to pay an amount of money which is 'extravagant and unconscionable' compared to the value of the contract may be an indication that a clause is a penalty clause.

Unliquidated damages are intended to compensate the victim and it would be reasonable to assume that there is an assessment of loss and that this is the amount to be awarded. However, the court has a large role to play in assessment, and a fair amount of discretion. Although the basic principle of awarding damages is purely to compensate, the exact measure can also be used to express disapproval or to have a deterrent effect (although it could be questioned whether this should be the role of the criminal law).

Unliquidated damages can be divided into:

- substantial damages (a normal claim reflecting the loss as accurately as possible)
- nominal damages (a minimum amount, acknowledging merely that a party has won)
- exemplary damages (an unusually large amount, representing more than the actual loss, awarded to show the court's disapproval of the party at fault – these are not awarded very often).

Basis of assessment

The normal basis for awarding damages in contract is for loss of bargain, sometimes known as an expectation basis. The aim is *restitutio in integrum*, and this is best explained in the words of Parke B in *Robinson v Harman* (1848):

The rule of the common law is that where a party sustains a loss by reason of a breach of contract he is, so far as money can do it, to be placed in the same situation with respect to damages as if the contract had been performed.

This supports the view that the idea behind the law of contract is to uphold agreements where possible.

In some circumstances damages are awarded on a reliance basis. This is the basis used normally in tort, restoring the injured party to the position which would have existed if the contract had not been formed. This applied when damages are given for misrepresentation, both fraudulent and under the Misrepresentation Act 1967.

The 'market rule' is that for non-delivery a person can claim the difference between what would have been paid and what the item would now cost to buy on the open market.

Contributory negligence

While it is established that in tort damages can be apportioned by the court on the grounds of contributory negligence under the Law Reform (Contributory Negligence) Act 1945, this does not extend to breach of contract. This was made clear in the case of *Basildon D C v J E Lesser (Properties) Ltd* (1985). However, the Law Commission have reported that this could be a useful measure for the future. Note also that sometimes apportionment can be achieved via a different route, for example in capacity and frustration, by giving the courts discretion in awarding damages under a statute.

Mental distress and non-pecuniary loss

The situation has traditionally been that damages could not be recovered in contract for mental distress, the court requiring something tangible to be shown, such as pain and suffering from personal injury, or physical inconvenience. However, there are some contracts where the very nature of the contract indicates that the benefit is not of a tangible nature. The loss from a breach will then be non-pecuniary, or not a direct financial loss, such as loss of enjoyment of a holiday. Damages can in some circumstances be recovered for disappointment, vexation and mental distress, and the following are examples.

Jarvis v Swann Tours (1973)
The plaintiff was the only person in the holiday accommodation, when the holiday had been advertised as a 'houseparty'. Damages were given for loss of the enjoyment expected, and on appeal Mr Jarvis received twice the value of his holiday as compensation.

Jackson v Horizon Holidays (1975)
Damages were given to compensate for disappointment of the whole family at facilities on a holiday not being as advertised.

Chaplin v Hicks (1911)
Damages were awarded to compensate for the possibility of not winning a beauty competition, when the entry was not processed correctly. Clearly the actual amount was speculation but the court was prepared to make an assessment for both loss of earnings and disappointment.

Thake v Maurice (1986)
Compensation was given for the suffering of both husband and wife for a pregnancy and birth following a vasectomy operation because neither had been warned of the possibility of the operation not being effective.

It was stated in the case of *Addis v Gramophone Co Ltd* (1909) that damages would not be awarded for injury to feelings for wrongful dismissal under contracts of employment. After some uncertainty this was confirmed by the Court of Appeal in *Bliss v S E Thames Regional Health Authority* (1985).

Do you think that all of these awards are reasonable? Are there any circumstances when you feel that the award of substantial damages is unreasonable?

Remoteness of damage

The court has to decide if the expenses for which compensation is claimed are a direct result of a breach of contract. The principle is generally that losses are recoverable if they are reasonably within the contemplation of the parties as a probable result of the breach.

Hadley v Baxendale (1854)
A mill shaft was taken for repair, and it took longer than the expected time. It was held that losses caused by not being able to use the mill were foreseeable and therefore damages were awarded.

However, although normal loss of profit is usually foreseeable, particular losses which could not reasonably have been foreseen by the defendant will not be recoverable.

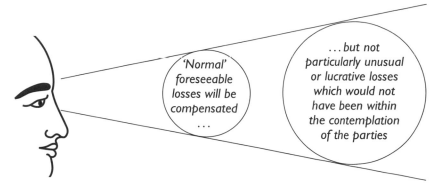

'Normal' foreseeable losses will be compensated ...

...but not particularly unusual or lucrative losses which would not have been within the contemplation of the parties

Figure 15.1

> *Victoria Laundry v Newman* (1949)
> A boiler was to be fitted in a laundry, and after delay a claim was made for loss of normal profit and for not being able to undertake a particularly lucrative dyeing contract for the Ministry of Supply. The claim for loss of normal profits was upheld but not the one for the extra work, as it could not have been foreseen.

Mitigation

The party claiming damages is expected to take steps to mitigate, or offset, loss where this is reasonable, but there is no obligation to take extreme steps, or to mitigate before the date of performance. It was said in *British Westinghouse Electric and Manufacturing Co Ltd v Underground Electric Railways Co of London Ltd* (1912) that the party claiming would not be expected to 'take any step which a reasonable and prudent man would not ordinarily take in the course of his business'.

Other remedies

Equitable remedies are available where common law remedies do not provide a just outcome.

*   Rescission has already been examined as a remedy for misrepresentation (see Chapter 11, p. 179 for more detail).
*   Specific performance may be ordered if the court believes that it is appropriate to force someone to fulfil an obligation under a contract. The sanction for not complying is a fine or imprisonment for contempt of court.
*   An injunction may be ordered to stop a person from acting in breach of contract where merely awarding damages is not appropriate. For example, if a factory begins to allow noxious fumes to escape from a chimney,

affecting neighbouring residents, damages would be inadequate as the residents would want to stop the fumes being emitted. An injunction may therefore be ordered not to emit the fumes. An injunction may be long-term or temporary (an interlocutory injunction) until a case goes to trial.

These equitable remedies, then, are added to the common law remedies generally available to give the courts a wide discretion in order to bring about justice.

Stop Now Orders

Sometimes, even though the law gives rights to consumers, it is difficult to enforce these rights against a business that persists in being unfair. A new recent measure, the Stop Now Orders (E C) Regulations 2001, made available as a result of a European Directive, allows the Office of Fair Trading to order a business to stop whatever they are doing that is regarded as unfair. The Regulations apply to ten areas of consumer protection, including sale of goods, unfair contract terms, doorstep selling, misleading advertising, package holidays, consumer credit and distance selling.

The OFT have said that their approach will be to ensure that action taken under the Regulations will be 'proportionate the circumstances', depending on such things as potential for harm to consumers. Businesses will be given a chance to rectify the wrong and efforts will be made to obtain agreement to stop the wrong action before legal action is taken. Help may be enlisted from other 'bodies', such as local authorities, in the enforcement of orders. One of the first Stop Now Orders issued was against Craftsman Kitchens. They were ordered to stop supplying goods not of satisfactory quality or as described, and breach of this order would be regarded as contempt of court.

You can read more about Stop Now Orders on the internet at the website of the Office of Fair Trading http://www.oft.gov.uk

---

Summary

The usual remedies in contract law are:

- Damages (compensation in money for the loss suffered).
- Repudiation (ending the contract) – or its equivalent in equity, rescission, if the claim is made under an equitable doctrine, such as misrepresentation or undue influence.

Damages can be:

- Liquidated (where a fixed amount is set by the parties).
- Unliquidated (where the court decides the amount of the award).

But not a:

- Penalty clause (an amount agreed in advance which has a similar effect to a fine). Often the amount payable is excessive, and the courts hold these to be illegal – *Dunlop v New Garage*.

Regarding penalty clauses, note that:

- The use of the words 'penalty clause' or 'liquidated damages' is not conclusive.
- An obligation to pay an amount of money which is 'extravagant and unconscionable' compared to the value of the contract may be an indication that a clause is a penalty clause.

Liquidated damages may be:

- substantial (a normal claim)
- nominal (a minimum amount)
- exemplary (an unusually large amount).

Basis of assessment

Two different methods of assessment:

- Expectation basis: the normal contractual basis for breach of contract, which compensates for loss of bargain – *Robinson v Harman*.
- Reliance basis: the usual tort basis, found in misrepresentation, putting the claimant back to the position before the contract was formed.

The 'market rule' allows the difference between what would have been paid and what the item would now cost to buy on the open market. Contributory negligence does not apply to breach of contract – *Basildon D C v J E Lesser (Properties) Ltd.*

Mental distress and non-pecuniary loss

Damages are given for:

- Disappointment, vexation and mental distress, and when there is no precise measure of the amount lost – *Jarvis v Swann Tours, Jackson v Horizon Holidays, Chaplin v Hicks, Thake v Maurice.*
- But not awarded for injury to feelings for wrongful dismissal under contracts of employment – *Addis v Gramophone Co Ltd, Bliss v S E Thames Regional Health Authority.*

Remoteness of damage

* Losses are recoverable if they are reasonably within the contemplation of the parties as a probable result of the breach – *Hadley v Baxendale*.

* Losses for particular losses which are not foreseeable are not recoverable – *Victoria Laundry v Newman*.

Mitigation

Reasonable steps should be taken to mitigate loss, but this only need be reasonable – *British Westinghouse Electric and Manufacturing Co Ltd v Underground Electric Railways Co of London Ltd*.

Other remedies

Equitable remedies supplement common law remedies:

* Rescission has already been examined with respect to misrepresentation (see Chapter 11, p. 179 for more detail).

* Specific performance (to enforce fulfilment of an obligation under a contract).

* Injunction (stops a person from acting in breach of contract). May be long-term or temporary (an interlocutory injunction) until trial.

* Stop now orders.

Questions

1 What factors will the courts take into account when awarding damages for breach of a contract, where there is no provision for this in the contract?

2 Critically compare the award of damages with other remedies which may be available.

Part 5

Consumer protection

This area of law is of use to all students as a life skill, in that most people will find at some time that they are a victim of some problem regarding goods purchased, possibly as a result of faulty production. If you buy a new radio tomorrow and it proves to be faulty, what can you do about it? What rights do you have in law? These are the kind of questions that this aspect of law addresses.

This chapter contains the main statutory material on consumer protection, but for some topics it is necessary to look back a little. The following chapters of this book contain material which supports this unit:

Formation of a contract

Part 1 of this book provides the basic information that you will need on forming a contract. Whilst much of the protection for consumers comes from statute law, a lot of this still depends on there being a valid contract. You will find information on this in the following chapters: Chapter 2, Offer and acceptance; Chapter 3, Consideration; and Chapter 4: Legal intent. You may find the summaries at the ends of these chapters particularly helpful, especially as this is only part of the law needed for your unit of study.

Privity

The relationship between parties to a contract, which gives the right to sue, is very important in the protection of consumers. Some measures only apply if there is a relationship of privity, and you will find information on this in Chapter 9, Privity.

Exemption clauses

Exemption clauses are terms within a contract where a party attempts to exclude or limit liability. The expression can include exclusion clauses (where a party attempts to totally exclude liability) and limitation clauses (where a party limits liability to a certain amount). Information about these clauses can be found in Chapter 8, Exemption clauses.

Remedies

Once a breach of contract is found to exist a remedy is needed for the 'innocent' party. This may mean that the contract is to be ended, or it may be better for all if a certain amount of money is given to put right the defect. The issue of remedies can be found in Chapter 15: Remedies. Other areas of law should also be considered, such as criminal liability and liability in the tort of negligence, which is examined very briefly here. You may wish to refer to negligence in the companion book in this series on the law of tort.

16 Consumer protection

So far we have concentrated mostly on ensuring that the law works well for those who have negotiated agreements. Sometimes we have seen that one party may lack bargaining power, so needs extra protection, and often that party is a consumer. We have already seen some ways in which the law is effective in helping individuals who are not in a position to assess and modify the terms of a contract. This is a very important aspect of the modern law of contract, as it is there for all, not just as a framework for trading. This protection of the consumer has been accomplished in two main ways:

- through the common law, over a long period, as cases involving individual difficulties have been taken to court
- through Acts of Parliament, the law recognising that common law alone was not enough, and that the consumer needed clearer rights which were more easily enforceable.

There are various aspects to the protection of consumers. An incident may involve more than one aspect, particularly where goods bought are faulty and have caused injury.

- A fair contract must exist between the consumer and the retailer.
- There may be immediate liability on the retailer for defective products supplied under the Sale of Goods Act 1979 and the Sale and Supply of Goods Act 1994.
- There may be liability beyond the strict sale of goods, for example for services.
- There may be liability on the producer under the Consumer Protection Act 1987 and possibly in tort or in criminal law.

The contract

Many commercial deals take place between large organisations, which trade with each other in the supply of goods and services, and it is assumed that, on the whole, they have the resources to make fair bargains. However, a huge number of deals take place every day which form contracts between ordinary people and those in commerce in some way. All of these 'deals', involving the exchange of money for goods or services, form contracts, so you may like to read the chapters on the formation of a contract (Chapters 2–4) and on the incorporation of terms (Chapter 7).

If there is no contract, less protection is available, and in many cases, there is no protection. So if, for example, a person is given a hairdryer by a friend for a present, the contract of sale is between the buyer and seller. If the hairdryer does not work, the legal remedy is for the buyer to return it to the shop, not the friend (although in practice a shop will often give an exchange item or refund of money to maintain good customer relations).

Of course there may be other remedies both within and outside the field of contract law. If the buyer is misled into purchasing the hairdryer because of false statements by the shop assistant about its capabilities there may be a remedy in misrepresentation (Chapter 11). If the hairdryer not only malfunctioned, but also injured the user, there would be remedy not only in contract but also in the tort of negligence, in addition to any statutory protection.

The consumer

A person in a consumer situation often has little bargaining power and is less able to negotiate freely than is a person in a business situation. Recognising this, the courts have in many cases tried to protect individuals, but the great bulk of protection has come from Acts of Parliament, in an attempt to remedy the imbalance of power in consumer contracts. Some of the protection given by legislation only applies to consumer contracts.

The basis of a consumer contract is where an individual buys from a person in business.

This is important to establish, as there is a wealth of protection now in force for the consumer. If a person is not buying as a consumer, then the principle of *caveat emptor* applies, which means that the buyer takes responsibility for the state of the goods or services purchased (see below, Sale and Supply of Goods Act 1994, section 14). Of course an individual could be in business as a seller of goods, but at some times, such as at the weekend, be a consumer in shopping for the family or pursuing a hobby.

The Sale of Goods Act 1979 as amended by the Sale and Supply of Goods Act 1994

The Sale of Goods Act 1979 was a major step forward for the consumer, updating a previous Act passed in 1893. It applies to the sale of goods, defined in section 2(1) as a 'contract by which the seller transfers or agrees to transfer the property in goods to the buyer for a money consideration, called the price'. So some money, at least, must be given, and an exchange of goods for other goods is excluded from this law. Remember that most of the provisions in the Act apply to a consumer (see above).

The passing of property

The moment at which ownership of property transfers to the other party is very important in determining whether certain liability arises. The point at which property passes can be determined by the parties, providing the goods have been 'ascertained', or identified. If the point at which property passes has not been specified, then certain rules apply from sections 16 to 18 of the Act.

- Goods deliverable – property passes on contract.
- Specific goods not yet deliverable – property passes when the seller has them ready and tells the buyer.
- Goods on approval – property passes on acceptance by buyer or lapse of time.
- Unascertained or future goods – property passes when goods are 'unconditionally appropriated' to the contract.

Risk

The risk of some kind of damage to goods, or their loss, may be arranged specifically by the parties, but otherwise will normally pass when the property passes.

Terms implied by sections 12 to 15

The Sale of Goods Act 1979 implies five basic, but important, terms into contracts for the sale of goods to consumers in sections 12 to 15. Some cases quoted as examples were based on the sections of the 1893 Act but would not have changed significantly if they had arisen more recently.

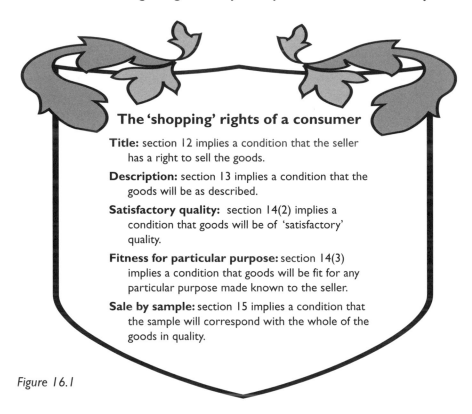

The 'shopping' rights of a consumer

Title: section 12 implies a condition that the seller has a right to sell the goods.

Description: section 13 implies a condition that the goods will be as described.

Satisfactory quality: section 14(2) implies a condition that goods will be of 'satisfactory' quality.

Fitness for particular purpose: section 14(3) implies a condition that goods will be fit for any particular purpose made known to the seller.

Sale by sample: section 15 implies a condition that the sample will correspond with the whole of the goods in quality.

Figure 16.1

The five main terms which affect consumers are:

- title
- sale by description
- satisfactory quality
- fitness for a purpose
- sale by sample.

Title

Section 12 implies a condition that the seller has a right to sell the goods. This is so fundamental to a contract of sale of goods that it is implied into all such contracts. Under the Unfair Contract Terms Act 1977 section 6(1) a party may not use a contract term to exclude liability under section 12.

> *Rowland v Divall* (1923)
> The plaintiff bought a car from the defendant but later found out that it was stolen. This meant that the defendant was not, at the time that the car was sold, the legal owner, so the plaintiff was entitled to the refund of the purchase price, even though he had used the car for a period of time.

Sale by description

Section 13 implies a condition that the goods sold will be as described. This applies to all contracts for the sale of goods. Under the Unfair Contract Terms Act 1977 sections 6(2) and 6(3), a party may not exclude the provision in section 13 if the buyer is dealing as a consumer, but can exclude it in other circumstances if it is reasonable to do so.

> *Beale v Taylor* (1967)
> An advertisement read 'Herald, convertible white 1961'. In fact the car consisted of two 'half cars' joined together, the back half of a 1961 model and the front of an older model.

However, there must be reliance on the description. There is likely to be important where the buyer selects the goods, as stated in *Grant v Australian Knitting Mills Ltd* (1936), and where the description itself was an important factor in identifying the goods: *Ashington Piggeries v Christopher Hill Smith* (1972). In *Harlingdon and Leinster v Christopher Hull Fine Art* (1990) there was no reliance on any claims about a painting, since it was bought at 'own risk'. This section is increasingly important in self-service shopping, with reliance on signs, packets, etc.

Satisfactory quality

Section 14(2) of the Sale of Goods Act 1979 implied a term that goods will be of 'merchantable' quality. From January 1995 the Sale and Supply of Goods Act 1994 section 1 has changed this to 'satisfactory' quality.

> What differences, if any, can you see between these two words?

This important term only applies to sales in the course of a business, not to private sales, so although a consumer is protected in buying from a shop or other commercial concern, there is far less protection when buying from an individual. The principle of *caveat emptor* will then apply, which literally translated means 'let the buyer beware'. This means, for example, that in a private sale the buyer must watch out for evidence of defects in products purchased, etc., as there will not be any protection under this section regarding quality, once the deal is done. This creates an anomaly between two different types of purchase by the same individual, but it could, on the other hand, be argued that the consumer would be paying more if purchasing from a business retail outlet, enabling the seller to provide for the cost of statutory protection. Despite this difference the section is nevertheless a very important measure in consumer protection.

Bernstein v Pamsons Motors (1987)
A new Nissan car was purchased, and after three weeks and 140 miles the engine seized up on the motorway. It was found that sealant had escaped into the lubrication system when the car was assembled and had caused a blockage, depriving the car of oil. It was held that a consumer who buys a new car is entitled to expect that the engine will not seize up after three weeks if the car is to be considered as 'merchantable' quality.

Rogers v Parish (1987)
This case concerned a new Range Rover. On delivery defects were found in the engine, gearbox, bodywork, and oil-seals. The plaintiff drove the car for six months, constantly complained, but drove 5,500 miles in between visits to the garage. There were still faults remaining with the car after six months, and it was held to be not of merchantable quality.

The change of wording from 'merchantable' to 'satisfactory' was made in an attempt to make the meaning of the section clearer, but it is arguable that on their own the words 'merchantable' and 'satisfactory' are equally vague. A slight change of emphasis *could* be implied, since 'merchantable' strictly would indicate fit to be sold, where 'satisfactory' may indicate a state in which the consumer is happy to receive the goods. Because of the difficulty of interpreting the word 'satisfactory' the Sale and Supply of Goods Act 1994 explains what may be taken into account:

Section 14
(2A) For the purposes of this Act, goods are of satisfactory quality if they meet the standard that a reasonable person would regard as satisfactory, taking account of any description of the goods, the price (if relevant) and all the other relevant circumstances. (2B) For the purposes of this Act, the quality of goods includes their state and condition and the following (among others) are in appropriate cases aspects of the quality of goods –

(a) fitness for all the purposes for which goods of this question are commonly supplied

(b) finish and appearance

(c) freedom from minor defects

(d) safety

(e) durability.

Section 14 (2C) adds that 'any matter specifically brought to the buyer's attention before making the contract will not amount to unsatisfactory quality, neither will any defect found, or which ought to have been found, if the buyer examines the goods'.

Jewson v Boyhan (2003)

In this case, concerning the efficiency of electric heating boilers, the Court of Appeal confirmed that the word 'satisfactory' in s.14(2) refers to general quality of goods and is quite distinct from a particular use that the buyer has in mind, which may come within s.14(3). The word 'satisfactory' in s.14(2) referred to whether the boilers worked in general for heating purposes, while s.14(3) referred to whether the boilers would be suitable to heat this particular property.

Fitness for a particular purpose

Section 14(3) implies a condition that goods will be fit for any particular purpose made known by the buyer to the seller.

Can you think of some special purposes for which products may be bought, which a buyer may wish to make known at the time of purchase?

Griffiths v Peter Conway (1939)

A buyer of a Harris tweed coat had a particularly sensitive skin and found that it caused dermatitis (even though it would not have done so to a normal user). She sued, claiming that the coat was not fit for her purpose, and failed because she had not made known her particular sensitivity at the time of forming the contract.

Why do you think that this particular buyer may not have made her requirements known more clearly?

Sometimes the purpose is implied because there is only one obvious purpose, as in *Priest v Last* (1903) where it was held that a hot water bottle which had a hole in it was only really designed for one purpose. The condition will not apply where it is not reasonable for the buyer to rely on the seller's judgement, or where the advice is not in fact relied upon: *Ashington Piggeries v Christopher Hill* (1972).

The Sale and Supply of Goods to Consumers Regulations 2002 give extra rights to consumers, including free repair. They also widen slightly the application of s.14 to include the effect of statements of an advertising nature made by the seller or producer.

Sale by sample

Section 15 implies a condition that the sample will correspond with the whole of the goods in quality. Just having an item on display does not necessarily make it a sample of what is bought. The sample must be used to show features of the goods actually purchased. In *Drummond v Van Ingen* (1887) it was said that the purpose of a sample is to 'present to the eye the real meaning and intention of the parties'.

In the case of *Rogers v Parish* (above) the Court of Appeal raised some other important points to take into account when applying these sections, such as:

- what will amount to acceptance (see below)?
- the external appearance (the case involved a new Range Rover)
- the effect of a repair being possible
- the manufacturer's warranty
- the use of the vehicle between periods of breakdown.

Exclusion

The old Sale of Goods Act 1893 could be excluded from contract, which was a reflection of the general freedom to contract which took priority over other principles at that time. Now, opting out of protective measures is much more difficult, and often not allowed at all. As stated above, under the Unfair Contract Terms Act 1977 the current Sale of Goods Act 1979 (as amended) section 12 cannot be excluded from any contract. Sections 13 to 15 cannot be excluded from a consumer contract (where a buyer is not 'in the course of a business'), and can only be excluded from other contracts if this is reasonable. This reflects a huge move toward the protection of consumers, and, far from being paternalistic, as may have been alleged by some when the 1979 Act was passed, is now no more than we have come to expect of a developed legal system in a modern society.

Acceptance of goods

If the goods are accepted this will normally mean that they cannot then be rejected by the buyer. However, the buyer should have a chance to examine the goods. Acceptance may be made by words or actions, or by lapse of time. The new Sale and Supply of Goods Act 1994 has attempted to improve the position of the consumer on acceptance of goods.

The Supply of Goods and Services Act 1982

Where goods are handed over, or services undertaken, but nothing is actually bought over a counter, as in a shop sale, a consumer could still be in need of protection, and yet would not fall within the definition of a sale under the Sale of Goods Act 1979. The case of *Samuels v Davis* (1943), see Chapter 6, p. 103, highlights the problem, raising the issue of whether the supply of a set of false teeth is a sale of goods.

The Supply of Goods and Services Act 1982 implies similar conditions into contracts as the Sale of Goods Act. Sections 2 to 5 cover the supply of goods (the 'materials' element) and sections 13 to 15 cover the supply of services (the 'work' element). The Act applies, for example, where goods are supplied by someone who essentially delivers a service, like a decorator who supplies paint and wallpaper and uses it to redecorate, and also gives similar rights to a consumer in hiring goods. It protects a consumer by implying conditions into a contract for services, such as one for servicing a car. This is a good example of a statute implementing changes demanded by the common law through cases.

These provisions are as follows:

- The service will be carried out with reasonable care and skill – *Wilson v Best Travel* (1993) regarding a holiday in Greece, where the customer fell through a glass door, which although ordinary glass, complied with local requirements, and was therefore held reasonable.

- The service will be carried out within a reasonable time, where a time limit is not specified in the contract.

- A reasonable price will be paid for the service, where this is not specified in the contract.

The Consumer Protection Act 1987

This Act was passed as a direct result of Britain's membership of the European Union, giving effect to the European Product Liability Directive, and section 1 provides that the Act should be construed in accordance with the Directive. Just as a claim in negligence may be made by a *user* of a product which causes harm, who is not necessarily the buyer, the Consumer

Protection Act 1987 gives protection to this person by legislation. It also creates criminal liability if certain safety procedures are infringed.

The producer

Strict liability for a defective product is placed on the producer, without having to prove fault. The producer will normally, but not necessarily, be the manufacturer, and in addition the retailer may be liable for 'own brand' products.

The defect

A product will be defective if the safety 'is not such as persons generally are entitled to expect'. The product may be defective because of a fault in the manufacturing process, a problem of design, or warning and instructions given to the consumer.

The Act covers liability for:

• death
• personal injury, and
• damage to property valued at over £275.

But it does *not* cover liability for damage to the product itself – see *Aswan Engineering Establishment v Lupdine* (1987) regarding a burst tyre causing damage to a car.

Defences

Certain defences are available under the Act, including the following:

• the producer is not in business (such as the sale of home-made products for charity)
• the defect did not exist at the time of manufacture
• that only the component was supplied, whereas the fault lay in the whole product design
• the state of scientific and technical knowledge was such that the producer would not be expected to have discovered the defect – a 'state of the art' defence. This last defence causes the most worrying problems, as it could mean that the manufacturer of a product such as the Thalidomide drug may not be liable for harm caused.

The Act then is not totally satisfactory, but takes consumer protection a further step forward – in fact for those who have relied on it, it is more like a huge leap in the direction of total consumer protection.

The Unfair Contract Terms Act 1977

This is not in the 'right' order chronologically in the list of statutes in this Chapter, as it protects the consumer in quite a different way from those above. The statutes examined so far have been concerned with implying terms into consumer sales, or giving the consumer rights within the contract formed. The Unfair Contract Terms Act 1977 operates by declaring certain terms which may already be within the consumer's contract to be so unfair that they are invalid. The Act stepped in largely to give protection where consumers found that they were not protected because of either:

- a term in written contract which they had not noticed or understood, or
- a notice which had become incorporated as a term of a contract, unknown to the consumer, and depriving the consumer of basic rights.

The kind of term which the Unfair Contract Terms Act 1977 addresses generally takes the form of an exemption clause, that is one which either limits liability (a limitation clause) or excludes liability (an exclusion clause). Because consumers, with little bargaining power, are not realistically able to negotiate over these terms, they are in an unfair position. The common law restricts the use of these to some extent by requiring fair incorporation as a term – see Chapter 8 for more detail concerning the points made here.

Figure 16.2

The term must not come too late – *Olley v Marlborough Court Hotel.*

- It must be brought to the attention of the other party – *Thornton v Shoe Lane Parking.*
- Construction (interpretation) must cover the damage caused.
- The term must not offend the main purpose rule or the *contra proferentem* rule.

Added to these requirements now are the two main provisions in the Unfair Contract Terms Act 1977.

1 An attempt to exclude or restrict liability for death or personal injury resulting from negligence is not allowed at all – section 2(1).

2 An attempt to exclude or restrict other liability caused by negligence will only be allowed if reasonable – section 2(2).

Schedule 2 of the Unfair Contract Terms Act 1977 makes some suggestions regarding reasonableness:

- the bargaining strength of the parties
- if any inducement was given to agree to the term
- if the customer knew of the term
- if the goods were specially manufactured.

For more detail see cases from Chapter 8 on reasonableness.

Can you find some examples of exemption clauses from real life? Try to decide whether they are fair and if they would be valid, should they be relied upon in court.

Other provisions in the Unfair Contract Terms Act 1977 which affect a consumer are as follows:

- A party can only exclude liability for breach of contract, non-performance or substantially different performance if this is reasonable – section 3(2). This applies when a person is dealing as a consumer and also when dealing on written standard terms.
- A party can only exclude indemnity for negligence or breach of contract where reasonable – section 4.
- A party can only exclude a manufacturer's guarantee where reasonable – section 5. Here the party claiming must be a purchaser of goods ordinarily supplied for private use or consumption. In a contract of sale or hire-purchase, a party may not exclude an implied condition as to title or description, and may only exclude liability regarding quality and fitness for purpose if reasonable – section 6. The provision regarding title applies to any contract, not just a consumer contract.

• A party may only exclude liability for misrepresentation where it is reasonable to do so – section 8, and also section 3 of the Misrepresentation Act 1967.

The Unfair Terms in Consumer Contract Regulations 1999

Again, Britain's membership of the European Union has had an effect on consumer protection, this time via the *European Directive on Unfair Terms in Consumer Contracts*. This was incorporated in the Unfair Terms in Consumer Contract Regulations 1999. Terms are considered to be unfair which are 'significant to the detriment of the consumer', and 'contrary to the requirement of good faith'.

Reasonableness is interpreted to mean fair given the circumstances known to the parties at the time, and given the resources to meet the liability. The possibility of insurance may also be taken into account. Other factors which the court may take into account include:

• the bargaining power of the parties, and whether an alternative source was available

• any inducement to agree to the term, such as a favourable price

• trade custom and previous dealings

• the difficulty of the task

• whether the goods are adapted to the order of the customer.

For more detail on cases concerning unfair terms and the new regulations, see Chapter 8.

Consumer protection other than through the law of contract

It should be noted that while much of the law of consumer protection is based in the law of contract, other measures exist to protect the consumer and may prove useful, particularly where a claim in contract law would be unsuccessful or inconvenient.

Negligence

For a claim in negligence it must be established that there was:

• A duty of care owed to the injured party: *Donoghue v Stevenson* (1932) – where a claim succeeded against a manufacturer of ginger beer by a consumer who became ill after drinking the remains of a decomposed snail. See also *Bourhill v Young* (1943) regarding forseeability of injury.

- A breach of the duty of care: this is viewed according to a 'reasonable man', so if the risk is very small, there is no liability – *Bolton v Stone* (1951). A professional will be judged by accepted standards, for example medical standard practice – *Bolam v Friern Hospital* (1957).

- Damage caused by the breach: this must be a direct cause, not as in *Barnett v Chelsea and Kensington Hospital* (1957) where a man died because of the amount of poison already in his system and not because of the negligent act of the doctor at the hospital.

The concept of contributory negligence must also be considered here, as a person may have contributed towards the damage caused, even thought they were not responsible for the initial problem. A common example is a claim for personal injury in a motor accident, where the compensation is reduced by a proportion representing the victim's contributory negligence in not wearing a seat-belt.

For more on the law of negligence see the companion book in this series on the law of tort.

Criminal liability

Another area of law where liability may arise is criminal law. This does not necessarily result in any compensation for the victim, but acts as a deterrent to prevent further wrongs taking place. Criminal liability may arise alongside civil claims. So, for example, if a seller of goods describes them wrongly, liability may arise under Sale and Supply of Goods Act 1994, in misrepresentation, directly through the contract as a breach, and also under criminal law. This criminal liability derives from two main sources:

- The Trade Descriptions Act 1968 – this contains penalties for statements which falsely describe goods or services, such as quantity, size, method of manufacture, composition. Liability under this Act arose when a watch was described as 'waterproof' and a 'diver's watch' in *Sherratt v Geralds* (1970), but was found to leak after one hour in a bowl of water. The Act also applies to description of services, an example being a description of a hotel's air conditioning – or the lack of it – in *Wings v Ellis* (1985).

- The Consumer Protection Act 1987 – this contains penalties for misleading statements about the price of goods and services. A statement of price would be misleading if it was marked on the product as £15 but £15.50 was charged by the cashier. A code of practice has been issued with the Act, which does not incur liability if breached, but may be used as evidence of a breach.

The current state of consumer protection

The general trend in protecting the consumer, then, can be seen as a still growing area of law, particularly in light of our membership of the

European Union. It is obviously an important area of general concern, for a number of people. Consumers themselves are becoming much more aware of their rights, and have come to expect extremely high standards in this field compared with consumers in many other countries. Legal advice is sought more readily than twenty years ago, especially since solicitors are now allowed to advertise services (following the Courts and Legal Services Act 1990), and there is much greater competition in the legal market place. There is material freely available to advise people of their rights as citizens, and these matters arise commonly in school education programmes.

On the other side of the coin, manufacturers are very conscious of the high standards of production expected of them, and need to account and plan for this. The more the consumer expects, the higher the price paid. On the whole, the consumer is probably happy to pay a little more on the unit price of an item, in the assurance of the right to a high quality product.

The media acts as a watchdog, to some extent, in the many consumer programmes that have been broadcast over recent years. In addition, consumers are also the voting public, so some issues may have some political merit. Ultimately, we have a set of laws concerning individuals who trade with businesses which now are of an extremely high calibre, and although they may need fine tuning in individual cases, the statutes in this area form a comprehensive package of protection for the consumer.

Summary

Consumer protection ensures support for a purchaser of a product or service who lacks bargaining power. This is normally an individual buying from a person in business.
Protection is available:

- through common law as cases arise in court
- through statute law, e.g. Sale of Goods Act 1979.

The contract

- Be clear about the formation requirements – see Part 1 of this book.
- Note the relationship between the parties – see Chapter 9 on privity of contract.
- Refer to Chapter 8 on exemption clauses (or exclusion clauses).
- Refer to Chapter 15 on remedies.

Sale of Goods Act 1979 as amended by the Sale and Supply of Goods Act 1994

Passing of property: determined by the parties, providing the goods have been 'ascertained', or identified. If not then sections 16 to 18 apply.

Risk: may be negotiated by the parties, but otherwise will pass when the property passes.

Terms implied by sections 12 to 15:

*   Title: section 12 implies a condition that the seller has a right to sell the goods – *Rowland v Divall*.

*   Sale by description: section 13 implies a condition that the goods sold will be as described – *Beale v Taylor, Harlingdon and Leinster v Christopher Hull Fine Art*.

*   Satisfactory quality: section 14(2) (amended by section 1 of the Sale and Supply of Goods Act 1994). Only applies to sales in the course of a business – *caveat emptor* applies to private sales. See *Bernstein v Pamsons Motors, Rogers v Parish*. See section 14 (2C) *re.* matters specifically brought to the buyer's attention.

*   Fitness for a particular purpose: section 14(3) implies a condition that goods will be fit for any particular purpose made known by the buyer to the seller – *Griffiths v Peter Conway, Priest v Last, Ashington Piggeries v Christopher Hill*.

*   Sale by sample: section 15 implies a condition that the sample will correspond with the whole of the goods in quality – *Drummond v Van Ingen*.

Exclusion: under the Unfair Contract Terms Act 1977, section 12 cannot be excluded from any contract. Sections 13 to 15 cannot be excluded from a consumer contract and can only be excluded from other contracts if reasonable.

Acceptance: the buyer should have a chance to examine the goods. Acceptance may be by words or actions, or by lapse of time.

The Supply of Goods and Services Act 1982

The Act implies similar conditions into contracts as the Sale of Goods Act. Sections 2–5 cover the supply of goods (the 'materials' element) and sections 13–15 cover the supply of services (the 'work' element). The work must be done with reasonable care and skill, within a reasonable time, and at a reasonable price.

The Consumer Protection Act 1987

Imposes liability on the manufacturer for defective products and on the retailer for 'own brand' products.

- The defect may arise from the manufacturing process or a problem of design.
- The Act covers liability for death, personal injury or damage to property valued at over £275, but not for damage to the product itself – *Aswan Engineering Establishment v Lupdine.*
- Defences include: producer not in business, defect arising after manufacture, fault with the whole product design, not this component, 'state of the art'.

Exemption clauses

See also Chapter 8, Exemption clauses. An exemption clause is a term of a contract either limiting liability (a limitation clause) or excluding liability (an exclusion clause). There are three stages to considering validity:

- Is the term incorporated? *Olley v Marlborough Court Hotel*, *Thornton v Shoe Lane Parking*, etc.
- Docs the term, when construed (interpreted) cover the damage caused? Main purpose rule and *contra proferentem* rule.
- Does legislation apply to the term? Unfair Contract Terms Act 1977 and Unfair Terms in Consumer Contract Regulations 1999.

The Unfair Contract Terms Act 1977

The main provisions in the Unfair Contract Terms Act 1977:

- Exclusion or restriction of liability for death or personal injury resulting from negligence is not allowed – section 2(1).
- Exclusion or restriction of other liability caused by negligence will only be allowed if reasonable – section 2(2).

Under Schedule 2 in assessing reasonableness the court may consider: the bargaining strength of the parties, any inducement given to agree to the term, the customer's knowledge of the term, any special manufacture.

Exclusion of implied terms is only allowed in limited circumstances and often subject to a test of reasonableness.

The Unfair Terms in Consumer Contract Regulations 1999

Implemented the *European Directive on Unfair Terms in Consumer Contracts (93/13)*. Terms are unfair which are 'significant to the detriment of the consumer', and 'contrary to the requirement of good faith'. Reasonableness includes circumstances, resources to meet liability and possibility of insurance. Bargaining power of parties, any alternative sources, any inducement, trade custom and previous dealings, the difficulty of the task, and adaptation to the order of the customer may also be considered. Again, for more detail on cases concerning the new regulations, see Chapter 8.

Consumer protection other than through the law of contract

To claim in negligence a party must establish a duty of care owed to the injured party, a breach of the duty of care, and damage caused by the breach. Contributory negligence should also be considered. For more on the law of negligence see the companion book in this series on the law of tort. Criminal liability may arise from the Trade Descriptions Act 1968 or the Consumer Protection Act 1987.

Questions

1 The ideas of laissez-faire in the law of contract have been gradually eroded by statute. Discuss some of the incursions of statute law to control contractual agreements.

2 Explain and evaluate the concept of 'product liability' as introduced by the Consumer Protection Act 1987 and the way that it has been applied.

Part 6

General questions on contract law

17   Additional questions

The 4-module examination paper for OCR includes a section of 'dilemma'-style questions. These are intended to focus on one or more topics within the law of contract and require very brief, but logical, explanations as answers. Some examples of these questions follow.

In answering the questions remember that the statements that you are evaluating may or may not be true. You do not, therefore, necessarily have to agree with them. Your aim should be to apply the law as it has been decided by courts, and if there is a 'grey' area, so that a statement may be either true or false, say so, with reasons.

1   Spencer has purchased a car from Belinda after being told that it had done 20,000 miles. Belinda relied on the recorded mileage on the car. Shortly after buying the car Spencer sets out on a journey to his friend's house 80 miles away. As he starts out on the journey the car breaks down and he has to call a mechanic to fix it. The mechanic informs Spencer that there are a lot of faults with the car and it has probably done 120 000 miles. Spencer is annoyed at this and, after completing the trip to see his friend, drives the car to Belinda to complain about it.

Evaluate the accuracy of **each** of the four statements A, B, C and D individually, as they apply to the facts in the above scenario.

Statement A: If Spencer is able to prove misrepresentation he will have a remedy in rescission.

Statement B: Spencer will have a remedy under s.2(1) Misrepresentation Act 1967.

Statement C: Belinda has made a misrepresentation in not informing Spencer about the other faults with the car.

Statement D: Belinda has made a fraudulent misrepresentation to Spencer.

OCR 4-module specimen paper

2   Sue owns a hotel and is having 20 rooms redecorated before the summer season. The work is to be completed by Hamish at a cost of £400 per room. Hamish completes 12 of the rooms and then informs Sue that he is unable to purchase materials he needs in order to complete the other 8 rooms. Sue does not have time to look for another decorator and is worried that she will have unfinished rooms for the summer season. She offers Hamish an extra payment of £600 to help pay for the materials. Hamish accepts and continues with the work. As Hamish is grateful he also promises to paint the entrance hall. Some time later Sue is refusing to pay the extra £600 and Hamish has not painted the entrance hall.

Evaluate the accuracy of **each** of the four statements A, B, C and D individually, as they apply to the facts in the above scenario.

Statement A: Hamish has provided good consideration for the extra payment.

Statement B: Sue would be estopped from going back on her promise to pay the bonus.

Statement C: Sue can avoid paying the extra £600 on the basis of economic duress.

Statement D: Sue has not provided any consideration for Hamish's promise to paint the entrance hall.

OCR 4-module specimen paper

3   Rosie notices an advertisement in the window of Best Bargains Store which states, 'All MP3 players at £10 to the first twenty customers on Monday morning.' Rosie queues all night on Sunday and is customer number seven in the queue on Monday morning. When she enters the store and selects her MP3 player, she is told that the management has decided to end the promotion.

While in Best Bargains Store, Rosie buys a pair of shoes. The label on the shoes states the price to be £25, but the cashier, Tom, tells her that the shoes are wrongly priced and that the correct price is £35. Rosie believes that she should be allowed to buy the shoes for the advertised price.

Having finished her shopping, Rosie notices a wallet in the bushes at the exit of the shop and returns it to Nick at the address which she finds in the wallet. On the way home, she sees on a notice board a poster requesting the return of Nick's lost wallet and offering a reward of £50 to the finder. Rosie returns to Nick's house to claim the reward, but Nick tells Rosie that he is not going to pay her.

Evaluate the accuracy of **each** of the four statements A, B, C and D individually, as they apply to the facts in the above scenario.

Statement A: Rosie has responded to an offer to sell the MP3 player for £10 and therefore has a binding contract on the price.

Statement B: The label on the shoes in the shop is a statement of the contracted price.

Statement C: Rosie's claimed acceptance of a reward for finding the wallet was carried out before she knew of the offer and is not therefore binding.

Statement D: Any consideration that Rosie has provided in order to claim the reward is in the past and not therefore valid.

4   Tom invites two friends, Dana and Harry, to his house for the evening, saying that he will provide the drinks if they bring the food. The friends arrive, but, having been busy, have not brought food. Tom decides to buy some food instead.

A local pizza supplier advertises 'free dessert with each pizza ordered'. Tom orders three pizzas, but on paying he is told that they are no longer giving free desserts because they are busy.

Tom and his friends then decide to complete a football pools coupon and enter the competition together. Each pays towards the entry fee and they agree to share any money which they may win. The friends prove to be lucky, and find a week later that they have won £1,500 in the football pools competition. However, the football pools organisers refuse to pay out due to low funds.

Evaluate the accuracy of **each** of the four statements A, B, C and D individually, as they apply to the facts in the above scenario.

Statement A: The agreement of Dana and Harry to provide food to eat at Tom's house lacked legal intent and was not, therefore, a binding contract.

Statement B: The pizza supplier, as a commercial organisation, has legal intent and has therefore breached a contract in not supplying the 'free dessert'.

Statement C: There is never legal intent between friends in entering a competition.

Statement D: Pools coupons contain honourable pledge clauses and are never binding.

5 Pippa visits her local skating rink, pays to skate on entry to the rink and takes a ticket. She has a bag with her which is too big for the lockers provided, so she hands the bag to an attendant, Will, who takes a payment of £1 and assures Pippa that he will take good care of the bag.

  A steward skates past Pippa very fast and collides with her, causing her to fall into a barrier and injure her mouth. Pippa is helped from the rink. She is further dismayed to find that the attendant, Will, has given her bag to another skater.

  Pippa later contacts the manager, saying that she will claim compensation for the injury and the loss of her bag. The manager points out a large notice at the corner of the rink, to which reference is made on the back of Pippa's admission ticket. The notice reads as follows:

  'The management of the skating rink will not be responsible for any injury to users of the premises, however caused. Similarly the management will not be held responsible for any damage to, or loss of, personal property belonging to users of the rink.'

Evaluate the accuracy of **each** of the four statements A, B, C and D individually, as they apply to the facts in the above scenario.

Statement A: Any terms in a notice in the skating rink or on Pippa's ticket exempting the skating rink management from liability for injury will be automatically incorporated into the contract between Pippa and the skating rink managers.

Statement B: Any statements exempting the skating rink managers from taking care of Pippa's bag will be incorporated into the contract with the attendant.

Statement C: The skating rink management may not choose to exempt themselves from liability for personal injury.

Statement D: Whether the skating rink may exempt themselves from liability for the loss of Pippa's bag will depend on the court's view of it being reasonable.

6 Fola books a room, for one day, in the Hip hotel so that she and her friends can watch a festival due to take place one Saturday in May. Fola pays a deposit of £20 on making the booking in March, the remaining £100 to be paid on the day of the festival. The festival is unexpectedly cancelled on the Friday before the festival, due to storm damage in the area.

  Fola has also ordered a new dress for the festival from Bella's boutique. It is a particularly unusual dress, and is being made to order, to be ready in time for the festival. One week before the delivery date, Fola tells Bella that she will not need the dress, as her aunt has given her a similar one.

Fola also orders a luxury taxi from Supacars for a dance on the evening of the festival. When the taxi arrives Fola is told that Supacars are busy with other customers, so Quickcabs are to take her instead. The small taxi supplied is cold, noisy and dirty, and breaks down on the way to the dance, so that Fola and her friends arrive late.

Evaluate the accuracy of **each** of the four statements A, B, C and D individually, as they apply to the facts in the above scenario.

Statement A: The contract between Fola and the Hip hotel may be frustrated rather than breached.

Statement B: If the contract between Fola and the Hip hotel is found to be frustrated the Hip hotel may claim damages in compensation from Fola.

Statement C: The contract between Fola and Bella may be cancelled as it has not yet been completed.

Statement D: Supacars are entitled to send another firm of taxis to perform the contract on their behalf.

Part 7

Studying contract law

18   Contract law in context

The law is not a subject which can be studied in isolation with any degree of satisfaction. It is a living, changing body of knowledge, which, if somewhat slowly at times, evolves in response to changes and developments in society. This is an aspect of studying law that makes it interesting and exciting. It is not simply a set of static regulations which cannot be challenged, but a reflection of collective ethical, cultural, moral and political views. It is important, therefore, that throughout your study of contract law you continually consider the wider issues raised by the 'rules' themselves.

'The important thing is to not stop questioning.' (Albert Einstein)

For instance, taking the case of *R v Clarke* (Chapter 2), the theory of this may seem to be a straightforward rule, and a relatively small issue, that is, whether a person would be considered to have formed a contract if the actions required for acceptance were performed without knowing of the offer. We can learn the answer to this easily – the outcome of the case, that no contract is formed, is the 'rule'. However, further thought may stimulate the question of whether this is fair or sensible in every case.

In *Clarke* the defendant told the truth as evidence in court (presumably – it is an old case and we must go on what is reported). He said that he had forgotten about the offer of the reward. For telling the truth, he was penalised by not being given the reward money. Had he chosen to lie, and to say that he had indeed known of the reward, he would have received the money. This raises the issue of whether the court should punish those who tell the truth and reward those who lie. Furthermore, the reasoning for the decision, given by the judge, was that forgetting something (in this case, the reward) is the same as never having heard of it. Whilst we can perhaps understand what the judge was trying to achieve, the argument can be questioned if used in any other context (for example, forgetting an assignment is certainly not the same as never having known about it!).

However, in commenting on, or criticising, decisions in cases, especially where they took place some time ago, it should always be remembered that we may not know the whole picture. For example, going back to the scenario in *Clarke*, would there be, or should there be, the same amount of sympathy towards a defendant who was a known villain as there would be towards a known local person who genuinely tried to be helpful to the police?

'For every action, there is an equal and opposite criticism.'
(Harrison's postulate)

This kind of reasoning can be applied to many other cases, and throughout the book there are pointers to start you thinking in this way in the form of boxed questions. With some of these, suggested answers become obvious as you continue to read the text (although you should, by now, feel free to challenge, and to differ in opinion), and with others the answers are much more open to personal persuasion. There are also suggestions for you to find practical examples from everyday life to illustrate your work.

Fairness in contract law

Quite often, in contract law, the moral issue involved is simply one of fairness. Does the case bring about a just result, both for the parties involved at the time, and for those who depend on the legal authority of the case as it forms a precedent? This can almost always be used as a point of analytical comment when writing essays. This approach not only makes learning the rules of contract law much more interesting, but also earns extra marks in examinations.

An important area for analysis and comment is that of protection of the party with weaker bargaining power. When two parties meet with equal standing, such as two companies or two individual people in business, they negotiate on equal terms. They are both protective of their own position, either by earning money or in receiving goods of value. Both parties, therefore, have strength of argument, and are said to have equal bargaining power. It is quite different, however, if a person who is not involved in the business world, buys an item about which they know very little from a person who is in business. The buyer in this situation is said to lack bargaining power.

This is normally the position of the consumer, and that is why the law has been so pro-active in protecting the consumer. A vast quantity of statute law has evolved over the last twenty years or so, in an effort to ensure fair bargaining for all of us when we act as consumers, doing our shopping, travelling on public transport, and so on. We all pay for this, of course, indirectly. If we are able to reject faulty goods, and be certain of good service or a refund, then the cost is higher to the provider, and this cost is eventually passed on to the consumer. There is little doubt, however, that we would all rather pay a little more for the sake of this protection. In general the law of consumer protection is acknowledged to be much fairer now than thirty years ago, and is built upon strong moral arguments. In order to prepare for synoptic assessment using other areas of contract law, do consider all the issues raised in the main chapters. Where a question is posed, consider *your* response, before going on to read the rest of the chapter.

Law and morals

You may know about other areas of law, and you will be able to use them here in an overview of the system to distinguish between law and morals. A good distinction is to compare the following:

- a practical arrangement, such as the taxing of a motor car, which is purely a method of raising money to build and maintain roads, etc., and
- the law of murder, which is clearly based upon moral and religious beliefs.

There is obviously a great overlap between many areas of the law in general and major moral issues, for example in genetic engineering and the issue of the use of foetal material. However, there are also many cases in contract law which you can use to show the difference between law and morals.

For example, the case of *Carlill v Carbolic Smoke Ball Company* is so familiar that we may forget the good that it did in changing the face of Victorian advertising, and in trying to ensure that extravagant promises were not made to consumers unless they could be backed up. Consider also the area of legal intent. It is generally considered a moral duty for a person to keep a promise, especially if it is given in exchange for the promise of another, such as, 'if you clean my car I will buy your lunch'. However, if this is between friends or members of a family, there would be no legal obligation involved. There is only a moral duty. Read the case of *Jones v Padvatton* (see Chapter 4, p. 69) regarding this. However, wherever a binding contract exists, a legal duty arises, so the same promise made in the context of business would be binding. This would be a good place to discuss the idea of honorary pledge clauses, such as *Jones v Vernons Pools* (see Chapter 4).

Consider the 'reward' cases, if a person returns a lost dog in response to a reward notice, they are entitled to claim the reward money. If they return the dog anyway, without having known about a reward being offered, they are not entitled to claim any money, following the case of *R v Clarke* (see Chapter 2). Does the law follow moral principles here?

You could use the developments in statute law to illustrate the way in which Parliament has stepped in to support case law and to uphold morals. It would be very wrong if people were led into contracts through lies. So the Misrepresentation Act 1967 has provided a (relatively) easy route to a remedy for such people. Equally, the Unfair Contract Terms Act 1977 has provided protection for consumers who may be in an unfair bargaining position and therefore open to exploitation. European law has added another dimension to this in requiring 'good faith', in its directive which formed the basis of the Unfair Terms in Consumer Contract Regulations 1999.

When changes occur in society, the law generally changes in line with current thought. The changes in law may lag a little behind those in society, and this is generally not a bad thing, as it would be impractical to change the law with every fleeting fashion. Many examples can be found, and you may well use some from your knowledge of the English legal system. For example, in the case of *British Rail v Herrington* (1972) the House of Lords used their new Practice Statement powers to overturn previous law and encourage large organisations, like British Rail, to ensure that the environment was a safe place for everyone, including children. The Abortion Act 1967 (now modified by the Human Fertilisation and Embryology Act 1990) raised emotive concerns, but one thing which it accomplished was a reduction in the number of 'back street' illegal abortions, undertaken in dangerous conditions.

Policy issues

Policy is another area which you can illustrate by calling on material already studied in law. It not difficult to think of cases where the court wished to formulate and uphold 'rules', but at the same time bring about a result which reflected a certain line of thought or behaviour. In the performance of an existing duty, for example, the court in *Collins v Godefroy* would not have wanted to endorse the right of a lawyer to claim extra money for obeying the summons of the court to appear as a witness. However, they obviously felt in *Williams v Roffey* that it was important to support commercial arrangements made within the context of a building trade in recession. When the case of *Re Selectmove* raised a similar argument regarding payment to the Inland Revenue of outstanding tax, however, this more flexible approach was not evident, and one can only wonder whether the outcome would have been the same had the debt been owed to an individual rather than a government body. Lord Denning had, after all, stretched the idea of 'extra' duty to its limits in order to find payment for the single mother in *Ward v Byham*.

Such cases should follow a line of precedent, of course, but it is almost always possible to distinguish cases on the facts, if the courts so wish. How much they should do this is a debatable point. If they do not make decisions in cases which are acceptable to society, then it is a lengthy process to appeal to the House of Lords or to legislate to correct the mistake. However, the opposite argument is that we leave some important law-making in the hands of a small body of judges who are not democratically elected.

So, it can be seen, that to succeed in the kind of synoptic paper which asks you to make these links, what is needed is a good knowledge of your area of substantive law (contract law in this case), a working knowledge of the material studied on the English legal system, and the initiative to take an overview, combine the two, and apply what you know to the question under discussion.

Contextual skills in examination

When you learn about areas of the English legal system for examination at AS-level, the scene is set for then developing that body of knowledge and taking a look in depth at an area of substantive law – again, in this case, the law of contract. The wider context of contract law, however, should not be forgotten. The examination boards take that view too, and all boards include marks for analytical content in marking essay questions. This is nothing new, and has been happening for years. What is new, however, is that the new A2 specifications (for the full A-level qualification) must include a clear element of synoptic assessment – that is the law of contract set into the context of the English legal system.

Module 6: concepts of law, for AQA

Although this paper is 'new' to the A2 assessment pattern for A-level, the format of the paper is well established. The paper is 1 hour 30 minutes long, and contains four essay questions, of which you are required to answer two.

The issues are broad, and can be based on whatever areas of law you have already studied. In fact, you are particularly reminded in the instructions on the paper to 'illustrate your answers with relevant material gained in your study in any of the modules'. This does not just mean that you may do so – it means that to obtain a good mark you must do so. As you are studying contract law, make use of the cases and issues raised within this module.

Read the material on synoptic assessment, and the approach to the examination, and this will help you to form in depth analytical ideas about an area of contract law. Do consider the issues raised in the main chapters of this book. Where a question is posed, consider your response, before going on to read the rest of the chapter. Refer to the ideas above, add your own views and your own illustrations from studying contract law and possibly other areas of law too, and plan an answer to one or two of the questions which follow.

The questions below are examples of the kind of questions you should be able to answer to do well in this unit.

---

1 'Often judges have the difficult task of balancing the interests of one party with those of another'. Using cases from civil and/or criminal law, consider how effectively this is done.

2 The law needs to develop continually. To what extent are Parliament and the judiciary free to do this?

3 Using cases from any area of law to illustrate your answer, discuss the difference(s) between law and justice.

4 To what extent is fault a central feature in deciding liability or guilt in law?

5 An ordinary person, if asked, may expect the law to reflect moral values in society. To what extent does it do so?

---

19 Sources of contract law

Although as students of law we may often find out many of the rules of contract law by reading them in textbooks, these are not where the law was first formulated and are really the textbook writer's opinion of what they believe the law to be. These books are not, then, original or primary sources of law. So what do we mean by original sources?

Case law

Much of our modern law of contract is based on decisions in cases which have been heard in court, and these recorded decisions, the speeches of judges, form an important primary source of contract law. You may have encountered cases from contract law when studying judicial precedent, such as *Merritt v Merritt*, or the lines of cases involving attempts to avoid the doctrine of privity. For example, in *Port Line Ltd v Ben Line Steamers Ltd* the rules of precedent allowed the court to say that the decision in *Strathcona Steamship Co v Dominion Coal Co* was wrong (and statute law now covers the problem which arose). This idea of building up a body of law through decided cases is a practical one, founded in English common law. It provides solutions to problems when issues arise as society develops and changes, and these solutions can be tailored to the circumstances and to the situations of the parties. However, while there are great advantages to case law, there are drawbacks too, one of them being that the law can only change in this way if a suitable case is taken to an appropriate level of court.

Statute Law

A second source of contract law which is being used increasingly in the area of contract law is that of statutes. A statute, or Act of Parliament, is a decree from those running the country, and partly elected by the people of the country, as to how we should behave. The great advantage of a statute is that it can be planned, views and reports can be taken into account in forming it, and it can be considered and debated by a number of experts to form a comprehensive assessment of an area of law. This will then apply universally across the country from a date stated within the statute.

An interesting aspect of statute law is that although it is decreed by Parliament, it is still fine-tuned by the courts, as it is their role to interpret it on a daily basis. You may have come across contract cases when studying statutory interpretation, e.g. *Fisher v Bell* regarding whether a shop window display is an offer or an invitation to treat.

Examples of statutes affecting contract law include the Sale of Goods Act 1979, which made huge inroads into protecting the rights of consumers, and the Misrepresentation Act 1967, which provided a much needed remedy of damages for those suffering from misrepresentation. Another example is found in the Unfair Contract Terms Act 1977, and this statute is a particularly good example of a change which would have been much more difficult to achieve by case law. Many cases had appeared in court to decide whether particular exemption clauses were valid. Each time a decision was made on a particular exemption clause, those seeking to use such clauses would devise an alternative form of wording which would in turn need further consideration. Parliament, through statute, was able to make a decree which applied to all such exemption clauses.

European law

A further source of contract law which is becoming increasingly important is European law. While we do not study primary sources of European law as an integral part of A-level contract law, they abound in other areas, such as employment law, and are certainly of immense importance in the forming of new statutes and making decisions in cases. The Unfair Terms in Consumer Contract Regulations 1994, for example, is a direct result of a European directive. A directive must be implemented by individual countries within the European Union, and Britain chose to implement the directive via the Regulations. The detail on these, found in Chapter 8, will show the European nature of this piece of legislation.

The following section of this chapter concerns the use of original sources of law. It is good to read these sometimes, to understand the way in which ideas are formulated and to become used to this kind of research. The sources below are those used by the examination board and include primary sources (cases and statutes), and in addition material selected from reports and authoritative textbooks.

Special study: synoptic assessment based on legal sources

First of all, be reassured. The idea of synoptic assessment is not to catch you out. The examination board **wants** people who have worked during their course to have A-level awards. Also reassuring is the fact that in synoptic assessment you will only be expected to know about areas of law which are already included in the rest of the syllabus.

Synoptic assessment is a combination of skills, but it is not really new to you. You will have used these skills in answering questions in your studies at AS-level, and in answering questions on the main Contract Law paper, by analysing and commenting on issues in essay questions and by applying your knowledge of law to problem situations. Now, all you need to do is refine your technique to answer questions using sources in a slightly different way in the examination.

During the year, well before the examinations, you will be issued with a booklet containing a set of pre-released source materials. These materials will contain extracts from statutes, cases, academic articles, etc., and will be based on a theme, the new one for examination from 2007/9 being **consideration**. This means that *all* of the sources within the booklet concern some aspect of consideration, such as adequacy and sufficiency, past consideration and performance of existing duties as consideration. (*Note that from 2007 onwards, in the new 4-unit specification, there will* ***not*** *be a source directly based on AS material, as was the case in previous years.*) It should therefore be an encouragement to you to realise that in this examination you will sit a paper being absolutely sure of the topic on which you are to answer questions, i.e. consideration. This narrows the focus of your revision tremendously.

You are not allowed to take your own copy of the booklet into the examination room, but you will be issued with an identical 'clean' copy for the examination, which you can then use for reference in answering questions. You will not, therefore, need to learn a lot of new material off by heart – although, to enhance your answers, you will need to know about **some other** cases and materials on consideration, not included in the pre-released materials booklet.

It is vital that you are thoroughly familiar with the material before the examination and that you have thought about the kind of issues that could arise. In the examination you will be given a set of questions based on the pre-released material and you will need to refer to the source material in answering the questions. However, this is certainly not just a comprehension test needing no revision. You will be expected to bring into your answers your knowledge and ideas, as well as to respond to the material and the questions themselves.

The examination is *synoptic* – which means that although the materials are based on your A2 work, the questions are intended to bring together various strands of previous knowledge. You will need to revise Chapter 3: Consideration <u>very thoroughly</u>. It would also be good to recap the work you did for the AS paper on sources of law, especially the areas of judicial precedent and law reform. You may wish to refer to Chapter 6 of the companion book in this series, *AS Law*, in order to deal with the AS material.

The current pre-released source materials for OCR follow below, and we will examine some of the issues that are raised by these materials which could provide a useful basis of comment and analysis and help you to answer the questions on the Special Study paper.

SOURCE I

Consideration means some thing which is of some value in the eye of the law, moving from the plaintiff: it may be of some benefit to the plaintiff or some detriment to the defendant; but at all events it must be moving from the plaintiff. Now that which is suggested as the consideration here, a pious respect for the wishes of the testator, does not in any way move from the plaintiff; it moves from the testator; therefore, legally speaking, it forms no part of the consideration.

Adapted from the judgment of Patteson J in *Thomas v Thomas* [1842] 2 QB 851.

This is an extract from a judgment that highlights some principles of consideration. Revise the case – the one where a widow paid a very small amount of ground rent in order to stay in the family home after her husband died. The judgment concentrates on the meaning of consideration, i.e. the 'thing' given in exchange for the promise of the other party. The following points arise from this passage concerning two rules of consideration:

- **Consideration must be of 'some value'.** What exactly does this mean? It is a vague expression – it could relate to money, goods, something visible, etc. The phrase has, in fact, been explained and refined by the facts of the case, and in the cases which follow – *by the doctrine of precedent*, as various consideration cases have followed each other to court. In this particular case it was said that the wishes of the late Mr Thomas would not be 'of value', but that the money paid by his wife as ground rent, however small the amount, would form sufficient (valid) consideration. This clearly indicates that a monetary value, however small, would be sufficient consideration (although it is obviously not adequate). **Hint** – do remember to use the words **sufficient** (something recognisable) and **adequate** (market value) correctly!

- **Consideration must move from the promissee.** This means that the person wishing to enforce a contract must have given something to the bargain. The promissee in this case was Mrs Thomas who could not, then, claim that the wishes of her husband would amount to consideration as they came from her husband. However, she could claim that the money that *she* paid for rent was valid consideration to enforce the contract.

SOURCE 2

It has been settled for well over three hundred years that the courts will not inquire into the 'adequacy of consideration'. By this is meant that they will not seek to measure the comparative value of the defendant's promise and of the act or promise given by the plaintiff in exchange for it, nor will they denounce an agreement merely because it seems unfair. The promise must, indeed, have been procured by the offer of some return capable of expression in terms of value. A parent who makes a promise 'in consideration of natural love and affection' or to induce his son to refrain from boring him with complaints, as in *White v Bluett*, cannot be sued upon it, since the essential elements of a bargain are lacking. But if these elements be present the courts will not balance the one side against the other. The parties are presumed to be capable of appreciating their own interests and of reaching their own equilibrium.

A modern illustration of the premise that it is for the parties to make their own bargain is afforded by the current practice of manufacturers to recommend the sale of their goods by offering, as an inducement to buy, something more than the goods themselves. In *Chappell & Co Ltd v Nestlé Co Ltd* (1960) the plaintiffs owned the copyright in a dance tune. Nestlé offered records of the tune to the public for 1s 6d, but required, in addition to the money, three wrappers of their sixpenny bars of chocolate. When they received the wrappers they threw them away. Their main object was to advertise the chocolate, but they also made a profit on the sale of the records. The plaintiffs sued the defendants for infringement of copyright. The defendants offered royalty based on the price of the record. The plaintiffs refused the offer, contending that the money price was only part of the consideration and that the balance was represented by the three wrappers. The House of Lords by a majority gave judgment for the plaintiffs. It was unrealistic to hold that the wrappers were not part of the consideration. The offer was to supply a record in return, not simply for money, but for the wrappers as well.

Adapted from *Cheshire, Fifoot and Furmston's Law of Contract*, Furmston (1996) Butterworths: 84–7.

This extract is from a well-established textbook on contract law. It is about two cases, *White* v *Bluett* where a son promised to stop complaining about the distribution of his father's estate in exchange from being released from a debt, and *Chappel* v *Nestlé*, where chocolate wrappers were sent to the manufacturers and exchanged for a 'free' record. The extract deals with the issue of sufficiency and adequacy of consideration. You should remember the rule:

Consideration must be sufficient but need not be adequate

(Reminder – use these words correctly)

It could be said that these cases set the boundaries of what will be accepted as consideration. Whatever is given as consideration must be recognisable in some way (remember – it must be of 'some value') but need not necessarily be of monetary worth or market value – the price we would normally expect. This is a good illustration of later cases refining the principle of consideration through *precedent*. In *White v Bluett* it was decided that the son's promise was not of sufficient value to form valid consideration. Maybe it was too vague, or it could be that the court felt that promises within the confines of relationships in a family home were not appropriate. However, in *Chappell v Nestlé* it was held that chocolate wrappers of no apparent worth were part of the consideration.

Revise the facts of these cases so that you can compare them.

SOURCE 3

The question is whether the three wrappers were part of the consideration. I think that they are part of the consideration. They are so described in the offer. 'They [the wrappers] will help you to get smash hit recordings.' It is said that, when received, the wrappers are of no value to the respondents, the Nestlé Co Ltd. This I would have though to be irrelevant. A contracting party can stipulate for what consideration he chooses. A peppercorn does not cease to be goods consideration if it is established that the promissee does not like pepper and will throw away the corn.

Adapted from the judgment of Lord Somervell in *Chappell and Co Ltd v Nestlé Co Ltd* [1960] AC 87.

This is again about the case of the chocolate wrappers being exchanged for a 'free' record. From the actual words of this judgment in *Chappell v Nestlé* it could be argued that it really does not matter whether consideration is 'of value' at all. The judge seems to be saying that a party can request anything, even if it is of *no* value. On the other hand, if there is something recognisable in existence, even if it has no monetary value, surely it is of value to the person requesting it? Here it could be argued that the wrappers represented proof of increased sales and were therefore of some value to the party requesting them.

The case is a step forward in **precedent** in that the courts are taking the opportunity to further define what will amount to sufficient consideration. The peppercorn is a good example. It has little or no monetary worth. The person requesting it may not like pepper, and may not want to keep the 'corn'. However this does not matter if it can be seen and recognised as an item by the courts, just as clearly as a piece of jewellery or any other item, and if it is exactly the item requested by a party to a contract.

SOURCE 4

Although a nominal consideration will suffice at law, there are cases in which the act or forbearance, promised or performed, is of such a trifling character that it becomes doubtful whether it can be regarded as consideration at all.

The reason for this rule, however, is not to be found in the trifling value of the consideration, but in the requirement that it must be given in exchange for the promise. This last requirement also explains the general rule that 'past consideration' is no consideration. This means that an act done before the promise was made cannot normally be the consideration for it. Consideration is, for example, past where, after an employee has retired, his employer promises to pay him a sum of money in recognition of his past services. The same is true where goods are sold and at some later time the seller gives a guarantee as to their quality. But there is obviously some elasticity in the notion of past consideration. If the promise and the previous act are substantially one transaction, the consideration is not past merely because there is a (relatively short) interval of time between them.

An act for which no recompense was fixed before it was done can constitute consideration for a subsequent promise to pay for it if it was done at the request of the promisor, if the understanding of the parties when it was done was that it was to be paid for, and if a promise to pay for it would, had it been made in advance, have been legally enforceable. The rule covers the common case in which services are rendered on a commercial basis, but the rate of remuneration is only agreed after they have been rendered. On the same principle, a past promise made at the request of one party can constitute consideration for a counter-promise later made by that party.

Adapted from *An Outline of the Law of Contract*, G.H. Treitel (1995) Butterworths: 32–3.

This is an extract from a textbook and the writer, Treitel, is discussing the rule concerning past consideration. So at this point you should:

- be familiar with the rule **past consideration is no consideration**, i.e. an act which has already been completed at the time of contract will not amount to valid consideration;
- know that there are exceptions to this rule, e.g. if it was expected all along that payment would be made, or in an employment situation;
- revise the facts of some cases concerning past consideration, e.g. *Roscorla* v *Thomas* (promises were made *after* a sale had taken place that a horse was 'sound and free from vice'); *Re McArdle* (where money was promised *after* accommodation was renovated for an elderly relative); *Lampleigh v Braithwait* (a promise was made *after* a friend had obtained a pardon from the King, *but* payment of expenses had been expected); *Re Casey's Patents* (a promise was made to give a share of a patent as payment for work done *after* the work had been completed, *but* some kind of payment was expected all along).

SOURCE 5

The rule in English law is that 'past consideration is no consideration'. In defining consideration, consideration for a promise has to be given in return for a promise, in other words there has to be a causal link between the two promises in order for the contract to be enforceable. If a party makes a promise subsequent to some action carried out by the other party, then that promise can only be regarded as an expression of gratitude, a gift, and nothing more.

It should be noted carefully that past consideration means past in relation to the promise that the plaintiff is seeking to enforce and not in relation to the time at which the plaintiff is seeking to enforce the defendant's promise.

Two cases traditionally illustrate the principle as regards past consideration: *Roscorla v Thomas* (1842) 3 QB 234 and the modern authority *Re McArdle* (1951) Ch 669.

In *Lampleigh v Braithwait* (1605) Braithwait had killed another man and asked Lampleigh to secure a pardon. Lampleigh went to considerable effort to secure the pardon for Braithwait who subsequently promised to pay Lampleigh £100. Braithwait then failed to pay the £100 and was sued. Clearly on the basis of past consideration, the efforts of Lampleigh were in the past in relation to the promise to pay and he should have failed in his action. The court, however, held that the original request by Braithwait in fact contained an implied promise that he would reward and reimburse Lampleigh for his efforts. Thus the previous request and the subsequent promise were part of the same transaction and as such were enforceable.

It should be noted that the principle only applies if the plaintiff's services had been rendered at the defendant's request and that it was implicit that both parties must have understood that the plaintiff's services would have to be paid for. Further, the implication of the promise to pay normally only arises in a commercial relationship between the parties.

The principle in *Lampleigh v Braithwait* has been affirmed and restated by Lord Scarman in *Pao On v Lau Yiu Long* [1975] 3 All ER 65 as follows:

An act done before the giving of a promise to make a payment or to confer some other benefit can sometimes be consideration for the promise. The act must have been done at the promisor's request, the parties must have understood that the act was to be remunerated further by a payment or the conferment of some other benefit and payment, or the conferment of a benefit must have been legally enforceable had it been promised in advance.

Adapted from *The Law of Contract,* Paul Richards (1997) Pitman: 49–50.

This is another extract from a textbook. The writer, Paul Richards, provides further comment on the cases concerning past consideration. It is worth

---

spending some time working out *how* and *why* the rules have evolved through the precedent of cases so you can comment on them. For example:

- Are the exceptions to the rule an attempt, in individual cases, to bring about just results where otherwise a judgment purely following *precedent* may seem unduly harsh? It seems highly likely that the court thought so in *Lampleigh v Braithwait*.

- In the passage above importance is placed on the intentions, or request, of the parties. It is likely that whenever a person carries out work for another in a commercial context the parties themselves intend there to be payment for it. This would explain the decision in both *Lampleigh* and *Re Casey's Patents*.

- It could be argued, then, that these cases form a way of avoiding an awkward *precedent*.

SOURCE 6

In many contractual situations, it makes perfectly good sense for a party to promise an extra reward in return for the other party performing what he is already obliged to do. Provided that the promise is given freely, it is irrational for the law to obstruct the enforcement of the promise by insisting on the classical requirement of exchange (particularly in the light of the development of an independent doctrine of economic duress). Having greater regard for commercial considerations than for classical theory, in the landmark case of *Williams v Roffey Bros and Nicholls (Contractors) Ltd*, the Court of Appeal held that a promise by A to carry out his existing contractual obligations to B may count as good consideration in relation to a promise freely given by B to pay A an additional sum for the performance of these obligations.

Building on the analogous cases of *Ward v Byham*, *Williams v Williams*, and *Pao On v Lau Yiu Long*, Glidewell LJ summarised the legal position as follows:

(i) if A has entered into a contract with B to do work for or to supply goods or services to B in return for payment by B; and

(ii) at some stage before A has completely performed his obligations under the contract B has reason to doubt whether A will, or will be able to, complete his side of the bargain; and

(iii) B thereupon promises A an additional payment in return for A's promise to perform his contractual obligations on time; and

(iv) as a result of giving his promise, B obtains in practice a benefit, or obviates a disbenefit; and

(v) B's promise is not given as the result of economic duress or fraud on the part of A; then

(vi) the benefit to B is capable of being consideration for B's promise, so that the promise will be legally binding.

But in the light of (iv) what practical benefit did accrue to the defendants?

Given the long-standing interpretation of *Stilk v Myrick* in the standard textbooks how could the plaintiff be entitled to recover any part of the additional payments? It might be argued that in *Stilk v Myrick* the promise was gratuitous, or that the promisor derived no benefit, but these lines of argument seem to be question-begging, and unconvincing. The better answer, and the one most explicitly accepted by Purchas LJ, must be that *Stilk v Myrick* was a case involving what would now be recognised as economic duress. Even if we accept, however, that there was no economic duress in *Williams v Roffey* what consideration did the plaintiff provide?

Counsel for the defendants in *Williams v Roffey* conceded that the promise to pay additional sums secured some practical benefit. In particular, it improved the chances of the plaintiff continuing to work which, in turn, meant that the defendants might avoid having to pay liquidated damages for late completion, and might avoid the inconvenience and expense involved in engaging another carpenter to complete the sub-contract work. The point is that the defendants, guided by economic imperatives, preferred to cut their losses rather than gain a Pyrrhic victory by standing on their legal rights.

Adapted from *Key Issues in Contract*, John Adams and Roger Brownsword (1995) Butterworths.

This is an extract from another book on the law of contract. It focuses on the rule that the **performance of an existing duty does not normally amount to consideration**.

The source is a commentary on the rule using the case of *Williams v Roffey*. This is an important case in this area of consideration, so you need to know the facts well.

Reminder: Owners of property contracted with builders to renovate the property. They in turn contracted with carpenters, who were unable to complete by the original deadline for the price originally agreed. A further agreement was made in order to finish the work.

It may help you to draw a diagram something like this, showing exactly what consideration was agreed by each party:

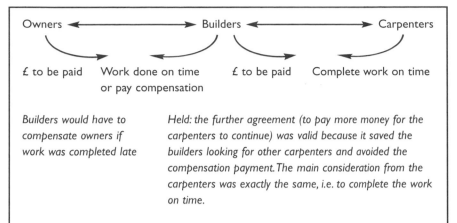

Builders would have to compensate owners if work was completed late

Held: the further agreement (to pay more money for the carpenters to continue) was valid because it saved the builders looking for other carpenters and avoided the compensation payment. The main consideration from the carpenters was exactly the same, i.e. to complete the work on time.

Note: *Williams v Roffey* is based on the principles in *Stilk v Myrick* (performance of an existing duty is not good consideration), *Hartley v Ponsonby* (performing more that the existing duty may be valid) and *Ward v Byham* (very little 'extra' may suffice). You should revise these rules and the facts of the cases, and reflect on how they have developed through precedent.
Remember that:

- The important case of *Williams v Roffey* is an existing *contractual* duty, as opposed to a duty owed under the law of the land. (Revise the facts of *Roffey* – what *exactly* was seen as a practical benefit or the avoidance of a disadvantage?)

- *Williams v Roffey* is an excellent example of the difficulties of the courts having to decide whether to follow the strict rules of precedent in order to maintain certainty, or to attempt to tailor the 'rules' to take into account commercial reality – a flexible approach.

- There was found to be no economic duress in *Roffey* (we take this as a finding of fact when the judges listened to the evidence). It would be good to compare this with the more recent case of *Carillion Construction v Felix* (see Chapter 10: Duress).

SOURCE 7

The Board agrees with the submission of counsel for the plaintiffs that the consideration expressly stated in the written guarantee is sufficient in law to support Lau's promise of indemnity. An act done before the giving of a promise to make a payment or to confer some other benefit can sometimes be consideration for the promise. The act must have been done at the promisor's request, the parties must have understood that the act was to be remunerated either by a payment or the conferment of some other benefit, and payment, or the conferment of a benefit, must have been legally enforceable had it been promised in advance. All three features are present in this case. The promise given by Fu Chip under the main agreement not to sell the shares for a year was at Lau's request. The parties understood at the time of the main agreement that the restriction on selling must be compensated for by the benefit of a guarantee against a drop in price: and such a guarantee would be legally enforceable. The agreed cancellation of the subsidiary agreement left, as the parties knew, the Paos unprotected in a respect in which at the time of the main agreement all were agreed they should be protected.

Adapted from the judgment of Lord Scarman in *Pao On v Lau Yiu Long* [1979] 3 All ER 65 PC.

Again, in this judgment emphasis is placed on the request of the promisor alongside the understanding that some benefit is being conferred. It is important to read the case and be sure that you can explain the principles involved, using *other cases that you know on existing duty to illustrate your answer.*

SOURCE 8

The colliery owners repudiated liability on the grounds that there was no consideration for the promise to pay for the police protection and that such an agreement was against public policy. The case was tried by Bailhache J and he entered judgment for the plaintiffs saying: 'There is an obligation on the police to afford efficient protection, but if an individual asks for special protection in a particular form, for the special protection so asked for in that particular form, the individual must pay.'

This decision was affirmed by a majority on appeal (Banks and Scrutton LJJ; Atkin LJ dissenting). The colliery owners now appeal and ask that judgment should be entered for them.

It appears to me that there is nothing in the first point made for the colliery owners that there was no consideration made for the promise. It is clear that there was abundant consideration. The police authorities thought that it would be best to give protection by means of a flying column of police, but the colliery owners wanted the 'garrison' and promised to pay for it if it was sent.

Adapted from the judgment of Viscount Cave LC in *Glassbrook Bros Ltd v Glamorgan County Council* [1925] AC 270 HL.

This is part of the judgment from the line of cases concerning existing duty owed under the law of the land rather than by contract. *Collins v Godefroy* (see Chapter 3) is a good example of the basic principle, concerning a lawyer who was already under an order to give evidence and could not, therefore, enforce payment from an individual for giving evidence in court. In the case here the police were under a duty to keep the peace, and the emphasis was on the 'extra' work undertaken by them in giving added protection to this colliery (although this was also at the request of the colliery owners). One of the problems with these cases is that there is no definition of how much 'extra' must be undertaken. *Ward v Byham* indicates that it may be very little indeed.

SOURCE 9

What consideration has moved from the plaintiff to support the promise to pay the extra £10,300 added to the lump sum provision? In the particular circumstances there was clearly a commercial advantage to both sides from a pragmatic point of view in reaching the agreement of 9 April. The defendants were on risk that as a result of the bargain that they had struck the plaintiff would not, or indeed possibly could not, comply with his existing obligations without further finance. As a result of the agreement the defendants secured their position commercially. There was, however, no obligation added to the contractual duties imposed upon the plaintiff under the original contract. *Prima facie* this would appear to be a classic *Stilk v Myrick* case. It was, however, open to the plaintiff to be in deliberate breach of the contract in order to 'cut his losses' commercially. In normal circumstances the suggestion that a contracting party can rely upon his own breach to establish consideration is distinctly unattractive. In many cases it obviously would be and if there was any element of duress brought upon the other contracting party under the modern development of this branch of the law the proposed breaker of the contract would not benefit. I consider that the modern approach to the question of consideration would be that where there were benefits derived by each party to a contract of variation even though one party did not suffer a detriment this would not be fatal to establishing sufficient consideration to support the agreement. If both parties benefit from an agreement it is not necessary that each also suffers a detriment. On the facts the judge was entitled to reach the conclusion that consideration existed. I would not disturb that finding.

Adapted from the judgment of Purchas LJ in *Williams v Roffey Bros and Nicholls (Contractors) Ltd* [1990] 1 All ER 512 CA.

This is also about *Williams v Roffey*, but is part of the judgment in the case. The judge (Purchas LJ) explains the outcome in *Roffey* by saying that where a contract of variation takes place (as it did in the further contract with the carpenters), then it is enough that both parties obtain *some* practical benefit. What was the benefit here? It was said in the case that because the carpenters were promised extra money (i) the builders avoided the need to obtain other carpenters, and (ii) by having the work completed on time they avoided a liquidated damages payment.

▶

> This extract is one of several speeches and does not set out the facts. You should therefore revise the facts of *Williams v Roffey* and know the basis of the decision, so that you can set it in the context of the precedent of the other existing duty cases and discuss its merits.

SOURCE 10

While consideration remains a fundamental requirement before a contract not under seal can be enforced, the policy of the law in its search to do justice between the parties has developed considerably since the early nineteenth century when *Stilk v Myrick* was decided. In the late twentieth century I do not believe that the rigid approach to the concept of consideration to be found in *Stilk v Myrick* is either necessary or desirable. Consideration there must still be but in my judgment the courts nowadays should be more ready to find its existence so as to reflect the intention of the parties to the contract where the bargaining powers are not unequal and where the finding of consideration reflects the true intention of the parties.

Adapted from the judgment of Russell LJ in *Williams v Roffey Bros and Nicholls (Contractors) Ltd* [1990] 1 All ER 512 CA.

> Another extract from the same case, this time from the judgment of Russell LJ. The fact that there is so much on this case in the booklet indicates the importance that lawyers have placed upon it. Note that the case reached the Court of Appeal but not the House of Lords. There is still, then, a possibility of it being overruled one day. However, many lawyers believe that it is time that the courts did not just rely on the precedent of *Stilk v Myrick* but review the area of existing duty, especially in the context of modern commerce, such as the building trade. This case is therefore welcomed by many as a modern approach to the practical difficulties encountered in such contracts.
>
> Russell LJ is of the opinion here that, especially where parties are of equal standing, the courts should be more willing to 'find' consideration in order to do justice and reflect the intention of the parties.
>
> A case that followed *Williams v Roffey* is *Re Selectmove*. It could have confirmed the decision but actually went against it. However, *Re Selectmove* concerned part payment of a debt of income tax to the Inland Revenue, so may be considered partly as a policy decision and to turn on its own particular facts.

SOURCE 11

If a party performs an act which is merely a discharge of a pre-existing obligation, there is no consideration, but where a party does more than he was already bound to do, there may be consideration. The pre-existing obligation may arise out of a contract between the same parties, under the public law or out of a contract with a third party.

In relation to the first category, the question to be asked is whether the party claiming to have given consideration has done any more than he was bound to do under a previous contract with the other party. If the answer is no, then there is no consideration furnished for the further promise of the other contracting party.

The third category which is traditionally examined under this heading considers the situation where one party is claiming to have given consideration by doing what he was already bound to do under a pre-existing contract with a third party. However, this category can be distinguished from the previous two in the sense that the performance of the pre-existing duty owed to a third party will invariably be regarded as sufficient consideration for a promise given by the promisee.

Shadwell v Shadwell and *Scotson v Pegg* are often stated as authorities for the principle although the reasoning in the judgments is not without some flaws. Nevertheless, any doubts regarding the validity of the principle were swept away in *New Zealand Shipping Co v AM Satterthwaite & Co* (1975), where on appeal to the Privy Council the rule in *Scotson v Pegg* was applied. It was held by Lord Wilberforce that 'An agreement to do an act which the promisor is under an existing obligation to a third party to do, may quite well amount to valid consideration and does so in the present case: the promisee obtains the benefit of a direct obligation which he can enforce.'

This decision was given further approval by the decision of the Privy Council in *Pao On v Lau Yiu Long* (1980).

Adapted from *Law of Contract,* W.T. Major and Christine Taylor (1996) Pitman: 53–7.

The last source is slightly different. In this extract from a book the authors discuss the obligation to perform an existing duty owed under a contract to a third party. The usual explanation for these contracts being enforceable is that the promisor runs the risk of being sued by two parties, and this amounts to 'extra' consideration. Revise this area from Chapter 3.

A strategy for using the material

The source material is original – that is the idea of it. It is not a neat potted summary of cases, but original judgments using the words of the judges sitting in the cases, original wording from statutes and analysis from legal authors. The sources are made a little more approachable by being selective, so that you only have to read certain parts which contain key issues, but even so, to a student who has so far only been reading user-friendly textbooks and a helpful teacher for their supply of information, these can seem a little daunting. You can help to ease yourself into these sources in various ways:

- Identify the topics involved – it is not the whole of the law of contract, but selected areas of the doctrine of consideration. Re-read Chapter 3 of this book and hopefully this will immediately help you to focus your thoughts.

- Do not try to read the whole booklet in one session at the beginning. Decide on a method of working through the articles one at a time – see the suggestions below. It is daunting to have a task before you which seems immense, but it can be much more encouraging to think that you have something achievable ahead and then to complete comfortably what you set out to do.

- When you have read an extract, refer to your textbook and revise the cases involved thoroughly, to help understand the context.

- Make notes on what you have read – both short jottings in the margin of the materials and then more formally on paper. If there are words or phrases that you find difficult because of the language, look up the words in a dictionary and rephrase them. Try to summarise the extracts in your own words (see the next point).

- Think about questions or issues which may arise in an examination. You may be asked to explain part of an extract *in your own words* – so make sure that you can do this. If you were asked to do so, you would not receive any marks at all for merely copying out the section.

- When you have read several extracts, consider why they were included, and what the connection may be between two extracts. In particular, look for the development of the law of consideration through precedent. It is usually very mark-worthy in an examination to make links between extracts.

- Finally, think about any extra issues which may arise, or any alternative ways of wording questions or issues.

The list of extracts

Scan through the source material, and make your own list of the extracts, possibly leaving a small gap between them, in case you want to add in any comments. You can then tick the extracts on your list as you work on them. The following items are included:

Adapted from the judgment of Patteson J in *Thomas v Thomas* [1842] 2 QB 851.
Adapted from *Cheshire, Fifoot & Furmston's Law of Contract* (ed. Furmston), Butterworths.
Adapted from the judgment of Lord Somervell in *Chappell & Co Ltd v Nestlé Co Ltd* [1960] AC 87.
Adapted from *An Outline of the Law of Contract* by G.H. Treitel, Butterworths.

Adapted from *The Law of Contract* by Paul Richards, Pitman.

Adapted from *Key Issues in Contract* by John Adams and Roger Brownsword, Butterworths.

Adapted from the judgment of Lord Scarman in *Pao On v Lau Yiu Long* [1979] 3 All ER 65 PC.

Adapted from the judgment of Viscount Cave LC in *Glasbrook Bros Ltd v Glamorgan County Council* [1925] AC 270 HL.

Adapted from the judgment of Purchas LJ in *Williams v Roffey Bros & Nicholls (Contractors) Ltd* [1990] 1 All ER 512 CA.

Adapted from the judgment of Russell LJ in *Williams v Roffey Bros & Nicholls (Contractors) Ltd* [1990] 1 All ER 512 CA.

Adapted from *Law of Contract* by W.T. Major and Christine Taylor, Pitman.

Initial thoughts

You will see from the list of sources that they are a mixture of case judgments and sections from books. They all concern the development of the doctrine of consideration. Each judgment or book extract concerns at least one 'rule' of consideration, or a modification of those rules, so you should make sure that you have a summary of **all** of the rules and a note of any cases which could be used to illustrate them. You may then like to go through the sources and note down which rules arise in each one.

Read and make notes

*   The key to doing well on this paper really is familiarity with both the area of study and the materials. In this new set of sources, none of the writing is especially complex in style, so it would make sense to read them in the order in which they appear in the booklet.

*   The case which possibly complicates consideration most of all, and which therefore needs full treatment, is *Williams v Roffey*. It is worth studying this in detail and examining exactly why it is so important. What exactly can be seen as consideration in this case? Why are opinions so divided on its merits? Some see the case as a welcome willingness on the part of the Court of Appeal to take a realistic view of the difficulties in business, especially in the building trade during a difficult time of recession. Others see it as a bad decision which goes against the rules of consideration. A third view is that there should not, in modern society, be a need for consideration, where there is clearly no evidence of duress and where legal intent exists, so there is therefore no need to 'find' it artificially. Any of these views is equally acceptable in analysing for examination purposes, but you should be able to consider more than one view, and be able to explain your opinions in relation to the case(s).

The questions which you may be asked

Read the question paper carefully (as you would, of course, in any examination – but here the timing and structure may be less familiar). Note the marks (out of the total) awarded for each question – this will help you plan out your time. You will need a little time to read the questions carefully, and then you should divide the time left to give a fair proportion to each question. Remember that although you do need to write fully on each part, you should definitely **not** be writing as much as in a full essay on the main Contract paper, where you would have 40 to 45 minutes per question. You may need to be quite brief, but to the point, in some questions worth fewer marks. This is particularly true of the problem/scenario type questions.

You are likely to be asked something on the 'rules' of consideration – so make sure that you know these, which cases they stem from and which of the source materials refer to them. Since the main theme is consideration, you are likely to need to examine how rules have changed through cases, for example:

- In *Roscorla v Thomas* the principle of past consideration was applied to find that there was no binding contract, whereas in *Re Casey's Patents* the 'rule' was modified to allow Casey to receive his share.
- In *Stylk v Myrick* an existing duty was not seen as valid consideration, in *Hartley v Ponsonby* the court modified the rule where a party could be seen to have exceeded their existing duty, and in *Williams v Roffey* some practical benefit or the avoidance of a disadvantage was seen as consideration.

If you can form links in this way between precedent and consideration you will really improve your chances of high marks in this examination. Remember that this unit is synoptic, which means that it is not simply testing your knowledge of consideration, but your understanding of the way in which the cases and rules fit together, and how the system of precedent has enabled this development to take place. You can use any cases that you know from your study of contract law to answer questions.

A reminder

Do re-read, and learn, the material in Chapter 3 of this book on consideration and the section in your notes, or in the companion book *AS Law*, on precedent. Also look out for any cases that arise in this area before you take the examination, and any articles in the newspapers and journals.

Be confident in your basic knowledge – be familiar with the case law and the synoptic material and develop your own analysis and ideas on these areas. Most of all – good luck!

20 Key skills

Be reassured – key skills are nothing new. They are really ongoing skills that you will have largely acquired in your journey through education. Just as it is expected that you can write an essay in order to pass A-level law, it is also expected that you can read, summarise, form an argument, present your work in a reasonable way, etc.

What is new, is the increasing requirement to show that you have achieved a reasonable level of proficiency in these skills. To a prospective employer, or a university admissions tutor, these skills are an integral and essential part of your attainment. This is an encouragement to think positively and enthusiastically about key skills, because if you are studying A-level subjects, you should find it a reasonably straightforward task to assemble the evidence needed.

The government and examination boards have set out guidelines on what is expected and how this can be achieved. There follow some suggested activities which can be included in your portfolio of key skills, and which can, as a routine part of your study, help you to provide evidence that you are working at an appropriate level in the particular areas of skill.

Key skills to be assessed

The main key skills at level 3 are:

- C3   Communication
- N3   Application of number
- IT3 Information technology

The wider key skills at level 3 are:

- WO3 Working with others
- LP3 Improving own learning and performance
- PS3 Problem solving

To achieve a qualification in key skills, both internal and external assessment is involved. You will have to compile a portfolio of tasks undertaken across your studies, showing evidence that you are competent in each area of skill. This need not be a particularly difficult task, or much more than you would do in the normal course of studying at A-level. The ideas here will provide opportunities for you to demonstrate that you have the skills within the various categories, which you can use to compile your portfolio. It is difficult in an essay-based subject to show evidence of the skill of application of number, but there are many opportunities of using the other skills in achieving your goal of success in A-level law. The following are suggestions, pointing you to an area of study covered in most cases by this book where you can find material to help you. A few suggestions go beyond this book a little, linking into areas useful as revision for the synoptic assessment at the end of your course.

Communication

C3.1a: contribute to a group discussion about a complex subject

- Is it always necessary to identify offer and acceptance? (Chapter 2)
- How could revocation take place in a unilateral contract? (Chapter 2)
- Do we need a doctrine of consideration? (Chapter 3)
- Are honorary pledge clauses fair to the consumer? (Chapter 4)
- Is the level of protection given to minors in forming contracts satisfactory? (Chapter 5)
- Is the *Hong Kong Fir* approach to innominate terms satisfactory? (Chapter 7)
- What level of responsibility should be taken by banks in ensuring that a person being granted a loan takes independent advice? Should the whole loan be set aside for a finding of undue influence in such cases? (Chapter 10)
- When should a person's silence amount to a misrepresentation? (Chapter 11)
- When should a mistake of quality of subject matter render a contract void? (Chapter 12)
- How difficult must a contract become for it to be frustrated through impossiblity? (Chapter 14)
- What level of legal protection ought today's consumer to expect? (Chapter 16)

C3.1b: make a presentation about a complex subject, using at least one image to illustrate complex points

- Explain an area of contract law, ready for use on an overhead projector, using a diagram – use some of the diagrams in this book as a starting-point for gathering ideas. You could explain: termination of an offer (Chapter 2), the principles of privity, illustrating *Dunlop v Selfridge* (Chapter 9). Both of these lend themselves to a flowchart-type of illustration (see diagrams in the chapters).
- Explain the limits to the doctrine of frustation, using a diagram to help illustrate *Tsakiroglou Noblee Thorl* and/or *Maritime National Fish v Ocean Trawlers* (Chapter 14).

- You could usefully work on your synoptic material by producing a flow chart of the hierarchy of the civil courts along with an explanation of the appeal route.

- Make a presentation on consumer rights for a group of non-lawyers, including a chart illustrating the terms implied by sections 12–15 of Sale of Goods Act 1979 and Sale and Supply of Goods Act 1994 (Chapter 16).

C3.2: read and synthesise information from two extended documentsthat deal with a complex subject. One of these documents should includeat least one image

- Reading an extended document is not a problem – choose any legal article or case report. The following would be particularly useful and interesting: *Thornton v Shoe Lane Parking Ltd, Esso v Commissioners of Customs and Excise* (Chapter 2).

- In addition there are articles in the *Times* Law Supplements and other leading newspapers. Other possibilities include reports of the Law Commission and articles in the *New Law Journal* or on the internet (see sites in the resources section at the end of the book). Here you may well find a graph or illustration included in a document.

C3.3: write two different types of documents about complex subjects.One piece of writing should be an extended document and include atleast one image

- Write a full essay on a subject of interest to you, e.g. misrepresentation when selling goods (Chapter 11), the capacity of minors (Chapter 5), rights under the Sale of Goods Act 1979 (Chapter 16), methods of communicating acceptance (Chapter 2). You could include a detailed account of some leading cases, and illustrate some of them using diagrams, e.g. acceptance by post (draw a map to show why the post was a reasonable method in *Henthorn v Fraser*).

- Draft advice to a client based on a scenario from a part of the syllabus, e.g. a claim in misrepresentation, using a diagram to show possible remedies, or a claim by a third party in privity, using a diagram to illustrate the relationship between the parties.

Information technology

IT3.1: compare and use different sources to search for, and select, information required for two different purposes

- There is a selection of internet web site addresses in the resources list of this book. Using these you can read the case reports of the House of

Lords, statutes passed recently, e.g. the Contracts (Rights of Third Parties) Act 1999 (Chapter 9), and legal articles.

- Search the internet for examples of e-commerce, to suggest where an offer and acceptance may have been formed (Chapter 2), or search for examples of exemption clauses, to consider if they are valid (Chapter 8).

- Use a CDROM to research a topic of contract law, e.g. the *Times* reports on CDROM, Lawtex (see resources list).

IT3.2: explore, develop and exchange information and derive new information to meet two different purposes

- Design a mini-project, involving the creation of a database of cases in contract law, using one field to contain a key word to identify the main topic of the case. You could work as a team on this, so that a larger number of cases can be entered. This could be used for:
  - fellow students to access a set of cases on a topic by performing a query
  - the production of a Law magazine (again, working as a team)
  - e-mailing a list of cases on a particular topic in response to requests by other law students.

IT3.3: present information from different sources for two different purposes and audiences. Your work must include at least one example of text, one example of images and one example of numbers

- Create a report for members of staff, describing how your compiled your database. Illustrate how the system works, and how it is possible to incorporate some of the results into a Law magazine. Show a table of cases requested, and construct a chart to show how many times they were requested.

- Create a presentation to explain the principles of part-payment of a debt to fellow students (Chapter 3). Use a diagram to illustrate a composition agreement of creditors.

- Going beyond contract into synoptic topics you could make a presentation for your fellow students on the funding of civil cases, and compare the likely number of people who would qualify for legal aid with those who may qualify under a new system.

Working with others

The evidence for this area of skill needs to be presented in at least two substantial activities that each include tasks for WO3.1, WO3.2 and WO3.3. You need to show that you can work in a group and in one-to-one situations. The aspects of activity for which you need to provide evidence are:

- *WO3.1*: plan a group activity, agreeing objectives, responsibilities and working arrangements.
- *WO3.2*: work towards achieving the agreed objectives seeking to establish and maintain co-operative working relationships in meeting individual responsibilities.
- *WO3.3*: review the activity with others against the agreed objectives and agree ways of enhancing collaborative work.

Suggested activities

The organisation of a moot based on a given scenario (many of the problem questions at the ends of chapters are suitable for this). The stages could be:

- Meet as a group and organise the breakdown of tasks, e.g. there will need to be agreement on pairs or small groups researching different legal aspects of the problem, including obtaining case details and references to be cited, and preparing speeches for presentation. Appoint a leader to co-ordinate the exchange of information and to coordinate communication. Establish a communication route – use e-mail if practical. Agree on deadlines, and on the method of recording the information.
- Carry out the research in agreed groups. Co-operate with members of the group in sharing information and the burden of recording, so that deadlines are met. Monitor problems with working relationships, to ensure that goals are achieved. Review progress and goals, changing plans by agreement if necessary.
- Hold the moot, inviting others to attend. You could ask a teacher or a fellow student to preside.
- Arrange a post-moot discussion group to give feedback. Encourage this to include positive criticism, with suggestions for improvement.

Make a presentation on a given topic of general interest from the syllabus, e.g. minors' contracts. This could be for presentation to the year group.

- Meet as a group and organise the distribution of tasks, e.g. there will need to be agreement on pairs or small groups researching different legal aspects of the problem, including obtaining case details and references to be cited, and preparing material for presentation, e.g. text of oral presentation, OHP (overhead projector) text, OHP illustrations (alternatively prepare text and illustrations for a Powerpoint presentation, if facilities for this are available on the computer network). Appoint a leader to co-ordinate the exchange of information and to co-ordinate communication. Establish a communication route – use e-mail if practical. Agree on deadlines, and on the method of recording the information.
- Carry out the research in agreed groups. Co-operate with members of the group in sharing information and the burden of recording, so that

deadlines are met. Monitor problems with working relationships, to ensure that goals are achieved. Review progress and goals, changing plans by agreement if necessary. Ensure that the style of presentation is consistent.

- Give the presentation, inviting others to attend.
- Arrange a post-moot discussion group to give feedback. Encourage this to include positive criticism, with suggestions for improvement. Alternatively this could be done by a questionnaire completed by those attending.

Problem solving

For this skill you need to follow through a complex activity which involves identifying a problem and providing a solution. The key skills syllabus requires you to implement a solution. You can easily find a problem scenario from contract law – most of the problems in the end of chapter questions would be suitable. The providing of a solution for this kind of theoretical problem is a feature of this course. You cannot, however, implement the solution, since the scenarios provided are hypothetical, not real cases to be taken to court, so your evidence here will be limited to PS3.1 and PS3.2.

- *PS3.1*: recognise, explore and describe the problem, and agree the standards for its solution.
- *PS3.2*: generate and compare at least two options which could be used to solve the problem, and justify the option for taking forward.

Suggested activity

Choose a problem question and research it in some detail. Compile your answer to the problem, and review the work done, considering any possible practical alternative solutions.

Improve own learning performance

To provide evidence of improvement you will need two examples of study-based learning, two examples of activity-based learning and one example of using learning from at least two different contexts to meet the demands of a new situation. For this assessment it is important to arrange to meet a tutor who will support you in providing the necessary evidence.
A plan could be drawn up to include the following steps:

- *LP3.1*: agree targets and plan how these will be met, using support from appropriate people.
- *LP3.2*: use your plan, seeking and using feedback and support from relevant sources to help meet your targets, and using different ways of learning to meet new demands.

- *LP3.3*: review progress in meeting targets, establishing evidence of achievements, and agree action for improving performance using support from appropriate people.

Suggested activity

You can monitor progress in many ways, but each should include appropriate feedback, recording of achievement and setting of targets:

- through essay-writing and solving scenario-type problems as homework assignments
- through timed essays
- through case tests
- through oral and practical contribution to group activities
- by extended work on an area of interest or one in which problems arise
- by attending court or student conferences, and writing appropriate notes and reports
- by aiming to improve hand written presentation or ICT skills.

Remember that the total portfolio of evidence that you compile for assessing key skills can come from any area of your studies – it does not all have to come from the study of law. However, your choice to study law as a subject will provide you with fine opportunities in the above categories.

Answers guide

Chapter 2: Offer and acceptance

Question 1

- Introduce the idea of Petunia making an offer and acceptance in forming a binding contract in shops.

- Explain the 'shopping' principles: display is invitation to treat, customer makes the offer, seller accepts – *Fisher v Bell, Pharmaceutical Society v Boots*.

- Discuss exceptions – *Carlill v Carbolic Smoke Ball Company, Esso v Commissioners of Customs and Excise*.

- Apply the shopping principle to Washwell and the exceptions to the promotional campaign.

- Consider the possibility of revocation – *Byrne v Van Tienhoven, Shuey v US* and apply this to the iron incident.

- Explain the 'reward' cases, especially *R v Clarke* – acceptance in ignorance of the offer – and apply this to Petunia and the watch.

- Consider what the outcome may be and whether it is fair / satisfactory.

Question 2

(a) Introduce the idea of offer and acceptance needed to form a binding contract, consideration being Bookworms' promise to supply certain books and Enrico's promise to pay. Back up your arguments with cases. Discuss which actions amount to an invitation to treat and where the offer and acceptance may have taken place.

- Discuss possible terms of the contract: express one, terms which may have been implied at common law and terms implied by statute.

- Consider whether there a breach of any term (do not discuss what kind of term, as this is the material for part (b).

- Consider possible remedies: termination or damages (depends on kind of term – do not go too far into this); equitable remedies do not apply here. Explain the provisions of the Distance Selling Regulations (cooling off period).

(b) Discuss the kind of terms within the contract.

- Has a condition or a warranty been breached? How do the courts decide?

- Are there any implied terms? If so, what type (statutory terms are likely to be conditions under the Sale of Goods Act 1979 / Sale and Supply of Goods Act 1994).

- Apply this to the facts.

(c) Consider the rules of offer and acceptance, quickly, to decide which ones you will describe and where you will suggest reform. For instance, you could describe the postal rule. You can refer back to previous material – do not waste time merely repeating it.

- You could suggest that the postal rule may not be valid now that communication can take a much faster (and reliable) route. This could be said to place an unfair burden on the offeror. If you can include any arguments by academics or judges, this would help.

- Use cases to illustrate your answer (e.g. *Household Fire Insurance v Grant*).

- Consider the arguments for and against whatever changes you suggest.

Question 3

- Very briefly explain the need for offer and acceptance in forming a contract.

- Explain what amounts to a counter offer – *Hyde v Wrench* – and apply it to Bert and Aman.

- Explain the need for communication of acceptance – *Felthouse v Bindley*.

- Explain the principles of lapse of time – *Ramsgate v Montefiore* – and revocation – *Byrne v Van Tienhoven, Dickinson v Dodds*. Apply this to Emma and Fred.

- Consider the 'rule' of acceptance by post – *Adams v Lindsell* – and discuss whether this applies to email.

- Apply the postal rule to Harry. Consider whether it would be fair to allow revocation of an acceptance by a faster method than the acceptance, and whether there is any disadvantage to the offeror – *Yates v Pulleyn*.

Question 4

- Very briefly explain the need for offer and acceptance in forming a contract.

- Explain the need for true agreement, and for communication of acceptance – *Felthouse v Bindley*, and the *Unsolicited Goods and Services Act 1971*. Apply this to Alex.

- Explain the main provisions of the Sale of Goods Act 1979, as amended by Sale and Supply of Goods Act 1994 and apply these to the sheepskin coat.

- Explain the principles of offer and acceptance in a shopping situation – *Fisher v Bell,* etc – and apply this to Cuteclothes.

Question 5

- The focus is on particular areas of offer and acceptance, so *very* briefly explain the need for a clear offer and acceptance, and the possibility of an offer being revoked.

- Regarding Logan and the auction, explain the principles of auctions and the status of an advertisement to hold one. As it is an invitation to treat there is no contract – *Harris v Nickerson*.

- Regarding Logan and Manesh, explain termination and consider that the offer to buy may have lapsed. In any case the Distance Selling Regulations may help Logan in giving him a cooling off period.

- Regarding Logan and Nigel, explain counter offers. As this cancels the original offer Logan is unlikely to be able to insist on forming a contract with Nigel.

Question 6

- Define an offer and explain the need for this to be clear.

- Compare an offer with an invitation to treat, using cases: shop windows, *Fisher v Bell*, supermarkets: *Pharmaceutical Society v Boots*, advertisements: *Partridge v Crittenden*, auctions: *Payne v Cave*, tenders: *Spencer v Harding*. Explain the reasoning: freedom to contract, exhausted stocks.

- Consider exceptions: *Wilkie v LPTB, Carlill, Thornton*, and why they arise.

- Consider non-standard situations: *Clarke v Dunraven, Esso*, and whether they are reasonable.

- Discuss the difficulty of identification of an offer in some situations, such as *Brogden*, and whether it actually matters (comments in *Gibson*).

- Consider the rather artificial nature of the rules in the general concept of *consensus ad idem*.

Question 7

- Think carefully about this question. You do not have time to write all you know on offer and acceptance *and* comment on it. Select areas that really answer the question.

- Very briefly explain the need for offer and acceptance in identifying the formation of a contract.

- Explain that, on the other hand, a clear acceptance is also needed to avoid imposing an unwanted contract on someone. Discuss how this may take place in a fair way – *Yates v Pulleyn*.

- Silence is not enough, and this supports the principles of freedom to contract – *Felthouse v Bindley*. Comment on this – the outcome may have been harsh in this case but it supports the principles of freedom to contract. *Confirmed in the Unsolicited Good and Services Act.*

- Discuss acceptance by conduct – *Carlill*, and ignorance of an offer – Clarke.

- Discuss the postal rule – *Adams v Lindsell, Holwell v Hughes*. Lots to say here. Use cases to illustrate.

- Consider established alternative methods of acceptance, such as telegrams (*Cowan v O'Connor*), telex (*Entores, Brinkibon*), and apply these to modern methods, e.g. fax, e-mail, courier. Consider the effect of distance and electronic trading.

Question 8

- Outline very briefly the need for an offer, and its role in forming a contract. Define offer and then explain that it must continue to the moment of acceptance to be valid.

- Consider each method of termination, explaining the straightforward issues quickly, and spending time on the more discursive areas. For instance, the following are not particularly contentious: refusal, death and failure of a precondition.

- Acceptance: define acceptance and very briefly explain one or two of the more discursive points, e.g. the problems with the postal rule and modern methods of communicating.

- Counter offer and its difficulties: *Hyde v Wrench, Stevenson v McLean, Butler v Ex-Cello*.

- Revocation and the difficulties it presents: *Byrne v Van Tienhoven, Dickinson v Dodds, Shuey v US, Errington*.

- Lapse of time and its inherent vagueness: *Ramsgate v Montefiore Hotel*.

Question 9

- Very briefly explain the need for offer and acceptance to form a contract.
- Define an acceptance.
- Explain the 'normal' principles of acceptance – *Yates Building v Pulleyn, Entores*.
- Explain why silence does not amount to acceptance – *Felthouse v Bindley*. Lots to comment on here.
- Discuss acceptance by conduct – *Carlill*; and in ignorance of an offer – *R v Clarke*. Comment on the case.
- Discuss the postal rule – *Adams v Lindsell, Holwell v Hughes*. Lots to say here, with cases to illustrate meaning of posting, unfairness, exceptions, etc.
- Consider other methods, established by cases: telegrams (*Cowan v O'Connor*), telex (*Entores, Brinkibon*), and speculate on modern methods, e.g. fax, e-mail, courier (see comments in *The Brimnes*) and distance and electronic trading.

Chapter 3: Consideration

Question 1

- Introduce the general idea of consideration, and define it. *Dunlop v Selfridge, Currie v Misa*.
- Discuss the need for Alan and Beth to provide consideration, and the relevant 'rules':
- Past consideration – *Re McArdle, Roscorla v Thomas*.
- Part-payment of a debt – *Pinnel's Case, Foakes v Beer*.
- Promissory estoppel – *Central London Property Trust v High Trees House*.
- Apply the principles of past consideration to David's offer.
- Consider whether the law is in line with morals here.
- Apply the principles of part-payment (in fact non-payment here) to Edmund's promise and consider whether promissory estoppel fits the facts given (again, matching the legal theory with moral principles).

Question 2

- Introduce very briefly the general principle consideration.
- Discuss the issue of consideration when performing an existing duty – *Stilk v Myrick*.
- Consider whether anything 'extra' to the duty has been given – *Hartley v Ponsonby, Ward v Byham, Williams v Roffey*.
- Apply the law regarding consideration, and *Williams v Roffey* in particular, to the facts of the problem, i.e. the payment to Kanbild, and

consider the particular problems that this may raise, e.g. the need to finish on time for the summer holiday trade.

- Identify the general issue of privity and/or consideration moving from the promisee – *Tweddle v Atkinson, Dunlop v Selfridge*.

- Apply the law on privity and/or consideration moving from the promisee to the facts of the problem, i.e. the payment to Mariner.

- Consider the Contracts (Rights of Third Parties) Act 1999 and conclude that it does not apply here.

Question 3

- Introduce the general need for consideration and define it.

- Show that it must be sufficient, even if not adequate – *Thomas v Thomas, Chapple v Nestlî_, Bainbridge v Firmstone*.

- Consideration: must not be vague – *White v Bluett*; must move from the promisee – *Tweddle v Atkinson*; must not be past – *Roscorla v Thomas, Re McArdle, Lampleigh v Braithwait, Re Casey's Patents*; may be in the form of forbearance to sue – *Haigh v Brooks*; and it must not be illegal – *Foster v Driscoll*.

- Discuss existing duty and doing more than the existing duty – *Collins v Godefroy, Stilk v Myrick,*

- Part-payment of a debt – *Pinnel's Case, High Trees,* etc.

Question 4

The Question is again about the nature of consideration, but you need to respond to the quotation. It would be a good idea to define consideration using the definitions from *Dunlop v Selfridge* so that you can explain benefit and detriment, and *Currie v Misa*, so that you can explain the idea of bargaining.

- Explain sufficiency and adequacy.

- Explain consideration moving from the promisee and the link with privity.

- Include some other rules on consideration, especially consideration not being vague or in the past.

- Discuss situations where there is very little, or no, consideration: promissory estoppel, *Williams v Roffey*.

- Conclude, referring back to the quotation.

Question 5

This is a narrower area of consideration, so you should know the facts and cases in detail.

- Explain, very briefly, the need for consideration. Outline the rule in *Pinnel's Case* (and *Foakes v Beer*), and show that generally part-payment does not discharge the debt.

- Discuss the exceptions in *Pinnel's Case*: something added, different place, early payment, etc.

- Explain promissory estoppel (as on of the exceptions to *Pinnel's Case*) and the circumstances where it will operate. Discuss its nature and the apparent lack of consideration.

- Discuss when, in the circumstances discussed, the debt may be discharged.

Question 6

- Explain briefly the nature of consideration.

- Define consideration, emphasising the idea of bargain in the *Currie v Misa* definition.

- Explain that for consideration to be sufficient it must be part of the current agreement.

- Explain the cases on past consideration – *Roscorla v Thomas, Re McArdle.*

- Develop this with cases which go beyond the basic 'rule' with an implication that something would be given in return – *Lampleigh v Braithwait, Re Casey's Patents*

- Speculate on other situations where this may arise, e.g. undertaking extra work for an employer, with the expectation of pay.

Question 7

- Introduce the traditional need for consideration and define it – *Dunlop v Selfridge, Currie v Misa.*

- Explain that performance of an existing duty does not normally amount to valid consideration (examine general duty – *Collins v Godefroy* – and contractual duty – *Stylk v Myrick).*

- Explain that work beyond the normal duty may be consideration, and why – *Glasbrook v Glamorgan, Hartley v Ponsonby.*

- Consider what might amount to 'extra' work – *Ward v Byham*

- Examine a duty owed to a third party – *Scotson v Pegg.*

- Examine the effect of *Williams v Roffey* on the existing case law, and discuss the circumstances in which it may apply in the future – *Re Selectmove.*

Question 8

- The question is about the 'rules' of consideration, and whether the exceptions indicate that it is time to review them.

- Discuss the principles outlined in the answer to question 3 and form a conclusion about whether the time has come to review the doctrine.

Chapter 4: Legal intent

Question 1

Introduce very briefly the need for legal intent as a formation requirement, along with agreement and consideration.

- Stress the importance of legal intent, to distinguish between various agreements, some of which may give rise to legal obligation, and others which do not.
- There are three incidents here: a group of friends providing food and drink for a social occasion, the promotional campaign with 'free' desserts, and the entry into the pools competition.
- The food and drink: Explain the presumption concerning social and domestic arrangements, and how it may be rebutted (unlikely here): various cases, but *Jones v Padvattan* and *Simpkin v Pays* are particularly relevant. Those involved here are just friends (there was a lodger in *Simpkin*). Note the extension of domestic arrangements to friends, rather than strict family relationships – see *Buckpitt v Oates*.
- The 'free' dessert: Refer to Chapter 4 regarding the situation in commercial situations, and use the *Esso* case to show the need for it in protecting the consumer.
- The pools entry: explain the presumption in commercial situations, and the honourable pledge clause as a way of rebutting this. Use a pools case, like *Jones v Vernons*. Consider the fairness of this, and whether the Unfair Terms in Consumer Contract Regulations 1994 may now apply.

Question 2

Introduce very briefly the need for legal intent as a formation requirement, along with agreement and consideration.

- Stress the importance of legal intent, to distinguish between various agreements, some of which may give rise to legal obligation, and others which do not.
- There are two incidents here, one set in a commercial context and one in a social context.
- Explain the presumption in a commercial context, then apply this to Franco and Grandstore – *Carlill v Carbolic Smoke Ball Co, Esso v CCE*.
- Consider whether the presumption can be rebutted.
- Discuss the idea of the presumption in social and domestic situations, and the extension of this to friends – *Merritt v Merritt, Jones v Padvatton, Buckpitt v Oates*.

- Consider whether the presumption may have been rebutted.
- Discuss briefly whether there is an issue of past consideration here regarding Franco and Hilary.

Question 3

Introduce very briefly the need for legal intent as a formation requirement, along with agreement and consideration.

- Explain the need for the courts to establish legal intent, to distinguish between various agreements, some of which may give rise to legal obligation, and others which do not.
- Explain the presumption in social and domestic arrangements. Explain how this can be rebutted, and why, using cases.
- Explain the presumption in commercial arrangements, and its rebuttal.
- Consider whether this brings about a fair result – you could examine some of the 'social' cases, a pools case and the *Esso* scenario.
- Would it be simpler for the courts just to make an enquiry? Would this be as certain, as a method of establishing intent? Would it give adequate protection to the parties involved? Consider the Unfair Terms in Consumer Contract Regulations 1994 and the possible impact on this area of law.

Question 4

This is similar in content to Question 3, but illustrates the need to address the question.

- Explain the law in a similar way, but raise the following issues:
- In social and domestic arrangements it is necessary to prove legal intent, because the presumption would be that there is none – why?
- How can this be proved? Use cases, like *Parker v Clarke*.
- In commercial situations there is no need to prove legal intent because it is presumed to exist – why? Use cases – *Carlill, Esso*. This can be rebutted: *Jones v Vernons Pools*. Is this fair?

Question 5

- Explain *very briefly* the general requirement of legal intent as a formation requirement.
- Explain the presumption of no legal intent in social and domestic situations: *Balfour, Jones v Padvation*, and its rebuttal in some cases: *Merritt, Parker v Clarke, Simpkin v Pays*.
- Explain the presumption of legal intent in commercial agreements: *Carlill, Esso*.

- Discuss honourable pledge clauses between companies: *Rose and Frank Co v Crompton Bros*, etc. and in consumer contracts: *Jones v Vernons Pools*, etc.

- Discuss the benefits that the principles give: thc benefit of certainty and the commercial expectation where both parties are in business – the need for certainty and commercial expectation; the protection of parties making informal family agreements, the extension of the principles beyond strict family.

Chapter 5: Capacity

Question 1

Introduce Anna as a minor who may be vulnerable in making contracts and therefore in need of protection. Explain that her capacity to make contracts is limited.

- Four areas of debate: the course, the books, the mobile phone and the loan.

- The course: contracts of education, training and employment – is this one? *De Francesco v Barnum, Doyle v White City*, etc.

- The books: necessaries or luxuries? Discuss them as a modern necessary: Sale of Goods Act 1979,. Discuss the mobile phone as a necessary or luxury: comments in *Chapple v Cooper, Nash v Inman*. Discuss restitution under Minors' Contracts Act 1987 s3.

- The loan: enforceable against the guarantor – Minors' Contracts Act 1987 s2.

- Consider whether the abovc arrangements are satisfactory.

Question 2

- Identify Ben as a minor, and therefore having limited contractual capacity.

- Explain the position regarding necessaries and non-necessaries – *Nash v Inman, Chapple v Cooper*.

- Explain the position regarding education, training and employment – *Doyle v White City Stadium, De Francesco v Barnum*, etc.

- Explain the circumstances of contracts of continuing obligation – *Edwards v Carter*.

- Explain the position regarding restitution of property (or any goods representing it) under an unenforceable contract and the position of guaranteed loans – provisions of the *Minors Contracts Act 1987*.

- Apply the law to each of the incidents in the problem, and whether the outcome is satisfactory for those concerned.

Question 3

Introduce the idea of protecting minors as an identified group of people in society who may be vulnerable in making contracts. Say who is a minor. Explain that capacity to make contracts is limited.

- Discuss the obligation to pay for necessaries, using cases. Explain how this is affected by the Minors' Contracts Act 1987 s3 provision of restitution.
- Discuss contracts of education, training and employment, using cases.
- Discuss contracts of continuing obligation.
- Discuss loans and the provision in s2 of the Minors' Contracts Act 1987.
- Consider whether the level of protection is right.

Question 4

This question is wider than the previous one, in that you need to consider contractual capacity in general, not just for minors (a good example of the need to read the question carefully).

- Discuss: corporations (registered business organisations), sovereigns and diplomats, persons of unsound mind and drunkards, and lastly minors (see the material above). This is where you are likely to have most knowledge, so you can use much of your time on minors (but leave some time to conclude).
- Consider whether the law is satisfactory and consider any areas of reform needed, e.g. the need to carry identity cards, the elderly.

Question 5

This is based on material broadly similar to that in Question 3, but the focus is much more on the balancing of fairness between adults and minors.

- Discuss the need to protect minors, and then consider whether any unfairness arises. You could consider the position of the tailor in *Nash v Inman*.
- Discuss the age of minors, and whether this is set at the right level.
- Consider whether there are occasions when the minor is too well protected.
- Discuss in detail the provisions of the Minors' Contracts Act 1987 and the attempt it makes to remedy any imbalance of protection.
- Consider what would be the outcome in *Nash v Inman* if the same case arose following the Act.
- Consider whether there are any further problems, e.g. the need to oblige the minor to hand over money, if this is available.

Question 6

The material to use here is similar to question 4. Phrase it in a way that answers the question.

Chapter 6: Incorporation of terms

Question 1

- Introduce the distinction between terms, which form part of a binding contract, and representations, which are merely pre-contractual statements.

- The distinction will be governed by: special knowledge of the representor – *Dick Bentley Productions Ltd v Harold Smith (Motors) Ltd, Oscar Chess v Williams*; importance placed on a particular issue – *Bannerman v White*; distance in time between statement and contract – *Routledge v McKay*; strength of inducement – *Ecay v Godfrey, Schawel v Reade*.

- Apply these factors to the incident between Smith and Jones regarding whether the claim over the age of the motor-cycle is a term of the contract. If it is, Jones may be able to claim breach of contract. If not, he may be able to claim misrepresentation.

- Discuss the importance of incorporation of terms into a contract. The following should be included: degree of notice – *Chapelton v Barry UDC, Parker v South Eastern Railway, Sugar v LMS Railway*; course of dealing – *Hollier v Rambler Motors (AMC) Ltd, McCutcheon v David MacBrayne Ltd, British Crane Hire Corporation Ltd v Ipswich Plant Hire Ltd*; time at which the notice was given – *Olley v Marlborough Court Ltd, Thornton v Shoe Lane Parking Ltd*.

- Apply these factors to the incident with Seaview Hotel. If the term on the back of the bedroom door is not incorporated, then the hotel will not be able to rely on its protection in a claim by Jones.

Question 2

- Explain that terms may be written, oral or a mixture of these, and that they may also be express (clearly expressed by the parties) or implied (incorporated in some other way, e.g. by statute).

- Distinguish between terms and representations (see the first part of Question 1).

- Explain how the difference between the two results in the different remedies, i.e. damages for breach of contract is the usual remedy for an term which is untrue or not performed, while the usual remedy for an untrue representation is rescission or damages for misrepresentation.

- Explain how terms are incorporated into an oral contract (see the second part of Question 1).

- Discuss how terms implied into certain contracts by custom, especially within a trade, as in a 'course of dealing', or in a geographical area.
- Discuss how terms are implied by statute, especially in consumer contracts, e.g. Sale of Goods Act 1979 (as amended) sections 12 to 15.
- Discuss how terms are implied by the courts on the facts – *Samuels v Davis*; or via the officious bystander test – *Shirlaw v Southern Foundries, Spring v National Amalgamated Stevedores and Dockers Society, Trollope and Colls Ltd v North West Regional Hospital Board*; or to give business efficacy to an agreement – *The Moorcock* (1889), *Liverpool City Council v Irwin*.
- Consider whether the approach taken by the law is satisfactory in producing the contract intended by the parties.

Question 3

- Introduce the idea of parties being bound by what they intended, but consider the need for external evidence of that intention.
- Explain the starting-point of a person being bound by what they 'see and sign' – use the rule in *L'Estrange v Graucob* and the parol evidence rule in *Goss v Lord Nugent*.
- Consider the ways in which terms may be incorporated, despite the two rules above (see material for Question 2 above).
- Relate this back to the quotation in the Question and conclude as to how far it is true.

Question 4

- Explain the general principles of terms being incorporated into contracts by the parties or the courts, and implied into the contract by statute, and explain the consequences of breach of these terms.
- Explain the common law principles on which terms will be implied into a contract and then explain the statutory provision regarding implied terms in consumer contracts found in the Sale of Goods Act 1979 sections 12 to 15 and the amendments found in the Sale and Supply of Goods Act 1994.
- Explain that Alex may need to rely on both the common law, regarding the motor cycle, and statute regarding the camera, and explain the difference in provision for a person purchasing in the capacity of consumer and a purchaser in a private sale.
- Apply the statutory provisions of the Sale of Goods Act 1979 and the Sale and Supply of Goods Act 1994 to the purchase of the camera and apply the common law to the purchase of the motor cycle.
- Consider whether the law in this area is satisfactory for those concerned.

Chapter 7: Types of terms within a contract

Question 1

The question invites you to consider whether it is an advantage to have the certainty of knowing whether a term is a condition or warranty, or whether the courts will be more likely to be flexible using the innominate term approach found in *Hong Kong Fir*. Make sure that you show that you know the different approaches taken by the courts in the past and use cases to illustrate this.

To most parties, the reason for examining the type of term is to find out what remedy is available – damages for breach of warranty or a choice of damages or repudiation for breach of condition. Explain this clearly.

- Discuss the need for certainty in some contracts, e.g. *The Chikuma, Bunge Corporation v Tradax* (1981), *Lombard North Central v Butterworth* – again, showing that you understand the question.

- Explain the two main types of terms and the traditional approach to differentiating between them: *Poussard v Spiers and Pond, Bettini v Gye*.

- Examine alternative approaches: when the parties label the terms: *Schuler v Wickman Machine Tool Sales Ltd*; statute may specify the nature of the term; a 'course of dealing' may exist: *British Crane Hire Corporation Ltd v Ispwich Plant Hire Ltd*.

- Examine the *Hong Kong Fir* approach, where the court examines the effect of the breach and treats the term **like** a condition or a warranty. Support this with cases like *The Hansa Nord* and *Reardon Smith Line v Hansen Tangen*.

- Conclude, referring to the wording of the question, on whether it is really important now to 'label' terms.

Question 2

This question raises similar issues to those in Question 1 (above), but the style of the question is different. The emphasis is on the use of the innominate term approach rather than the need for certainty, so you should respond to this in your answer.

- Explain the difference between the two main types of terms – *Poussard v Spiers and Pond, Bettini v Gye*.

- Discuss the approach to identifying terms taken in *Hong Kong Fir*, where the court examines the effect of the breach and treats the term *like* a condition or a warranty. Support this with cases like *The Hansa Nord* and *Reardon Smith Line v Hansen Tangen*. Consider whether this brings about the justice desired and whether it raises the level of uncertainty.

- Examine alternative approaches: whether the breach 'goes to the root of the matter' (Blackburn J in *Poussard v Spiers and Pond*); labelling the terms – *Schuler v Wickman Machine Tool Sales Ltd*; statute may specify; 'course of dealing' – *British Crane Hire Corporation Ltd v Ipswich Plant Hire Ltd*; the need for certainty between the parties (see Question 1 above).

- Conclude, referring to the balance of certainty and justice raised in the question.

Question 3

This question involves the same material as Questions 1 and 2 (above), but you need to arrange it to show that you understand the question.

- Show that the parties' intentions *could* be important, but there are other factors, too. A key case is *Schuler v Wickman Machine Tool Sales Ltd* which shows that the labelling of the parties is not necessarily conclusive.

- Examine alternative approaches (see previous answers). Conclude, responding to the question.

Question 4

Again, the answer to this requires the same basic material as the answers above, but it should be used in a way that shows the examiner that you understand the question.

- Show, using *Schuler v Wickman Machine Tool Sales Ltd*, that even where terms are set by parties, this general freedom may be overridden by the courts.

- Explain that statute may decide on the categories of terms, again overriding the freedom to contract.

- Consider other ways in which the court may intervene: 'course of dealing' – *British Crane Hire Corporation Ltd v Ipswich Plant Hire Ltd*; the need for certainty between the parties (see question 1 above); the *Hong Kong Fir* approach, supported by *The Hansa Nord* and *Reardon Smith Line v Hansen Tangen*.

- Conclude, responding to the question.

Question 5

The answer to this question is based on the same material as question 1, but the question is phrased differently. Use the same points and cases but adjust your comments, especially in the introduction and conclusion, to suit the question.

Chapter 8: Exemption clauses

Question 1

Identify the existence of exemption clauses in these incidents and explain, briefly, the nature of these clauses and the need to protect Kelly who, in this situation, is a consumer.

- Establish the factors which will be used to decide whether these clauses will be valid: incorporation – *Olley v Marlborough Court, Thornton v Shoe Lane Parking, Parker v South Eastern Railway, Chapelton v Barry, Sugar v LMS Railway, Hollier v Rambler Motors; construction – Glynn v Margetson,* etc.; legislation – the Unfair Contract Terms Act 1977 and the Unfair Terms in Consumer Contract Regulations 1994.

- Apply these to the facts regarding the injury and decide whether the clause used by the art gallery is likely to be binding.

- Apply these to the facts regarding the coat and decide whether the clause is likely to be reasonable – *Green v Cade, Smith v Bush, Photo Production v Securicor.*

Question 2

This question is also a problem involving an apparent exemption of liability for personal injury and an apparent exemption of liability for loss of a coat. Use the material in Question 1 and apply it to Alison's two problems.

Question 3

This question involves similar material to the above problems but is a straightforward essay on how the law deals with exemption clauses. You should therefore explain the law and develop a critique in order to answer the question.

- Explain the factors that are likely to be taken into consideration by the courts (as in Question 1). Remember that it must be established whether the person making a claim is a consumer.

- Consider the lengths to which the courts used to go in order to protect the consumer – it was out of these efforts that the 'rules' of incorporation and construction developed.

- Consider the role played by parliament in taking the lead (eventually) in protecting the consumer by the legislation on exemption clauses.

- Evaluate the continuing role of the courts, in that (i) there is still a need to enquire whether a term is incorporated, and (ii) the legislation regarding exemption clauses needs to be interpreted and applied (especially words such as 'reasonable').

Question 4

This question involves the same material as the answer to Question 3, but worded a little differently.

- Explain that although the area is now well controlled by legislation, there is still a need for incorporation and for interpretation of the legislation.

- Show how this works in practice (see some ideas from the two answers above).

Question 5

This question again involves the same material as the other questions, but asks you to consider whether there are, in addition to protecting the consumer, any occasions where an exemption clause may be justified (i.e. not against the law, or 'outlawed'). After having explained how the law decides the validity of exemption clauses, consider the following as possible arguments:

- There are occasions where, after going through the procedure outlined, the courts will decide that a clause is reasonable.

- There is a current trend to consider a clause reasonable if it is a limitation clause rather than an exemption clause (see Chapter 7).

- Consider the situation as described between Jenna and Lenton in Question 1 (above), where a restriction is accepted in exchange for a good price.

Question 6

Again, the basic material is the same as the questions above, but the question is a good revision exercise, as it requires you to form a critique on whether the measures taken by parliament, in addition to the approach of the courts, is satisfactory in protecting the consumer.

- You therefore need to combine the 'essay' type material from this chapter with an evaluation of the approach of both parliament and the courts towards protecting the consumer, who would otherwise be in a weak bargaining position.

Chapter 9: Privity of contract

Question 1

This question involves a number of issues.

- Firstly there is a requirement of consideration in proving that a valid contract exists, and Victor's work in the garden may amount to past consideration, which may not be valid (see Chapter 3).

- Secondly there is a question of whether legal intent exists, as Ursula and Victor are neighbours and there is a presumption of no legal intent in social and domestic arrangements, which can be extended to friends (see Chapter 4).

- The third issue is privity of contract, as Yolanda supplied Victor with the trees, not Ursula. The contractual relationship over the supply of the trees is therefore between Yolanda and Victor, and does not involve Ursula. Given the requirement for the contract to identify a person claiming a benefit under the recent Contracts (Rights of Third Parties) Act 1999, this is not likely to be of use to Yolanda.

Question 2

This is a good question to prompt you to revise the whole topic and develop a critique of your own on the recent reform. Note the following points:

- The need for reform was clear – see the various reports and cases.

- The legislation only applies to those who would benefit as third parties, not those would have a burden imposed under a three-sided arrangement.

- The legislation only applies where there is clear evidence of intention to benefit a third party, e.g. where that party is identified by name.

Question 3

- See the answer to Question 2 – the answer to this one will be similar in content, until some cases have come before the courts.

- The effect on the doctrine is to lessen its importance in relation to those receiving a benefit, but to leave it intact regarding the imposition of a burden. Even regarding those receiving a benefit, there may be situations where a person cannot prove that the intention to bestow the benefit was clear at the time of contracting, and there may be difficulties proving identity. It is not clear how precise this will need to be – a matter for statutory interpretation. See comments on this in Chapter 9.

Question 4

- This is similar to Question 2. Explain the background to privity, covering (briefly) the basic rule, its difficulties and established exceptions and the attempts to avoid the problems.

- Outline the provisions of the Act and explain the reason for it. This will involve going back to the reason for the rule of privity (to protect the contract and avoid imposing a burden unfairly on a third party), and, through cases, the hardships caused by it to those who would like to benefit as third parties.

- Develop a point of view on the way in which the Act enables most potential beneficiaries to obtain what they expect.

- Consider any problems with the Act, such as how clear the identification must be.

Question 5

The answer to this is based on material used to answer questions 2 and 4, reworded to answer the question.

Chapter 10: Duress and undue influence

Question 1

(a) Introduce undue influence as a vitiating factor which, like duress, deals with unfair pressure in forming a contract.

- Explain that there is not an automatic fiduciary relationship here giving rise to a presumption of undue influence, but that there may be on the facts (*BCCI v Aboody*) or by analogy (*Lloyds Bank v Bundy*). Consider the effect of Jake being a director.

- Consider whether there has been a manifest disadvantage – *National Westminster Bank v Morgan*.

- Discuss how Jake would be able to rebut the presumption – *Re Brocklehurst, O'Brien*, etc.

- Discuss the need to protect an individual in such a situation. *(b)* Explain that as an alternative to an action in the civil courts Kevin could us an alternative method of dispute resolution.

- Explain the advantages of conciliation and mediation: speed, low cost, informality (although they may not achieve the desired outcome).

- Explain the advantages of using arbitration: privacy and an enforceable award.

Question 2

- Introduce the idea of duress and undue influence as vitiating factors which occur when unfair pressure arises in forming a contract.

- Explain the original position of the court regarding duress (a narrow definition not including property) – *Skeate v Beale, The Siboen and The Sibotre.*

- Consider the need for a reform of this, and explain how it occurred through case law – *The Atlantic Baron, The Universe, Pao On v Lau Yiu Long* (factors which may help identify economic duress mentioned here – relate these to the question).

- Compare economic duress with legitimate commercial pressure – *Atlas Express v Kafco, Williams v Roffey*; again, relate this to the question.

Question 3

- Introduce undue influence as unfair pressure on a party when forming a contract, which does not amount to common law duress, and explain that it is an equitable doctrine, developed to provide relief in cases of injustice.
- Explain that a finding of undue influence renders a contract voidable, therefore the bars to rescission apply: lapse of time, third-party rights, restitution impossible and affirmation.
- Explain that the banking cases are situations where there is not normally a special or fiduciary relationship, but there *may* be in particular circumstances, such as: where the client 'crossed the line' into an area of confidentiality and undue influence is presumed – *Lloyds Bank v Bundy*; where the weaker party suffered manifest disadvantage – *National WestminsterBank v Morgan*; where there is a relationship of trust in the particular circumstances of the case – *BCCI v Aboody, CIBC v Pitt*.
- Explain how the presumption may be rebutted – *Re Brocklehurst*.
- Examine the state of the doctrine, firstly through *Barclays v O'Brien* which concerned a claim of undue influence. The court found that (a) there was a misrepresentation between husband and wife, and (b) the banks in these cases should be 'put on enquiry' (alerted, or informed). The whole loan was set aside. Secondly, consider cases which follow *O'Brien*, for example *Banco Exterior v Mann, Midland Bank v Massey, TSB v Camfield, Royal Bank of Scotland v Etridge, Bank of Scotland v Bennett*, especially regarding the extent of the duty to ensure that independent advice is given.

Question 4

This question combines the material from Questions 1 and 2, so you need to watch timing very carefully.

- Use the introduction to Part 4 of the book to explain the idea of duress and undue influence as vitiating factors.
- Practice using the outline answers to the above two questions to explain more fully how duress and undue influence operate, so that you have as full an answer as time will allow, keeping a reasonable balance between the two doctrines.
- Show the link between the two doctrines in that they have both developed through recent case law to take account of the problems of a modern society and sophisticated economy.

Question 5

The question uses the same material as Question 3, but takes a particular view, rather than asking you to just 'critically examine'. Remember that you do not have to necessarily agree with the view, but you must sustain an argument.

- Use the material from Question 3 to show how undue influence operates, and how the banking cases developed. Until *Barclays v O'Brien* it would have been very difficult to disagree with the opinion voiced, as apart from the initial shock caused by *Lloyds Bank v Bundy* banks had plenty of warning of the need to advise in a general way. *O'Brien* imposed a stricter duty, placing the bank 'on enquiry' and introducing the link with misrepresentation. This was particularly harsh on banks finally at House of Lords level (the Court of Appeal only intended to set aside part of the loan), so if you read a report make sure that it is at the right level.

- Examine cases which follow *O'Brien*, for example *Banco Exterior v Mann, Midland Bank v Massey, TSB v Camfield, Royal Bank of Scotland v Etridge, Bank of Scotland v Bennett*, especially regarding the extent of the duty to ensure that independent advice is given. Watch for further developments, such as further appeal regarding *Etridge* and any other relevant cases.

Question 6

- Introduce the doctrines of duress and undue influence as vitiating factors, explain the common law origin of duress and define it – *Cumming v Ince, Kaufman v Gerson*.

- Explain the original position regarding property – *Skeate v Beale* and the relaxation of that position in *The Siboen and the Sibotre*.

- Explain the development of economic duress as a justified limitation to the parties' freedom to contract – *The Atlantic Baron, Pao On v Lau Yiu Long, The Universel Sentinel, Williams v Roffey, Atlas Express v Kafco, DSND Subsea v Petroleum Geo, Carillion Construction v Felix*.

- Examine cases where economic duress was found and those where it was not – consider how ready the courts are to allow such claims, responding to the question.

Chapter 11: Misrepresentation

Question 1

- Identify misrepresentation as a vitiating factor, since Ben is induced into the contract by it, and the statements are made some time before the contract of sale is formed.

- Define misrepresentation and explain why it may help Ben.

- Deal with the claims made by Bill. There may be a mere commendation or a statement of opinion – *Dimmock v Hallett, Bisset v Wilkinson*. Consider silence and half-true statements – *Fletcher v Krell, Dimmock v Hallett*. The claim about the new clutch is likely to be a misrepresentation (even if you feel that it is not, you need to discuss what remedy may be available if it was held to be one, so that you can show the examiner that you know about the remedies).

- Consider the possibility of proving that the misrepresentation was fraudulent (according to *Derry v Peek*) – the options would be: rescission, or damages in the tort of deceit.

- If this is unlikely, or difficult to prove, then the options are: rescission, or damages under the Misrepresentation Act 1967 s.2(1). The burden of proof shifts to Bill to show innocence (difficult) – *Howard Marine v Ogden*.

- Discuss the basis of assessment and loss of profits – *Royscott v Rogerson, East v Maurer*. If the court decided not to allow rescission, damages may be possible under the Misrepresentation Act 1967 s.2(2).

- The use of the car raises the issue of common law bars to rescission, especially affirmation – *Long v Lloyd*, although a defence would be the need to fulfil obligations to clients.

- Conclude as to whether the remedies are satisfactory for Ben.

Question 2

This kind of question involves several issues. Part (a) involves the claims made by Conn about the computer, and therefore raises the issue of misrepresentation. Part (b) concerns the discharge of the contract by frustration following Bill's accident. Part (c) considers the remedies for breach of contract.

- Part (a) should be answered in a similar way to question 1, bearing in mind that you have about 25 minutes, this being one third of a question.

- Define misrepresentation and apply this to Conn's statements – he is acting on behalf of the seller and misleads the buyer, Bill – see *Esso v Mardon*.

- Likely to be fraudulent misrepresentation (*Derry v Peek*) as you are told that Conn knew that his statements were not true. Therefore rescission is possible, unless barred (see Chapter 11), as Conn knew that his statements were not true. Damages for fraudulent misrepresentation are available in the tort of deceit.

- If it is difficult to prove fraud, or the statements are not thought to be fraudulent, rescission is available (again, unless barred) under the Misrepresentation Act 1967 s2(1). The burden of proof shifts to the misrepresentor to prove innocence, and this is a heavy burden to discharge (*Howard Marine v Ogden*). See Chapter 11 for the measure of damages.

- Apply these principles to the facts of the situation involving Bill and Conn.

Part (b) involves the doctrine of frustration (see Chapter 14).

- Define frustration and explain that it is used as a defence to an allegation of breach of contract. Bill could therefore claim frustration if he no longer required the computer, did not pay for it, and breach of contract was alleged.
- Explain the operation, using cases like *Taylor v Caldwell, Morgan v Manser, Krell v Henry*, then consider the effects of a finding of frustration: Law Reform (Frustrated Contracts) Act 1943.
- Apply this to the contract between Bill and AB Computers. Part (c) involves an explanation of the remedies available for breach of contract.
- The main remedies are damages and repudiation depending on the type of term breached, but see Chapters 7, 14 and 15 for fuller details.
- Consider the choice of different remedies and whether they would be suitable in different circumstances.

Question 3

This question concerns the kinds of pre-contractual statements that may amount to misrepresentation. The discussion will centre on the first part of the chapter, and not really involve remedies.

- Define misrepresentation.
- Discuss the kinds of statements that will not amount to misrepresentation, such as mere commendation, opinion, etc.
- Discuss the general principle of remaining silent (*Fletcher v Krell*), and show that there are occasions where apparent silence can amount to a misrepresentation.
- Conclude, referring back to the question.

Question 4

This question focuses wholly on remedies. Although it may be useful to define misrepresentation, or to explain it very briefly, this should amount to no more than a couple of lines at the most, as you need to be selective, and use your time to launch directly into the remedies issues.

- Explain the remedy of rescission – an equitable remedy which restores the parties to original position unless barred by: affirmation – *Long v Lloyd*; thirdparty rights – *White v Garden*; restitution impossible – *Vigers v Pike*; lapse of time – *Leaf v International Galleries*; or statute – s.2(2) Misrepresentation Act 1967. Damages may be awarded in lieu

– *Zanzibar v British Aerospace*. Available for both fraudulent and non-fraudulent misrepresentation.

* Explain the remedy of damages. If fraudulent misrepresentation can be proved, damages via the tort of deceit – *Derry v Peek*. If fraudulent misrepresentation cannot be proved, damages available under *Hedley Byrne v Heller* if a 'special' relationship exists; otherwise damages under the Misrepresentation Act 1967 s.2(1) without the need to prove fraud.

* Consider the following points: the Misrepresentation Act 1967 is now the normal route to a remedy, and the most widely used; the burden of proof shifts to the misrepresentor to prove innocence; this is a heavy burden and it is difficult to avoid liability – *Howard Marine v Ogden*; damages are assessed on a tort basis putting the injured party into the position which they would have been in had the wrong not happened – *Royscott v Rogerson*; loss of profits may also be recoverable in some circumstances – *East v Maurer*.

* Conclude by observing that the remedies for non-fraudulent misrepresentation are now more or less equivalent to those for breach of contract or fraudulent misrepresentation.

Question 5

This is another question on remedies. Use the material from Question 4 (above) and tailor it to respond to this question (see comments on the end of Chapter 11 on misrepresentation).

Question 6

* This is similar in content to Question 5. Use the same material but respond to the statement in the question.

* You could point out that the net result of suing for breach of contract may be very similar to the result of suing in misrepresentation – and that this is fair, since an untrue statement in either situations could have serious consequences.

You could discuss the differences in the routes to obtaining the remedies.

Chapter 12: Mistake

Question 1

This problem question concerns unilateral mistake over identity, and you need to show at the beginning that you recognise that. It is fine to introduce mistake generally as a vitiating factor, negating true consent, but do not waste valuable time on detail of other types of mistake.

- Explain the nature of unilateral mistake and what is needed for it to be operative. Remember the requirement that one party has made a fundamental false assumption and the other is aware of this.

- Explain the difference between *inter absentes* and *inter praesentes* situations and identify that this is an example of the second situation.

- Explain that an apparent mistake over identity may be seen as one of creditworthiness and will often leave the contract intact.

- Explain the situation of the third party who has possession of the goods, in this case the violin.

- Relate the details of the chain of relevant cases – *Phillips v Brooks, Ingram v Little, Lewis v Averay*.

- Apply this knowledge to the facts of the case and form some conclusion over the likely outcome.

Question 2

In this problem question the issue centres on common mistake. Two incidents invite discussion: the purchase of a painting which turns out to be worth less than the amount paid, and the purchase of a chair which turns out to be worth more than the amount paid.

- As with Question 1 (above), you can explain, generally, the issue of mistake, but do not waste time on other types of mistake. Remember that this is where both parties are in agreement, but both have made the same false assumption.

- Differentiate between mistakes which concern the existence of the subject matter (*Couturier v Hastie, Galloway v Galloway, Scott v Coulson*), and those which concern the quality of the subject matter (*Bell v Lever Bros, Leaf v International Galleries, Associated Japanese Bank Ltd v Credit du Nord, William Sindall v Cambridgeshire County Council*). Consider especially *Leaf*, as it is particularly relevant to the facts of the problem.

- Examine both of these areas, relating them to the facts of the problem. Remember that Adrian will probably want a remedy in respect of the painting, but will not wish to take the chair back – can, or should, the law deal satisfactorily with both situations?

- Consider an alternative way of resolving the case – *McRae v Commonwealth Disposals Commission*.

Question 3

- Explain that there may be a mistake and/or a misrepresentation. Outline briefly the operation or both of these and explain that if Pauline cannot be found then a finding of misrepresentation by the court is not very helpful.

- Then consider the issue of mistake over identity and whether this might make the contract void.

- Refer to cases such as *Phillips v Brooks, Ingram v Little, Lewis v Avery* and *Shogun v Hudson*.

- Apply the principles to the characters and decide if Nazir can take any action.

Question 4

This question concerns the same material as Question 2 (above), i.e. common mistake, but in essay style.

- Introduce mistake as a vitiating factor, but focus clearly on common mistake.

- Remember that in this kind of mistake both parties are labouring under the same false assumption, so there is agreement, but over the 'wrong' subject matter. It is only where the *court* finds this so fundamentally different from that agreed that the original subject matter does not really exist that the contract is void.

- Explain that where there is genuine mistake over existence of the subject matter the court will generally declare the contract void – *Couturier v Hastie, Galloway v Galloway, Scott v Coulson.* Compare *McRae v Commonwealth Disposals Commission*, which appeared to be an issue of mistake but was held to be a breach of warranty, bringing about a more appropriate remedy.

- Examine mistake over title, which may invoke an equitable remedy – *Cooper v Phibbs*.

- Examine in some detail mistake over the quality of the subject matter (i.e. the value of the bargain). This will leave the contract intact if the mistake is not 'fundamental' – *Bell v Lever Bros, Leaf v International Galleries, Associated Japanese Bank Ltd v Credit du Nord, William Sindall v Cambridgeshire County Council*.

- Consider exactly what is 'fundamental'. Should there be a remedy more easily available? Should people not be held to what they bought (see the issue raised in Question 5)?

- Look back at Question 2 for ideas of the kind of issues to discuss – can the law deal effectively with those who have lost and those who have gained? Is it possible to share the burden of loss in a fair way between two innocent parties?

Question 5

The question again concerns common mistake, and covers the same theoretical ground as Question 4 (above).

- Use the material in the answer to Question 4 to answer this question, but tailor your argument to respond to the issue raised, i.e. that it may not be possible to have one single, comprehensive doctrine that suits all. In that case the law generally leaves people with their bargains, unless the subject matter no longer exists.

Question 6

This is a theoretical question concerning unilateral mistake over identity. Like the other questions, do introduce the idea of mistake possibly vitiating the agreement, but do not spend too long on other types of mistake.

- Remember the requirements for unilateral mistake to be operative: where only one party is working under a false assumption and the other is aware of this (and may have deliberately planned the situation).
- Explain that mistake over quality will generally leave the contract intact – *Smith v Hughes, Scriven v Hindley, Hartog v Colin and Shields.*
- Explain that mistake over identity *inter absentes* (not in each other's presence) may render the contract void – *Cundy v Lindsay.* Do you consider this to be a fair outcome? Is there a fair alternative?
- Develop the idea that mistake over identity *inter praesentes* (in each other's presence) may be seen as one of creditworthiness and will often leave the contract intact – *Phillips v Brooks, Ingram v Little, Lewis v Averay.*
- Consider whether there is in reality any difference between identity and creditworthiness. What factors may the courts have taken into account in deciding each of these three cases?
- What should the law be in this area in future?

Question 7

This is an alternative theoretical question on common mistake.

- Use the material from Question 4 and tailor your arguments to address the question.
- You may wish to consider the following cases – *McRae v Commonwealth Disposals Commission, Sheik v Oschner, Amalgamated Investment and Property Co Ltd v John Walker and Sons Ltd.*

Chapter 13: Illegality

Question 1

- Identify illegality as an undesirable element of a potential contract, and therefore a vitiating factor.

- Explain that the issue with illegality is often whether the contract formed was illegal at the outset by its very nature, or illegal in its performance.

- Explain that here we have two examples of illegality. The garden plants could be delivered in a legal manner; there is nothing illegal about buying them or supplying them, it is merely the way in which the contract is performed that makes it illegal – *Anderson v Daniel*.

- With the fireworks, if the company is operating without a licence when one is required, then the whole nature of the contract is illegal – *Re Mahmoud and Ispahani*.

- Consider the effect of this illegality on the contract for each of the incidents.

Question 2

- Explain that a contract may be illegal when formed or performed – *Re Mahmoud and Ispahani*; *Anderson v Daniel*, and explain the different causes of the illegality; statute – *Re Mahmoud and Ispahani;* common law – *Everet v Williams*.

- Explain that another division arises over the undesirable nature of contracts. They may be: illegal in the criminal sense, as in *Everet v Williams;* not in the interest of society, and therefore unenforceable, as in *Parkinson v College of Ambulance*.

- Explain that a further division arises over the undesirable nature of contracts. They may be: illegal in the criminal sense, as in *Everet v Williams;* not in the interest of society, and therefore unenforceable, as in *Parkinson v College of Ambulance*.

- Contracts in restraint of trade also come into this last category, so could be considered as time allows.

- Consider the extent to which the law should be controlling what is desirable in this way.

Question 3

- Introduce the idea of restraint of trade. A clause in a contract which is in restraint of trade is at first sight void, since it is against public policy to restrict a person's freedom to trade or earn a living.

- Explain that the clause may be justified by: protection of a trade secret – *Forster v Suggett;* protection of a range of clientele – *Mason v Provident Clothing, Fitch v Dewes;* the need to enable business to be carried on – *Nordenfelt v Maxim Nordenfelt;* showing reasonableness in exclusive dealing arrangements – *Schroeder Music v Macaulay, Esso v Harper's Garage*.

- Examine the effect of a restraint of trade clause: the clause itself is void, or unenforceable, if against public policy and not proved reasonable;

the whole contract is not necessarily void, and severance may be possible; the court may strike out offending words leaving the rest intact; a slightly more relaxed approach may now interpret the clause in a way that makes it reasonable – *Littlewoods v Harris*.

- Examine the effect of European Law.

Chapter 14: Discharge of a contract

Question 1

(a) This is a question on discharge. You should briefly introduce the topic of discharge, and point out that, as a starting-point, there may in each case be a claim of breach of contract. The idea of frustration is, then, an alternative to breach, where neither party is at fault – where the event causing the discharge is outside the control of the parties.

- Define frustration and give an example, such as *Taylor v Caldwell*.
- Explain that frustration can occur through radical change in circumstances (*apply Knell v Henry*.)
- Consider the alternative argument where a contract still has some point (*Herne Bay*) or is self-induced.
- Discuss the legal effect of frustration in the provisions of the Law Reform (Frustrated Contracts) Act (1943).
- Consider how breach of contract operates and compare this with a claim of frustration in Fern's case.
- Explain vicarious performance. Would this be satisfactory for Fern?

Question 2

Identify the issue of discharge of a contract and discuss the ways in which this may occur: performance, agreement, breach, frustration.

- Discuss Andrew's proposal of an alternative as not amounting to performance or agreement.
- Explain that Bruce may be able to claim breach of contract, and that Andrew may wish in turn to claim frustration.
- Explain frustration more fully (*Taylor v Caldwell, Krell v Henry*) and the restrictions on the doctrine, e.g. *Herne Bay Steam Boat Co v Hutton, Tsakiroglou v Noblee Thorl, Maritime National Fish v Ocean Trawlers*.
- Consider whether these apply to the facts of the problem.
- Compare frustration and breach as two methods of discharge, and examine the consequences of each. To do this you will need to explain the provisions of the Law Reform (Frustrated Contracts) Act 1943.
- Apply this to the facts of the problem.

Question 3

This question is a good one to use in order to practise an essay type answer, and also to ensure that you know about the different ways of discharging a contract. Refer to the summary at the end of Chapter 14.

- Ensure that you include some critical analysis, e.g. a party wish to claim frustration rather than be sued for breach if the provisions of the Law Reform (Frustrated Contracts Act) 1943 would mean that less money would be due (examine the provisions); a provider of services, such as a decorator, may wish to claim that substantial performance has taken place if it would mean that payment was made on the basis of the complete amount less a deduction for remedying the defect.
- Explain that the limits on the use of the doctrine of frustration are intended to prevent its misuse.

Question 4

- Explain the principles of total performance: exact (*Re Moore and Landauer*) and complete (*Cutter v Powell*). Discuss the outcome of these cases and whether (a) the decisions were fair and (b) whether they establish a good basis of law.
- Consider the exceptions to the general rule, substantial performance and partial performance, and whether they alleviate any potential unfairness. Use cases to illustrate, e.g. *Hoenig v Isaacs, Bolton v Mahadeva, Sumpter v Hedges*. Do the exceptions themselves raise uncertainty?
- Explain the operation of severable contracts.
- Consider the principles of time of performance, vicarious performance and prevention of performance.

Question 5

Introduce the doctrine of frustration and define it.

- Show when frustration can be used through case examples, and then explain why the limits are needed (see Chapter 14).
- Examine each limit in turn, using cases to illustrate: There may still be *some* point to the contract – *Herne Bay Steam Boat Co v Hutton*; where a contract is merely more onerous it will not be frustrated – *Tsakiroglou v Noblee Thorl, Davis Builders v Fareham UDC*; self-induced frustration (may be a choice of action or control over the circumstances) – *Maritime National Fish v Ocean Trawlers*.
- Explain that the Law Reform (Frustrated Contracts Act) 1943 also imposes limits by giving the courts discretion as to whether to order payment for expenses incurred and benefits obtained.

Question 6

This question concerns the reason for the doctrine of frustration, and focuses on the legal effects of it.

*   Define frustration, explain why it is needed as a doctrine, and briefly examine the circumstances when it has arise in cases.

*   Examine the effects in detail, using the provisions of the Law Reform (Frustrated Contracts Act) 1943 as a focus.

*   Compare this with the alternative of breach of contract.

Question 7

This question covers all of the material in Questions 5 and 6 (above), but you will need to arrange it in two parts.

(a) Define the doctrine of frustration and use cases to illustrate its operation. Explain when it can arise and how it is limited (Question 5 material) – remember to refer to the quotation used in the question.

(b) Explain what happens when a contract is frustrated, with the focus on the provisions of the Law Reform (Frustrated Contracts Act) 1943 (Question 6 material).

Question 8

*   Explain briefly the ways in which a contract may be discharged: performance, agreement, breach and frustration.

*   You are asked to discuss the liability of the English company, so payment of a lesser amount on signing is not of immediate importance, although it may be discussed in applying statute later.

*   The English company sends the first instalment of machine parts but then the rest of the work becomes illegal. This is at the fault of neither party, so they may wish to claim frustration.

*   Outline the factors that may lead to a claim of frustration: impossibility, illegality, radical difference in circumstances – illegality is particularly relevant.

*   Apply the provisions of the Law Reform (Frustrated Contracts) Act 1943 regarding money already paid, money due, expenses and valuable benefits.

*   Compare this with the alternative for the English company of compensation for breach.

Chapter 15: Remedies

Question 1

- Explain that the usual remedy for breach of contract is damages, and that these may be liquidated (where a fixed amount is set by the parties) or unliquidated (where the court decides the amount of the award) but must not be a penalty clause (generally an amount included in the contract which is oppressive). You are asked only to discuss unliquidated damages in detail.

- Explain that unliquidated damages may be substantial, nominal or exemplary.

- Explain the basis of assessment: expectation basis and reliance basis. Discuss the 'market rule'.

- Discuss contributory negligence, which at present does not apply to breach of contract – *Basildon D C v J E Lesser (Properties) Ltd*, but has been suggested as a possible area of reform.

- Consider mental distress and non-pecuniary loss and when there is no precise measure of the amount lost – *Jarvis v Swann Tours, Jackson v Horizon Holidays Ltd, Chaplin v Hicks, Thake v Maurice*.

- Consider remoteness of damage: losses recoverable if reasonably within the contemplation of the parties as a probable result of the breach – *Hadley v Baxendale*; losses for particular losses which not foreseeable not recoverable – *Victoria Laundry v Newman*.

- Explain that reasonable steps should be taken to mitigate loss – *British Westinghouse Electric and Manufacturing Co Ltd v Underground Electric Railways Co of London Ltd*.

Question 2

- Introduce damages as the usual remedy for breach of contract (see Question 1 above), and compare this common law remedy with others available, especially the equitable remedies.

- Explain what is meant by repudiation (ending the contract) – see material in Chapter 7 and 14.

- Consider the equitable remedies which supplement common law ones: rescission (see Chapter 11, as this is a remedy for misrepresentation); specific performance (to enforce fulfilment of an obligation under a contract); injunction (stops a person from acting in breach of contract).

- Discuss whether these remedies provide a satisfactory solution for a claimant.

Chapter 16: Consumer protection

Question 1

- Explain (briefly) the development of contract law through cases, based on the principle of freedom to contract. Consider the lack of statutory intervention for several centuries.

- Examine some of the cases where the courts have attempted to provide protection before statute intervened, for example in the area of exemption clauses – *Olley v Marlborough Court Hotel, Chapelton v Barry*; and in the area of sale of goods – *Samuels v Davies*. Show how the statutes were then introduced to cover the area that was causing problems to consumers.

- Consider that in protecting the consumer the statutory intervention increased the restriction on parties and reduced the general freedom to contract.

- Examine some provisions in detail. These could come from a variety of sources, e.g. Sale of Goods Act 1979, Sale and Supply of Goods Act 1994, Unfair Contract Terms Act 1977, Unfair Terms in Consumer Contract Regulations 1994.

- Discuss the effect of membership of the European Union, especially on the increasing concern for fair bargaining.

Question 2

- Explain the concept of product liability and discuss the need for provision in statute. Include some discussion of the problems in previous cases of no provision.

- Consider the problems of the consumer in establishing negligence against a manufacturer.

- Consider the protection given by statute. Consider exactly who may be liable under statute, what they may be liable for and what defences may be available, particularly that of 'development risk'.

- Discuss cases which have arisen and the way in which statute has applied.

Chapter 17: Additional questions

Question 1

Statement A

- Rescission is generally available for any misrepresentation unless barred, e.g. by lapse of time, third-party rights, affirmation, etc.

- By continuing to use the car Spencer may have lost the right to rescind but may be awarded damages in lieu under s.2(2) of the Misrepresentation Act.

Statement B

- Section 2(1) gives a general right to damages following a misrepresentation but the burden is on the other party to show reasonable grounds for belief in their statements.
- Spencer, then, only has to show that a false statement has been made, and it is up to Belinda to show that it was reasonable to believe in what she said. This is a heavy burden to discharge.

Statement C

- Silence generally does not amount to a misrepresentation, but there are exceptions, such as a half true statement.
- Spencer will have to try to show that one of these situations exists (which is unlikely).

Statement D

- Fraudulent misrepresentation is based on dishonesty – see the definition in Derry v Peek.
- There is no evidence in the question that Belinda acted dishonestly, as it says that she relied on the mileage counter. It would be up to Spencer to prove fraud.

Question 2

Statement A

- Generally the performance of an existing contractual duty does not amount to consideration (*Stylk v Myrick*). However, since *Williams v Roffey*, a practical benefit may be enough to enforce an agreement to pay extra money.
- It could be argued that Hamish is doing no more than his original duty, but on the other hand Sue is saved the trouble of finding other contractors and gets her work done for the summer season.

Statement B

- Promissory estoppel arises when there is a promise not to enforce a contract and this is relied upon by the other party.

- It does not arise here – neither Sue nor Hamish have made any such promise.

Statement C

- Economic duress can arise from a threat to breach, but it has to be substantial and under more than usual commercial pressure. It was found not to exist in *Roffey*.
- The situation is like *Roffey*, and this is not a threat to Sue's livelihood. She could presumably obtain the services of another contractor.

Statement D

- When a party undertakes a task spontaneously and then asks for payment afterwards this is generally seen as past consideration and not valid. If it is expected all along that payment would be made, e.g. if painting had been done before for payment, this *may* be different.
- This is likely to be seen as past consideration and therefore not valid.

Question 3

Statement A

- Generally a customer makes an offer in a shopping situation. However, where there is a promotion and all terms are clear, a general offer may have been made by the shop (*Lefkowitz*).
- In this case Rosie has responded by conduct to all the terms of the offer (*Carlill*) and should be entitled to the item at the advertised price.

Statement B

- Within the 'normal' shopping situation a customer makes an offer. The seller is entitled to refuse to sell and to make a counter offer.
- The label on the shoes is an invitation to treat. Rosie has made an offer to buy that has not been accepted. The seller is not obliged to sell at that price.

Statement C

- Any acceptance (or an action that is claimed to be acceptance) must be made in response to an offer.
- Rosie's action in returning the wallet was not initially in response to the offer. Strictly she is not therefore entitled to the reward.

Statement D

- Any act that is claimed to be consideration must be carried out at the time of contract, not previously.
- Rosie's act in delivering the wallet is therefore past consideration and not valid.

Question 4

Statement A

- Social and domestic arrangements are presumed not to have legal intent. The presumption may be rebutted.
- The agreement to provide food was a social event and it does not appear that there is anything in the situation to rebut the presumption.

Statement B

- A promotion made in a commercial context is likely to be presumed to have legal intent (*Carlill*, *Esso*). Very clear evidence would be needed to rebut this.
- The pizza/dessert promotion falls within this category, and there is apparently nothing to rebut the presumption.

Statement C

- A game between friends could be seen as lacking legal intent, being a social occasion (*Buckpitt v Oates*).
- However, this could be rebutted if very clear rules were drawn up between them concerning what they would do with any prize money.

Statement D

- Pools coupons do contain honourable pledge clauses which have in the past been upheld and agreements have been found not to be binding (*Jones v Vernons Pools*, etc.).
- However, these go against the Unfair Terms in Consumer Contract Regulations and could be challenged.

Question 5

Statement A

- Terms in a notice will be incorporated into a contract if they are brought to the other party's attention in a reasonable way and in good time.

- Terms at the skating rink would be incorporated into Pippa's contract only if she was made aware of them before or at the point of contract.

Statement B

- Statements will only be incorporated if they are brought to the other party's attention and do not go against the relevant legislation on unfair terms. A statement made by an assistant may be part of a contract.
- Any statement made by the attendant will form part of Pippa's contract.

Statement C

- A notice may be put up saying that a party denies liability, but this will still be scrutinised by the courts to see if it is incorporated and to see if it offends statute.
- Statute does not allow a party to exempt themselves from liability for personal injury or death.
- Pippa may therefore make a claim against the management for her injury.

Statement D

- Exclusion of any liability other than personal injury or death will only be allowed under statute if reasonable.
- The court will therefore have the right to decide whether denial of liability for Pippa's bag is reasonable.

Question 6

Statement A

- A contract is frustrated when it becomes impossible to perform and neither party is at fault. It may also arise if the contract is radically different and now has no point.
- Fola's stay at the hotel was to see a festival that was cancelled. It is not impossible for her to stay at the hotel, but the stay is pointless. The outcome will probably depend on whether she made the purpose of her visit clear.

Statement B

- If frustration is found, the sharing of loss follows the prodecures in the Law Reform (Frustrated Contracts) Act. Damages are given for breach.

- If Fola's contract is frustrated, the hotel may not claim damages, but may be able to claim for any specific expenses incurred under the Act.

Statement C

- A contract is binding at the moment of formation, not when performed.
- Fola made the contract with Bella when ordering the dress and will be bound by it.

Statement D

- Vicarious performance is allowed, but must be of a similar standard to the original agreement.
- Supacars are entitled to send a taxi from another firm, but not one that is cold, noisy and dirty.

Legal terms and expressions

Note about the use of legal expressions

It has been declared by Lord Woolf, Lord Chief Justice, that, with a view to making the Law more user friendly, certain terms will change to eliminate Latin expressions and to use more widely understood English words. So, for example, a pleading will become a statement of case, and a plaintiff will become a complainant. Welcome though the user-friendly approach is, the changes will take some time to become widespread. A few have not met with wide approval, such as a change from 'minor' to 'child' for someone under 18 – this does seem to be a strange move backwards, almost to the pre-1969 state. Whatever changes do take place, cases already reported and statutes already in existence will, of course, contain the previously established language. In this book the words and expressions widely known in the study of law have been retained, as you will continue to meet these at in your present studies, The 'new' terms are included in the glossary for reference. Do feel free to use them – you are a generation of new lawyers!

acceptance – agreement to the terms of an offer

accord and satisfaction – where a party agrees to obligations being replaced by new ones

Act of Parliament – a declaration of law by Parliament

adequate – market value (when referring to consideration)

affirm – indicate willingness to continue with a contract

agent – one authorised to act on behalf of another

arbitration – resolving a dispute by a person (usually an expert) as an alternative to court

authority – a declaration of the law, usually by case or statute

bilateral contract – a contract in which both parties negotiate the terms

bill – a proposal for a new Act of Parliament

bona fide – in good faith, or genuine

breach of contract – where obligations of a contract are not fulfilled

capacity to contract – the status to form a contract

caveat emptor – literally, let the buyer beware (let the buyer make his own enquiries)

charterparty – contract of hire of a ship

child – a person under 18 (the 'new' term for a minor)

claimant – the person taking a civil case to court (the 'new' term for plaintiff)

civil law – law involving disputes, usually between individuals, which do not amount to crimes

collateral contract – a secondary contract which stands beside the main contract

common mistake – where both parties make a contract based on the same false assumption

condition – a major term of a contract

consensus ad idem – literally the meeting of minds, or genuine agreement

consideration – the 'thing' (usually goods, money, service or promise) given by a party to a contract

consumer – an individual buying from someone in business

context – surrounding circumstances

construction – interpretation

contra proferentem – a clause interpreted against the person relying on it

contract – an agreement between two parties enforceable by law

corporation – an organisation with its own separate identity

course of dealing – series of similar transactions between the same parties

criminal law – law regulating wrongs so serious that society feels there is need for punishment

cross-purpose mistake – (an alternative term for mutual mistake – see that entry)

damages – money awarded as compensation

defendant – a person defending, or answering, a claim in court

directive – a European ruling to member states to bring about a particular law in their own country

discharge – the ending of a contract

dissenting – a judge who does not agree with the others

duress – a threat of violence or the unlawful restraint, used to make a person enter into a contract

economic duress – a serious threat to wealth forcing a party to enter into a contract

exclusion clause – a complete denial of an obligation within a contract

exemption clause – a limitation or denial of an obligation within a contract

freedom of contract – the idea that a person is free agree to anything they wish

frustrated contract – where a contract ends through the fault of neither party

gratuitous promise – a promise given without any obligation in return

honourable pledge clause – a clause stating that an agreement is not intended to be legally binding

implied term – a term which is included in a contract even if the parties did not negotiate it

incorporation – inclusion
indemnity – repayment of necessary expenses
injunction – an order to stop some event
innominate term – a term which cannot easily be labelled as a condition or a warranty
inter absentes – at a distance (not in each other's presence)
inter praesentes – in each other's presence, or face to face

judiciary – a body of judges

legislation – a body of statute law
liable – responsibility
liability – legal duty or responsibility
limitation clause – a clause limiting a party's obligations under a contract
liquidated damages – an agreement to pay a reasonable agreed sum on breach

mediation – where someone tries to obtain agreement between parties as an alternative to court
minor – a person under 18 (now to be referred to as a child)
misrepresentation – a misleading claim which leads a person into a contract
mistake – a false assumption in forming a contract
mitigate – to take reasonable steps to offset any loss
mutual mistake – (cross-purpose mistake) where two parties make different false assumptions

necessary – an item without which a person cannot reasonably exist and suited to their way of life
non est factum – literally 'this is not my deed' (a claim that a contract was signed in ignorance)

objective – a view which is not personal opinion
offer – an expression of willingness to contract on certain terms with serious legal intent

parol evidence rule – the rule that a written contract cannot be changed by oral evidence
party – a person, group or organisation who forms one 'side' of a contract
penalty clause – an agreement in a contract to pay money (usually a large amount) if there is a breach
plaintiff – a person bringing a civil claim to court (now called the claimant)
policy – a principle view of what the law should be
precedent – a ruling from case law which binds other cases
prima facie – at first sight
privity – the relationship between the two parties to a contract
prosecution – a person bringing a criminal case to court

quantum meruit – literally 'as much as is deserved' – payment for the amount of work done

registered company – a company with a legal structure, registered under the Companies Act 1985

remedy – a way of putting right a wrong, or a legal solution for that wrong

representation – a casual statement made before a contract is formed, which does not form a term

repudiate – end a contract under common law (as in breach)

res extincta – the thing is destroyed (referring to the subject matter of the contract)

rescind – end a contract under equity (as in misrepresentation)

right – something to which a person is entitled

severable – obligations in a contract which can be separated

severance – the deletion of a clause which is not allowed by the court

statute – an Act of Parliament

subject to contract – indicates that negotiations have not yet reached the stage of a binding contract

sue – make a civil claim in court

sufficient – recognisable (when referring to consideration)

term – a section, or clause, of a contract

uberrimae fides – literally, 'utmost good faith' – when one person places great trust in another

ultra vires – literally 'outside one's powers' – acting beyond the allowed limits

unanimous – with the agreement of everyone involved

undue influence – unfair pressure to enter a contract

unilateral contract – where one party lays down the terms and the other agrees

unilateral mistake – where one party to a contract is aware of the false assumption of the other

unliquidated damages – damages not pre-estimated by the parties, but assessed by the court

vitiating factor – something which makes an otherwise well formed contract not binding

vicarious performance – performance on behalf of another

void – when a contract ends completely under common law

voidable – the equitable right to end a contract, normally subject to bars to rescission

warranty – a minor term of a contract

Legal resources

Books

Cheshire, Fifoot and Furmston, *The Law of Contract:* Butterworth (an authoritative university text). Stone, R., *Principles of Contract Law*: Cavendish Publishing (a university text).

Vanstone, Sherratt, and Charman, *AS Law:* Willan Publishing (useful for review of material covered in the first part of the course, especially when studying for the synoptic examination).

Hodge, S., *Tort Law:* Willan Publishing (useful for overlap of some areas of consumer law, e.g. negligence).

Newspapers and journals

The Times (always good for current developments and articles, particularly in the supplement on Tuesdays, and a good source of current cases).

Student Law Review: Cavendish Publishing (published three times each year – useful for recent developments – see below for on-line version).

The New Law Journal (the major journal for current developments and academic articles on civil law issues).

See below (The Internet) for journals available on-line.

The internet

If you have access to the internet a new world of legal information is available to you. I have collected here a selection of addresses of sites which may be of interest and which should be useful to you in your studies. They are arranged into categories, very broadly, according to content, although some sites will contain material which belongs to more than one category.

This is a fast developing and changing resource, so the content of a site may not be the same from one visit to another. The addresses on page 333 were all accurate and operational at the point of publication.

Parliament and legislation

http://www.parliament.uk (for general information on Parliament)
http://www.legislation.hmso.gov.uk (for Acts of Parliament and other
  legislation)
http://www.swarb.co.uk (for Acts of Parliament and other resources)

Case law

http://www.parliament.the-stationery-office.co.uk/pa/ld199697/ldjudgmt/
ldjudgmt.htm (for House of Lords judgments since November 1996)
http://www.the-times.co.uk (for articles and law reports from The Times)
http://www.bailii.org/recent-decisions-ew.html#ewcases/EWCA/Civ (for
  recent Court of Appeal cases)
http://www.lawreports.co.uk (for sample reports of the Incorporated
Council of Law Reporting for England and Wales)
http://curia.eu.int/en/index.htm (for recent cases and information on the
  European Court of Justice)
http://www.courtservice.gov.uk (for selected judgments and news items)

Articles and news

http://www.lawzone.co.uk (for recent cases and articles)
http://www.cavendishpublishing.com (for recent cases and articles and
  back issues of *Student Law Review* useful to students – registration
  required (currently free of charge)

General interest

http://www.venables.co.uk (for a huge collection of legal resources)
http://www.the-lawyer.co.uk (for general legal news)
http://www.lawgazette.co.uk (for general legal issues)
http://www.lawcom.gov.uk (for reports and information on the Law
  Commission)
http://www.infolaw.co.uk (for general legal material)
http://www.e-lawstudents.com (law resources for A-level students-
  subscription needed for full access)

Index